The Scratch of a Pen

Also by Colin G. Calloway

Crown and Calumet: British–Indian Relations, 1783–1815

The Western Abenakis of Vermont, 1600–1800:
War, Migration and the Survival of an Indian People

The American Revolution in Indian Country:
Crisis and Diversity in Native American Communities

New Worlds for All: Indians, Europeans,
and the Remaking of Early America

First Peoples:
A Documentary Survey of American Indian History

One Vast Winter Count:
The Native American West before Lewis and Clark

PIVOTAL MOMENTS
IN AMERICAN HISTORY

Series Editors
David Hackett Fischer
James M. McPherson

James T. Patterson
Brown v. Board of Education:
A Civil Rights Milestone and Its Troubled Legacy

Maury Klein
Rainbow's End: The Crash of 1929

James M. McPherson
Crossroads of Freedom: The Battle of Antietam

Glenn C. Altschuler
All Shook Up: How Rock 'n' Roll Changed America

David Hackett Fischer
Washington's Crossing

John Ferling
Adams vs. Jefferson: The Tumultuous Election of 1800

Joel H. Silbey
Storm over Texas:
The Annexation Controversy and the Road to Civil War

Raymond Arsenault
Freedom Riders:
1961 and the Struggle for Racial Justice

The Scratch of a Pen

1763

AND THE
TRANSFORMATION
OF
NORTH AMERICA

COLIN G. CALLOWAY

OXFORD
UNIVERSITY PRESS

2006

OXFORD
UNIVERSITY PRESS

Oxford University Press, Inc., publishes works that further
Oxford University's objective of excellence
in research, scholarship, and education.

Oxford   New York
Auckland   Cape Town   Dar es Salaam   Hong Kong   Karachi   Kolkata
Kuala Lumpur   Madrid   Melbourne   Mexico City   Nairobi
New Delhi   Shanghai   Taipei   Toronto

With offices in
Argentina   Austria   Brazil   Chile   Czech Republic   France   Greece
Guatemala   Hungary   Italy   Japan   Poland   Portugal   Singapore
South Korea   Switzerland   Thailand   Turkey   Ukraine   Vietnam

Copyright © 2006 by Colin G. Calloway

Published by Oxford University Press, Inc.
198 Madison Avenue, New York, NY 10016
www.oup.com

Oxford is a registered trademark of Oxford University Press

Library of Congress Cataloging-in-Publication Data
Calloway, Colin G. (Colin Gordon), 1953–
The scratch of a pen : 1763 and the transformation of North America /
Colin G. Calloway.
p. cm. — (Pivotal moments in American history)
ISBN-13: 978-0-19-530071-0
ISBN-10: 0-19-530071-8
1. North America—History—Colonial period, ca. 1600–1775.
2. Frontier and pioneer life—North America.
3. Land tenure—North America—History—18th century.
4. Treaty of Paris (1763)
5. Great Britain—Colonies—America.   6. France—Colonies—America.
7. Indians of North America—History—Colonial period, ca. 1600–1775.
8. North America—Ethnic relations.   I. Title.   II. Series.
E46.C35 2005   973.2'6—dc22   2005020201

Design and typesetting: Jack Donner, BookType

1 3 5 7 9 8 6 4 2
Printed in the United States of America

To my American family—Marcia, Graeme, and Megan—
and in memory of the British family I lost while doing this book:
Ronald Keith Calloway (1920-2003)
Neil Graeme Calloway (1949-2004)
Anne Elizabeth Calloway (1918-2005)

Contents

Editor's Note

*W*E STILL CALL IT THE FRENCH AND INDIAN WAR, but it was much more than that. This half-remembered event was a great world war, fought on four continents and three oceans around the globe. For millions of people it was an agony of suffering and loss. The savage forest fighting in North America allowed no safety for noncombatants, no pity for the wounded, and no mercy for prisoners. Even more cruel was the war in central Europe, where absolute monarchs hurled large armies at one another, heedless of the human cost.

The world war ended with the Treaty of Paris in 1763, and we are still living with the consequences. Six men made the critical decisions: young King George III of Britain and old King Louis XV of France; their chief ministers the Earl of Bute and Duc de Choiseul; and their negotiators the Duke of Bedford and Duc de Nivernois. They argued for months over the fate of a few small islands. Then, with what Francis Parkman called a "scratch of a pen," they casually disposed of continents that they had never seen, and could scarcely imagine. It was one of the great moments of contingency in modern history, and the starting point for this remarkably fresh and original book.

The author, Colin Calloway, tells us that this "is not a book of diplomatic history. . . . Rather it surveys the enormous changes generated by the Peace of Paris and assesses their impact on many societies and countless lives." In that purpose, it represents a new trend in historical scholarship. It links the events and contingencies of political and diplomatic history to the processes and structures of social and cultural history.

This book reads so fluently that readers may miss the many years of research and reflection on which it rests. Every chapter makes a contribution. The book begins by surveying the condition of America in 1763, and it does so in a new way. In the nineteenth and early twentieth centuries, Whig historians centered that subject on British Americans and celebrated them as "a people instinct with the energies of ordered freedom," in the words of Francis Parkman. Indians, Africans, French, and Spanish were banished to the margins of history.

In the late twentieth century, another generation of historians took a broader view of the many populations of North America, but they combined that broad approach with a deep hostility to Anglo-American culture.

Colin Calloway's understanding of America in 1763 combines the strengths of these two approaches and corrects their weaknesses. It gives much attention to the Indians. The author writes that "it spends more time in Indian country than in colonial capitals, more time in Indian councils than colonial assemblies." But he also writes of European settlers with sympathy, understanding, and respect. The book is remarkable for its balance, depth, and maturity of judgment.

After that beginning, the author sets his many populations in motion. The second chapter is about hunger for land and a torrent of migration that followed the treaty of 1763. He follows the movements of many Indian nations, and the migration of the Spanish and French. In that context, the more familiar stories of English, Scottish, German, and Dutch pioneers take on new meaning.

The third chapter is about the collision of these many ethnic movements, in an explosion of violence with great kinetic force. Many historians have written about "Pontiac's Rebellion," but Calloway's account gives us a larger story of what he calls the first American War of Independence. He also gives us a stronger sense of individual agency in these events. We meet actors who are unfamiliar even to experts on the subject: Teedyuscung, chief of the eastern Delaware, and Reuben Cognehew, the Wamponoag teacher who after unimaginable adventures won rights of self-rule for the Mashpee Indians of Massachusetts. We get a new understanding of Pontiac, the great Ottawa war chief and one of the most able leaders of his age. And at the same time we are invited to empathize with colonial leaders and British soldiers. The moving account of Captain Donald Campbell is a case in point.

Chapter 4 centers on a sustained effort by British leaders to control these conflicts, by creating a reserve for the Indians beyond the Appalachians in the Proclamation of 1763. Frederick Jackson Turner believed that this was a major event in American history and a leading cause of the American Revolution. Other scholars have disagreed. Here again, Colin Calloway takes a new approach by enlarging the subject across national boundaries. A surprise to serious readers is his account of the great gathering at Niagara in 1764, where 2,000 Indians from twenty-four nations assembled to discuss the Proclamation of 1763. Historians of the United States will be startled by the Canadian history of the Proclamation of 1763 and by instructive parallels to the Maori gathering at Waitangi in New Zealand.

The last three chapters take a fresh approach to the French and Spanish populations in North America, and they develop a double theme of change and persistence after 1763. The history of the Acadians is handled brilliantly and in a very original way. So also is the history of the French and Spanish in Louisiana, Florida, and the lower Mississippi.

Altogether this book gives us a new understanding of its subject. Many historians have found large meanings in these dramatic events. In the nineteenth century, Whig historians such as Francis Parkman interpreted them as the grand design of Providence for a new world founded on ideals of liberty, freedom, and self-government. In the late twentieth century, academic iconoclasts made them into a dark story about the destruction of Indian nations and the expansion of African slavery by evil and rapacious European settlers. In the twenty-first century, Colin Calloway leads us to a deeper understanding of a pivotal moment, from which we all have much to learn.

David Hackett Fischer

Acknowledgments

I AM GRATEFUL TO EDITORIAL DIRECTOR Peter Ginna for inviting me to write something for the "Pivotal Moments" series and for watching over the evolution of this book. Joseph Cullon at Dartmouth College, Gregory Evans Dowd at the University of Michigan, and Daniel K. Richter at the University of Pennsylvania all read earlier versions of the manuscript, and Greg O'Brien at the University of Southern Mississippi read the sections relating to southern Indians. Anna Fleder, Dartmouth College class of 2004, also contributed to the project by her enthusiastic work as presidential scholar and research assistant.

Several individuals were particularly helpful in locating and providing illustrations: Brian Leigh Dunnigan of the William L. Clements Library, Isabelle Fernandes of Library and Archives Canada, Holly Frisbee of the Philadelphia Museum of Art, Megan Gillespie of the Albany Institute of History and Art, Thomas Lanham at the Louisiana State Museum, David Miller at Bushy Run Battlefield, Diane Reed of the Pennsylvania Historical and Museum Commission, and Michael Sherbon of the Pennsylvania State Archives. As always, at Dartmouth College I am indebted to the staff of Baker Library and to my colleagues in History and in Native American Studies.

1763 Timeline

FEBRUARY 10:	Peace of Paris
APRIL 8:	Lord Bute resigns as prime minister of England and is succeeded by George Grenville
APRIL:	Spanish citizens begin to evacuate St. Augustine
APRIL 19:	Teedyuscung murdered
APRIL 27:	Pontiac's war council
MAY 9:	Indians begin siege of Detroit
MAY 16:	Indians capture Fort Sandusky
MAY 25:	Indians capture Fort St. Joseph
MAY 27:	Indians capture Fort Miami
MAY 29:	Indians begin siege of Fort Pitt
JUNE 29:	Governor d'Abbadie arrives in New Orleans
JUNE 2:	Indians capture Fort Michilimackinac
JUNE 16:	Indians capture Fort Venango
JUNE 18:	Indians capture Fort LeBoeuf
JUNE 22:	Indians capture Fort Presqu'Isle
JUNE 24:	British give blankets from smallpox patients to Indian delegates at Fort Pitt
JULY 9:	Superior Council of Louisiana approves dissolution of Jesuit Order
JULY 20:	British take over St. Augustine from the Spanish

JULY 31:	Indians defeat British at Battle of Bloody Run
AUGUST 5–6:	Henry Bouquet fends off Indian attack at Battle of Bushy Run
AUGUST 6:	British take over Pensacola from the Spanish
AUGUST 10:	Bouquet relieves Fort Pitt
SEPTEMBER 3:	Spanish residents evacuate Pensacola
SEPTEMBER 14:	Indians defeat British at Devil's Hole, Niagara
OCTOBER 4:	British take over Mobile from the French
OCTOBER 7:	Parliament passes the Proclamation Act
OCTOBER 28:	James Murray appointed Governor of Quebec
OCTOBER 30:	Indians end siege of Detroit
NOVEMBER 9:	Treaty of Augusta with the Southern Indian Nations
NOVEMBER 21:	James Grant appointed Governor of East Florida; George Johnstone appointed Governor of West Florida
DECEMBER:	Smallpox hits Boston
DECEMBER:	Pierre de Laclède and Auguste Chouteau select site for trading post at St. Louis
DECEMBER 27:	Paxton Boys murder Indians in Lancaster County, Pennsylvania

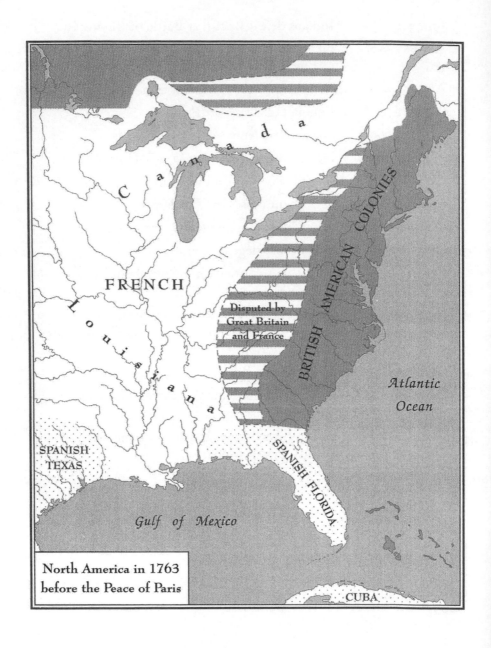

North America in 1763
before the Peace of Paris

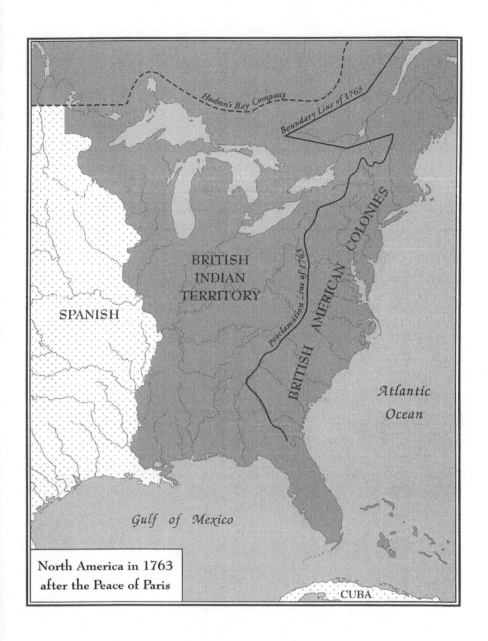

North America in 1763
after the Peace of Paris

The Scratch of a Pen

Introduction:
War, Peace, and Revolution

EMEMBER THE YEAR 1763," the celebrated stage actor David Garrick told James Boswell. He predicted great things for the twenty-two-year-old Scot. Boswell, however, seemed more interested in picking up prostitutes from the night streets of London than in striving for great things. The first four months of his year would be memorable mainly for the disease he caught from "the fair Louisa," an actress whom he had courted for several weeks and then quickly tired of once his amorous conquest was complete. He had "expected at least a winter's safe copulation" with Louisa and thought himself the injured party. But in May Boswell met Dr. Samuel Johnson and began a relationship that was to secure him lasting literary fame. Johnson encouraged Boswell to keep a journal of his life. Boswell was already doing so, recording "all sorts of little incidents" in it. "Sir," said Dr. Johnson "there is nothing too little for so little a creature as man."[1]

Johnson doubtless meant his comment to apply to the issues of empire with which kings and ministers were busying themselves that year as well as to Boswell's petty doings. While Boswell confided his conquests and affairs of the heart to his journal, the nation's conquests and affairs of state were debated publicly in Parliament and pamphlets, in newspapers and coffee houses. London in 1763 was abuzz. On February 10, 1763, Britain, France, and Spain, the superpowers of the time, signed the Peace of Paris. The Seven Years' War was over and the world breathed a sigh of peace. Nowhere was peace more welcome than in North America where the conflict, usually known as the French and Indian War, had lasted for nine years.

"[S]o LONG AS THE WORLD HAS STOOD there has not been such a War"; this is how the conflict was described to Delaware Indians by Christian Frederick Post, a Moravian missionary serving as an ambassador from Pennsylvania to the tribes in the Ohio Valley.[2] British and French, Americans and Canadians, American Indians, Prussians, Austrians, Russians, Spaniards, and East Indian moguls fought the war, and conflicts had been waged on land and sea, in North America, the Caribbean Islands, West Africa, India, and continental Europe. Britain executed global strategies at enormous costs financed by unprecedented levels of taxing and borrowing. In 1763 Britain had won an empire greater than that of imperial Rome but the nation was on the verge of bankruptcy.

For more than half a century, Britain and France had competed for domination in North America. Previous imperial conflicts—King William's War, Queen Anne's War, King George's War—had begun in Europe and spread to North America. But the French and Indian War began with bloodshed around the Forks of the Ohio. Britain and France each believed that whoever controlled the Ohio country would win the continent. The French feared British expansion there would threaten their position in the West; the British feared the French were building a line of forts that threatened to strangle Britain's seaboard colonies. The Indian peoples who lived in the Ohio country, meanwhile, endeavored to preserve their lands, cultures, and communities against outside pressures.[3] The fighting began when twenty-one-year-old Major George Washington, a novice in Indian diplomacy and frontier warfare, ambushed a French platoon but then was compelled to surrender to a superior French and Indian force.[4]

At first the war went badly for the British. In 1755 General Edward Braddock marched against Fort Duquesne at the Forks of the Ohio with more than two thousand troops. He hacked a road through the mountains and forests of western Pennsylvania, crossed the Monongahela River, and had the fort almost within his grasp when a sortie of Indians and French attacked his columns and routed the army, inflicting almost 1,000 casualties.[5] News of Braddock's defeat and escalating Indian attacks sent backcountry settlers scurrying east for safety.[6]

The next year, the French and their Indian allies captured the British fort at Oswego, and with it took control of Lake Ontario. In 1757, the Marquis de Montcalm took Fort William Henry on Lake

George. His Indian allies attacked the surrendered garrison, perpetrating a slaughter made famous by the book and movie versions of James Fenimore Cooper's *Last of the Mohicans.* Montcalm scored another victory in 1758, inflicting heavy losses on British troops who mounted a head-on assault against Fort Ticonderoga. The war went equally badly in Europe where Britain's allies suffered defeats in battle and the island of Minorca in the Mediterranean was lost.

William Pitt turned the tide. Taking office as Secretary of State for the Southern Department after a period of ministerial instability, Pitt effectively functioned as Britain's prime minister for the next four years. He pursued the war with new vigor and a simple strategy: reduce France from an imperial power to a continental power by stripping away its colonies, especially in North America. In Europe, Britain increased its subsidies to German allies, and Frederick II of Prussia embroiled French, Austrian, and Russian armies in recurrent bloodbaths. In America, British soldiers adjusted to forest fighting and began to win victories.[7]

In July 1758, British regulars and New England militia captured Louisbourg, overlooking the mouth of the St. Lawrence River. In August, Colonel John Bradstreet captured Fort Frontenac on Lake Ontario, severing French supply lines to the West. That fall, Ohio Indians made peace with the British at the Treaty of Easton, leaving Fort Duquesne, the prize that had cost Braddock so dearly, virtually undefended. The French blew up the fort before the British, led by dying General John Forbes, could seize it.[8]

In 1759, Britain won victories everywhere. British forces captured the slaving station of Goree in Africa and the rich sugar island of Guadeloupe in the Caribbean. In Europe, British and allied troops defeated the French at Minden. In July, the British captured Fort Niagara. France could no longer control the West or supply its Indian allies. The Franco-Indian alliance unraveled and Indians began to mend fences with the British, encouraged by promises of trade and protection for their lands.[9] In September, General James Wolfe turned a stalled siege at Quebec into a dramatic victory: his redcoats scrambled up the cliffs during the night and routed the French army in the morning on the Plains of Abraham. Wolfe died in the battle; so did Montcalm.[10] The British hung on to Quebec in the face of a French countersiege, and the first ship to appear in the St. Lawrence the following spring flew the Union Jack: the Royal

Navy had destroyed the French Atlantic fleet in November. Britain ruled the waves; beleaguered French forces in Canada were cut off from reinforcements, and France's remaining overseas empire could be picked apart. Horace Walpole said English church bells were worn thin ringing for victories.[11]

In 1760, British power converged on Montreal and the defeat of New France was complete. "I believe never three Armys, setting out from different & very distant Parts from each other[,] joyned in the Center, as was intended, better than we did," wrote commander-in-chief General Jeffery Amherst.[12] Montcalm's former aide-de-camp, Louis Antoine de Bougainville, carried the articles of Montreal's surrender to Amherst. Bougainville was an asthmatic, plump little man who could quote the classics and had written a book on calculus by the time he was twenty-five. He hardly seemed cut out for soldiering or frontier life, but he saw plenty of both. He fought at Fort Oswego in 1756 and at Fort William Henry in 1757, and was wounded at Fort Ticonderoga in 1758. He sat in council with Indian allies, sang the war song with them, and was adopted by them. He witnessed the fall of Quebec in 1759. He also left a vivid account of the war France lost in North America, a view from inside a crumbling empire. The French lacked the manpower and resources to hold back the British. British naval power deprived New France of reinforcements, news, and supplies. Waste, inefficiency, and corruption pervaded the French system. Personal rivalries and petty jealousies diverted energies and hampered defense efforts. Famine and disease stalked the land. French officers held endless councils with their Indian allies but felt less and less sure of their allegiance. (The tribes of the St. Lawrence, formerly France's most steadfast Indian allies, switched their allegiance in 1760.)[13] "What a country! What a war!" Bougainville exclaimed in frustration as the war slipped away from the French. Taken prisoner with the rest of the army, he was shipped back to France. (He later led a scientific expedition around the world and explored the South Pacific, introduced the Bougainvillea flower to Europe, was imprisoned for a time during the French revolution, and became a count during the Napoleon regime).[14]

Carlos III became King of Spain after his half-brother, Fernando VI, died in August 1759. He was on his way to Madrid to assume the throne when he heard about Britain's capture of Quebec. The news is said to have caused his blood to run cold. With French power removed, what was to stop British imperial ambitions reaching to Florida, Mexico, and even into parts of South America?[15] Spain had stayed out of the war, and for a time, William Pitt had even courted Spain in the hope that if it did fight, it would do so on the side of Britain, not of France. But the string of British victories removed Britain's need for Spanish allies, and at the same time pushed Spain to abandon its policy of neutrality.

Carlos renewed the Family Compact, the old alliance between the Bourbon monarchies of Spain and France, and in January 1762 joined France in a futile effort to avert total British victory in North America. It was a disastrous decision. Spanish privateers preyed on British shipping but Creek and Yuchi Indians harried the Spanish frontier in Florida. The British had been waiting for an opportunity to pounce on Havana, the hub of Spain's Caribbean empire and western Atlantic trade system—Admiral George Anson had drafted plans the year before for an amphibious attack. In June 1762 a British force comprising 40 warships, 135 transports, and 15,000 troops landed in Cuba and laid siege to Havana. Havana's fort was supposed to be impregnable, but the arrival of the British fleet caught the garrison off guard: the British had captured their mail ship and the Spaniards were unaware that a state of war existed. Despite appalling casualties to gastric disorder and yellow fever, the British captured Havana after a two-month siege. Britain had penetrated the outer defenses of Spain's American empire and merchant ships from England and the American mainland colonies hurried to Havana to expand their commercial activities. One Englishman called it "the most momentous acquisition we had til then ever made in America"; Benjamin Franklin called it "a conquest of the greatest importance." Havana's loss sent shock waves to Madrid.[16] Two months later, in October, British regulars and sepoys from India captured Manila in the Philippines. Spain's brief involvement in the war cost it heavily and caused massive adjustments in North America in the peace that followed.

EVEN AS BRITAIN WAS WINNING VICTORIES everywhere, William Pitt predicted that "peace will be as hard to make as war." The French foreign minister, the Duc de Choiseul, agreed; indeed he began the peace process almost as soon as he took office. "Since we do not know how to make war," he said, "we must make peace."[17] He dedicated himself to extricating France from the war on the best terms he could get. Pitt wanted to continue the war to inflict maximum damage on the French, whom he regarded as Britain's natural and permanent enemy. Others, however, feared that Pitt's strategy would guarantee future war by alienating all of Europe. Pitt had won the war but now he had to leave office to make way for peace. Despite Pitt's huge popularity with the people, the king forced him to resign.

In May 1762, the king appointed John Stuart, the Earl of Bute, a leading proponent of peace and a royal favorite, to serve as prime minister. In September, the Duke of Bedford crossed the Channel to restart peace negotiations in Paris; the Duc de Nivernois headed for London for the same purpose. Preliminary peace terms were agreed to on November 3. The next day Louis XV secretly ceded Louisiana west of the Mississippi, together with New Orleans, to Spain. Britain, France, and Spain signed the definitive Treaty of Paris on February 10, 1763. The same month, Austria and Prussia signed the Treaty of Hubertusburg, essentially restoring the *status quo ante bellum* in central Europe. By contrast, in North America, where the war began, the Treaty of Paris redrew the map.

As historical geographer D. W. Meinig observes, the contrast between "niggling negotiations over little islands and harbors and the casualness with which huge continental expanses were transferred from one flag to another" is difficult for the modern mind to comprehend.[18] In Britain, a long debate and a pamphlet war raged over the wisdom of holding on to snowy Canada, with its annual exports of £14,000, and returning Guadeloupe, which produced more sugar than all the British West Indies combined, with exports of £6,000,000. But the war had been fought for North America: "you must keep Canada, otherways you lay the foundation for another war," argued one pamphleteer. "If we do not exclude [the French] *absolutely* and *entirely* from that country we shall soon find we have done nothing." By the final round of the peace talks it was clear that Britain placed North American security over West Indian sugar.[19] Britain returned Guadeloupe, Martinique, and St. Lucia to France. It also returned the fishing islands at Saint Pierre and Miquelon in the Gulf of St. Lawrence and fishing rights on the Grand Banks off Newfoundland, a concession whose importance is difficult to fathom today but which was massive in the cod-consuming eighteenth century: the Grand Banks—the shoals of the edge of the North American continent where the waters of the Gulf of Mexico meet the waters of arctic Greenland—are teeming in phytoplankton and are the richest cod grounds in the world.[20] Gorée in West Africa and Belle-Île-en-Mer in the Bay of Biscay were also handed back. Britain returned Havana, captured with massive loss of life, to Spain, along with the Philippines, news of whose capture arrived too late for them to be included in the peace negotiations.

Out of office and in failing health, William Pitt gave an impassioned three-hour speech in the House of Commons, denouncing the treaty concessions as a betrayal of all he had worked for. France threatened Britain primarily as a maritime and commercial power, he argued, "and therefore by restoring to her all the valuable West Indian islands, and by our concessions in the Newfoundland fishery, we have given her the means of recovering her prodigious losses and of becoming once more formidable to us at sea."[21] John Wilkes, then a member of Parliament, attacked the peace, and the Earl of Bute as the man behind it, in the famous issue No. 45 of *The North Briton*. The preliminary articles, he said, "have drawn the contempt of mankind on our wretched negociators" [*sic*].[22] Crowds rioted in the streets of London, even stoning the king's coach.

Nevertheless, the merchants of London supported the peace and the House of Commons approved its terms by 319 to 65 votes.[23] Britain's gains were enormous: Canada "in its utmost extent," all French territory east of the Mississippi, Grenada, Saint Vincent, Dominica and Tobago, Senegal in West Africa, Minorca restored. In India, where British and French trading companies had competed for domination of Bengal and the Carnatic coast, the French were now restricted to trading stations, unable to stop British expansion in the subcontinent. Spain yielded Florida in partial payment for the return of Havana. Britain's North American possessions now stretched from the Atlantic to the Mississippi and from Hudson Bay to the Gulf of Mexico. *The Annual Register*, the year-by-year record of British and world events that began publication in 1758, declared that the gains "made our American empire compleat [*sic*]. No frontiers could be more distinctly desired, nor more perfectly secured." The challenge for Britain in North America, it seemed, was how to make profitable "an immense waste of savage country."[24] In his detailed chronicle of *The Late War in North-America*, Thomas Mante (who served in both the Seven Years' War and Pontiac's War and later acted as a double spy for

England and France) said that the Peace of Paris "was justly deemed, by the bulk of mankind, a happy event."[25]

The enormity of Britain's victory seemed to herald a new world order. "No prince had ever begun his reign by so glorious a war and so generous a peace," Lord Egremont was reported to have said to George III as they looked over the terms of the Peace of Paris.[26] But what would the new world order look like, and how would it be governed? After the vigorous wartime leadership of William Pitt, England now faced the future, and its new empire, with a new government and a young king. George III was twenty-five and had been on the throne little more than two years. He relied heavily on the Earl of Bute, the unpopular Scottish minister who was denounced for selling out the country in his rush to make peace and also rumored to enjoy intimate relations with the king's mother, the Dowager Princess of Wales.[27]

"It is truly a miserable thing," the Reverend Samuel Johnson of Connecticut wrote in December 1763, "that we no sooner leave fighting our neighbours, the French, but we must fall to quarrelling among ourselves."[28] His comment proved as apt for British North America as for English politics. The Peace of Paris brought little peace to North America, where Indian war dominated 1763 and where turmoil and movement led, ultimately, to civil war and revolution. George III became remembered as "the king who lost the American colonies." The seeds of that loss were planted in the Peace that he and his ministers celebrated.

IT HAS BEEN SAID, quite often and with good reason, that "Americans were never more British than in 1763."[29] They relished their part in the defeat of the old enemy and looked forward to a golden age in which the blessings of British political civilization would be extended west. On both sides of the Atlantic, newspapers and pamphlets, speeches and addresses, poems and plays, songs and sermons all celebrated Britannia's victory and the dawn of a new age of liberty. In May 1763, in a sermon preached before the governor and the House of Representatives of Massachusetts, the Reverend Thomas Barnard savored the victory. A new era was at hand. With God on its side and a generous king on the throne, Britain had reached "the Summit of earthly Grandeur and Glory." After long years of suffering, New Englanders could expect a bright future. Their Indian and French enemies were vanquished, their liberties were unequaled and intact:

Now commences the Era of our quiet Enjoyment of those Liberties, which our Fathers purchased with the Toil of their whole Lives, their Treasure, their Blood. Safe from the Enemy of the Wilderness, safe from the griping Hand of arbitrary Sway and cruel Superstition; Here shall be the late founded Seat of Peace and Freedom. Here shall our indulgent Mother, who has most generously rescued and protected us, be served and honored by growing Numbers, with all Duty, Love and Gratitude, til time shall be no more.[30]

The freest people in the world, their rights secure under a constitutional monarchy, had defeated the forces of absolute monarchy and the controlling hand of Roman Catholicism. As Linda Colley has shown, wars—and especially victories against France—played an important role in forging a national, British, identity. The Seven Years' War and the empire it brought helped bind English and Scots in a common imperial venture. But in America, it helped drive Britons apart. It was not the victory itself but the scale of the victory that "subsequently inflamed the peace." In 1763 Britain's North American empire was huge: more than thirty colonies on the mainland and in the Caribbean as well as vast territories in the interior of the continent. Sustaining it required money and military force. Britons, writes Colley, "were perplexed by the problem of having acquired too much power too quickly over too many people." The challenges of governing a continent from an island strained British politics and relations between Britain and its colonies.[31]

   ONCE THE DEFINITIVE TREATY was concluded, Bute resigned, and George Grenville, William Pitt's brother-in-law, formed a new cabinet as First Lord of the Treasury. The new government's major goal was to regulate and protect the new North American empire and to pay for that protection. Grenville's ministry, in historian Jack Sosin's words, "was to be one of the most momentous in the history of the first British Empire."[32] The government in 1763 began to impose order, controls, and limits on its colonies at the very time when colonists hoped for increased freedom, opportunities, and expansion. Britain was confronted with a new geographic space that lay beyond the reach of effective British control. By trying to bring colonies more closely into the empire, Britain produced American reactions that split the empire.[33] To extricate itself from the financial crisis caused by winning a world war, the government attempted to reduce expenses by cutting costs and to increase revenue by raising taxes. The first sparked an Indian war of independence immediately; the second ignited a controversy that would culminate in the American war of independence a dozen years later.[34] Victory in the great war for empire generated wars against empire.

Conquests cost money, and someone had to pay for them. Britain's national debt at the start of the Seven Years' War was £74,600,000. On January 5, 1763, according to Exchequer records, it stood at £122,603,336 and carried an annual interest of £4,409,797. A year later the debt had increased by another £7 million. The annual national budget was only £8 million. In 1754, revenue had exceeded expense in Great Britain (£6.8 million in revenue to £6 million in expenditure); in 1763, expense exceeded revenue (£14.2 million in expenditure to £9.8 million in revenue). Taxes in Britain had increased sharply during the war years. In 1763 imperial taxation in Britain averaged 26 shillings per person; in the colonies it averaged just 1 shilling per person. It seemed reasonable to expect the colonists to bear some of the expense of victory—after all, British ministers pointed out, the war had been fought for them.[35]

American colonists were not inclined to see things that way. As colonial historian Jack Greene reminds us: "Citizens expected little from government; budgets and taxes were low; paid officials were few; civil and judicial establishments were small, part-time, and unprofessional; and the maintenance of order devolved very largely upon local units of government, which had few coercive resources *vis-à-vis* the free population."[36] It was a huge step from this to sharing the burden of financing and administering an empire. Indeed, as an article printed in the *New Hampshire Gazette* in March 1763 demonstrates, many people were looking for ways to pay fewer taxes, not more. The writer, who called himself "Timothy Meanwell," acknowledged the necessity of taxes, "yet there is nothing against which, there is a more general, and louder clamor." One could hardly cross the street without hearing people complain about the increasing burden of taxes. Considering "how high taxes run at present ... and what an utter aversion people have to them," Meanwell offered a solution. Because a large part of a community's taxes went to pay the minister's salary, why not, Meanwell asked tongue-in-cheek, let communities vote whether to retain or dismiss their ministers? The outcome was hardly in doubt. Once the ministers were out of a job, they should be encouraged to open taverns, where they could preach to their customers as they served them liquor, thereby serving two functions simultaneously and costing the public nothing![37]

But the British government had to do something. Grenville realized he could generate some increase in revenue just by tightening up customs laws that were already on the books. Royal customs collectors were ordered to do their jobs (rather than sit back and accept bribes) and Royal Navy warships patrolling American waters were ordered to clamp down on smuggling. Ignoring the Molasses Act of 1733, colonists had routinely evaded the high rates the act had placed on the importation of sugar, rum, molasses, and other West Indian products to the North American colonies. To remove the incentive for this smuggling, Grenville recommended actually reducing the duty on foreign molasses, from 6 pence to 3 pence a gallon, a measure he believed would benefit both trade and the Treasury. He presented his recommendations to Parliament in March 1764. The resulting Sugar Act, however, caused consternation and protest in the colonies. Molasses is the key ingredient in rum and, Boston merchants declared, the act would "give a mortal Wound to the Trade of these Colonies." The assemblies of Massachusetts and Rhode Island protested immediately against enforcing the payment of even the much-reduced duties.[38] In seaports like New York, Philadelphia, and Boston, wartime prosperity had given way to postwar slump. British ministers might consider the tightening up of existing legislation and imposition of a few new taxes as sensible and equitable measures to help meet the financial costs of victory, but these measures struck a further blow to already ailing urban colonial economies. Laborers, artisans, and merchants in the colonies perceived the government as tightening the screws and being insensitive to their hardships.[39]

American colonists in 1763 took pride in being British but "their rights in relation to the mother country had never come up for close examination, and hence no one knew exactly what they were." They had not raised a constitutional challenge to Great Britain before, but the financial and imperial crisis of 1763 forced the question of "who had what rights and what authority."[40] Colonial assemblies had been created by royal and proprietary charters to rubber-stamp executive recommendations, but during the long struggles against France they had been left pretty much to their own devices and had acquired a fair amount of local autonomy. By 1763 they had evolved into "miniature parliaments, jealous of their privileges and immunities, proud of their power to initiate and pass legislation."[41] Colonists expected to share the rights and privileges of British subjects, including the right to resist taxation. The colonial assemblies in New York and Massachusetts denied the right of Parliament to tax Americans because they were not represented there. Parliament passed the Stamp Tax in 1765 in part to affirm its legislative supremacy over the colonies.[42] New taxes were bad enough, but a government that affirmed its right to impose taxes threatened to deprive Americans of their rights as British subjects. The issue of taxation became a question of the colonists' place in the imperial system. The new legislation generated protests, challenges to authority, and resistance in the streets. As tensions escalated and divisions widened, many Americans wished the clock could be turned back to the days before 1763, "a date," writes Simon Schama, "that began to assume scriptural significance as the first year of inequity.[43]

Governor Francis Barnard told the Massachusetts legislature in 1763: "That Enemy who hath so long stuck like a Thorn in the Sides of our Colonies is removed; and North-America is now become intirely [*sic*] British." He proclaimed December 8 a day of public thanksgiving to celebrate the birth of another son to the king and to thank God for the blessings of "that Peace which he hath been graciously pleased to grant unto us."[44] Two years later, the governor watched helplessly as an angry mob took to the streets of Boston in protest against the Stamp Act. They hanged the stamp officer in effigy and broke into his house, and they pelted the lieutenant governor and sheriff with stones. The governor ordered the colonel of the Regiment of Militia to beat an alarm, but the colonel replied that probably all the drummers were in the mob.[45] The costs of victory in 1763 had set Britons in America on the road to civil conflict and revolution.

THE PURPOSE OF THIS BOOK is not to retell the familiar story of the growing rift between Britain and the thirteen colonies, nor simply to narrate the events of just one year. Rather it surveys the enormous changes generated by the Peace of Paris and assesses their impact on many societies and countless lives in North America. Any given year will represent a snapshot of the triumphs and tragedies of the human condition. It is not unusual for a single year to be remembered for notable events or as marking the beginning of a new era. Some years—1492, 1776, 1863, 1917, 1945, 1968—stand out as pivotal, albeit for very different reasons.[46] 1763 was a year during which times turned, setting North America on a new course. More American territory changed hands at the Peace of Paris "than by any other international settlement before or since." To steal a phrase from nineteenth-century historian Francis Parkman, "half a continent ... changed hands at the scratch of a pen."[47] The Mississippi River had formerly run down the middle of French Louisiana and unified the colony; now it split the continent between Britain and Spain. Yet the Peace of Paris did more than shift cartographic boundaries; it set people and events in motion.

In 1763, flags were raised and lowered. There were celebrations of peace and outbreaks of war. Colonial officials of three European nations scrambled to adjust to new situations, to organize the migration and resettlement of their subjects, and to pursue effective relations with Indian nations. European migrations to North America and, within North America, to the backcountry, aggravated old tensions and generated new struggles—between settlers and colonial elites, between elites and the imperial government and, of course, between Indians and non-Indians. Traders pushed deep into Indian country to deal with new customers and tap new sources of furs; land speculators looked to Indian country to make new fortunes; Indians adjusted to new political and commercial conditions. In London and Madrid, imperial governments attempted to reorganize empires to reflect new realities; in North America, colonial governments confronted new imperial demands. Britons, French, Spaniards, and Indians migrated, to build new lives in new lands. In some places—Nova Scotia and Florida—the human geography of the region was largely remade. In others—Quebec and Louisiana—imperial and commercial takeover left regional culture and population largely intact.[48]

The year 1763 was ostensibly one of peace but for Indians and whites peace proved more elusive than ever. Indians and colonists had clashed in conflict virtually from first contact, but they also forged alliances and built patterns of coexistence. Such negotiated "middle grounds" were breaking down by the early 1760s. Political, social, and economic arrangements between Indians and European colonists, "painfully shaped by decades of contention and cooperation," were altered and rebuilt.[49] The fighting in the French and Indian War had been vicious and often intensely personal. Like King Philip's War in New England in 1675–76, the French and Indian War eroded possibilities of peaceful coexistence, left a bitter legacy, and assured a bloody future.[50] Despite efforts to preserve harmony, Indians and whites fell on each other with renewed fury in 1763 and the violence was increasingly racial. As European nations drew new boundaries in North America, Indians and whites built increasingly rigid, and increasingly bloody, ethnic and cultural boundaries between themselves. Indians went to war to try to rid Indian country of the British. The British government tried to clear Indian country of settlers. The Royal Proclamation of October 1763 recognized the need to separate Indians and whites. Few Indians and colonists disagreed with the principle, but they disagreed mightily about where the line of separation should be. Pennsylvania settlers calling themselves the Paxton Boys murdered pacifist, Christian Indians in an effort to purge the land of any Indians. Historian Daniel Richter sees two events of 1763—Pontiac's War and the Paxton Riots—as "parallel campaigns of ethnic cleansing." Not for the first time, but more than ever before, Indians and whites in 1763 killed people because their victims were, respectively, whites and Indians. Old hatreds crystallized "into explicit new doctrines of racial unity and racial antagonism" that shaped Indian-white relations for generations to come.[51]

Books about international peace settlements normally discuss tortuous negotiations, diplomatic maneuverings, and detailed terms. Accompanying maps illustrate changing political boundaries with shaded blocks of territory as if territories changed hands neatly in some kind of epic board game. This is not a book of diplomatic history. The Peace of Paris provides the context for the book but is not its subject. It is less concerned with changing colors on the map of North America than with the effects of changing circumstances on the various peoples living there and with how the events of 1763 radically altered the meaning of the Peace in North America. The book is less concerned with colonial administration than with colonial lives, as much concerned with individual experience as with imperial expansion: the events of 1763 mattered for the various peoples who inhabited North America as well as for the powers that exchanged territories at the peace settlement. It spends more time in Indian country than in colonial capitals, more time in Indian councils than in colonial assemblies, a focus that reflects American realities as well as the author's predilections: "Indian Measures for Some time Past have Engross'd all our Attentions in this Part of the World," Colonel William Eyre wrote from New York the following April.[52]

Historians have long recognized the significance of 1763 in setting America on a course to revolution a dozen years later, but they have often neglected actors and scenes that did not contribute directly to this central plot. America in 1763 was a crowded and often confused stage. The actors on stage did not have a script spelling out how the story would unfold, nor did they even have a clear view of everything that was going on. In time, the stage cleared, leaving key players with clearly defined roles, but that was long after 1763. Different people experienced the same events, the same year, in different ways. Three imperial powers responded to the dramatic realignments of 1763 in different ways, making the year a case study in comparative colonialism. Dissenting voices, unforeseen responses, racial conflicts, and human dislocations produced turmoil. Consequently, the book does not present a single narrative but rather multiple, often overlapping, narratives. The first chapter offers modern readers glimpses of what life was like in 1763 in America—its pace, character, concerns, and diversity—and introduces some of the central figures and places in the events of that year. Chapter 2 shows that although the Peace of Paris settled the Anglo-French contest for North America, contests for the land increased, as settlers and speculators cast covetous eyes on Indian homelands. Indian resistance exploded in Pontiac's War, which dominated the year from spring to fall, and Chapter 3 surveys the experiences of Indians, settlers, and soldiers in the war. As the war wound down, the British attempted to separate Indians and whites and define boundaries. Chapter 4 shows how the Royal Proclamation of October and the Treaty of Augusta in November attempted to control a volatile situation but ultimately widened the gulf between British officials and colonial Americans. The book then shifts attention in Chapter 5 to French America, first in Quebec, then in the Illinois country and the Mississippi Valley. Chapter 6 examines imperial and tribal adjustments in the lower Mississippi Valley and Louisiana, where several years passed before people felt the effects of the peace made in 1763. Some Frenchmen and some Indians lived their lives and went about their business with little change, but Spanish acquisition of Louisiana and British entry into the Mississippi Valley unsettled relations between colonists and colonial authorities, between colonists and Indians, and between Indians and Indians. The movement of Indian peoples and the movement of British settlers onto Indian land are recurrent themes in the book, but the final chapter deals with some of the other population movements that occurred as a result of the changes in French and Spanish North America. Spanish withdrawal from the Southeast opened the way for Anglo-American occupation and also for the expansion of African American slavery, while Spanish efforts to attract settlers to Louisiana prompted renewed movement by previously displaced French-speaking Acadians.

The year 1763, then, brought an end to an era of world war but initiated an era of upheaval that remade America. The epilogue looks ahead twenty years to another Treaty of Paris that shaped a very different American world from that delineated in 1763. The events of 1763 ensured that America would be English speaking, not French speaking, but they also divided the British Atlantic community and ensured that ultimately most of America would not be British. Redrawing the political map of North America in 1763 transformed the continent in ways the peacemakers and mapmakers could barely have imagined.

CHAPTER I

America and Americans
in 1763

EWS TRAVELED SLOWLY IN 1763. Communication occurred over months and weeks rather than in minutes and seconds. The express packet, which carried passengers and mail across the Atlantic, took about a month to travel from New York to Falmouth in England; the westward voyage, against the prevailing winds, usually took six to eight weeks. A copy of the definitive treaty of peace signed in Paris on February 10 did not reach the British commander-in-chief in North America, Jeffery Amherst, until May, arriving on a packet that had left Falmouth on March 27. In Charles Town, South Carolina, the Peace of Paris was proclaimed on August 25, six and a half months after it occurred.[1] Correspondence between Francis Fauquier, governor of Virginia, and Charles Wyndham, the Earl of Egremont, William Pitt's successor as Secretary of State for the Southern Department, illustrates the delays and uncertainties surrounding communication, even at the highest levels. On February 18, Egremont wrote a circular to colonial governors, informing them that the Peace of Paris, perhaps the most momentous event of their public lives, had been signed. Twenty-six days later, "the mail for North America not being yet dispatched," Egremont added a postscript. Governor Fauquier communicated the letter to the Virginia council on May 23. On August 16, Egremont wrote another circular, announcing the birth of Frederick Augustus, second son of King George III and Queen Charlotte. A week later, Egremont dropped dead "from an Apoplectick Fit," probably a massive heart attack. The news did not reach Virginia quickly. Three months later, Governor Fauquier was still writing to a dead man.[2]

Travel and trade between the cities and colonies of the seaboard was by river rather than by roads, which were few and poorly maintained. It would be another three years before a regular stagecoach line ran between New York and Philadelphia, a journey that took three days. Mail was carried by postriders who traveled not by a regular schedule but when they had enough mail to pay for the costs of the trip. News seeped slowly into the interior of America. It might take a year for Spaniards in New Mexico to hear about events in eastern Canada, and the news might reach them via Europe rather than being transmitted across the continent. Alternatively, officers at remote colonial outposts might hear news of events in Europe from passing Indians before they received word from their home government. "News flys swift among the Indians," said Charles-Philippe Aubry, the last acting governor of French Louisiana.[3]

Even though news unfolded at an eighteenth-century, not a twenty-first-century, pace and the impact of events was not always immediately apparent, people in 1763 understood that public events impinged on their private lives and that much changed that year. Although the first daily was not printed until 1784, there were newspapers—four in Massachusetts, four in Pennsylvania (two of them in German), three in New York, two in Rhode Island and Connecticut, and one each in New Hampshire, Maryland, Virginia, South Carolina, and Georgia—as well as pamphlets and broadsides.[4] Perennial shortages of paper meant that colonists often read their news on paper imported from England.[5] People who did not themselves read the newssheets often heard them read and discussed in taverns, where they drank prodigiously. There was plenty to toast in 1763, and plenty to talk about, and more in the years to come.

MOST AMERICANS IN 1763—Indians and Europeans—inhabited a world of villages rather than of empires and they thought locally rather than globally. The rhythms and rituals of planting and harvesting meant more to most people than did timetables for the transfer of territory. That is not to suggest they lived in idyllic rural communities unaware of their place in a larger world, only that communities were small by modern standards and paid most attention to the things that most immediately affected them. The regions people inhabited set them apart from and sometimes set them in tension with other regions, but their

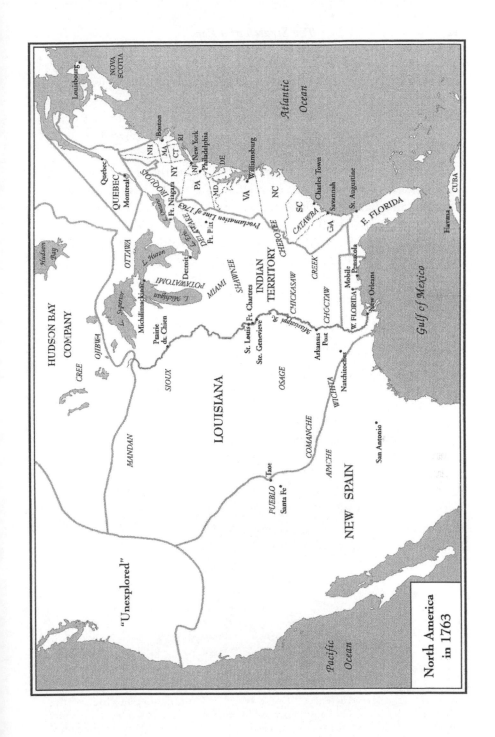

North America
in 1763

orbits overlapped and the lines between them proved porous and malleable. Coastal towns connected to the backcountry as well as to the Atlantic, and eastern elites experienced tensions with back-country settlers as well as with London. Backcountry communities connected to Indian country as well as to longer-settled regions further east and sometimes were in contest with both.

Many people were born, lived, and died in the same place, but America in 1763 was a world of movement, not of stasis. Emigrants from Europe landed in Philadelphia and other ports; migrants from coastal areas moved west. Some people moved back and forth between regions and some created their own borderland worlds in the interstices between regions. People traveled the Atlantic. Sailors carried news and ideas as well as goods across the ocean.[6] Fifty-seven-year-old

Atlantic Traveler: "Austenaco, Great Warrior, Commander-in-chief of the Cherokee Nation." This engraving of Ostenaco (d. ca. 1780) wearing court regalia while he was in London in 1762 appeared in two London magazines. National Anthropological Archives, Smithsonian Institution, Neg. 1063 G.

Benjamin Franklin had just come home after five years in London as agent for the Pennsylvania Assembly; he would return to London the next year and remain until 1775. (His wife Deborah stayed home—they spent eighteen of their forty-four married years apart). Also just back from a visit to England in 1762 was a delegation of three Cherokees—Ostenaco (also known as Judd's Friend), Oconostota, and Cunneshota or Standing Turkey—who had crossed the Atlantic with Lieutenant Henry Timberlake. They saw the sights and met the king, although they had to wait three weeks for an audience—Indian delegations were not *that* uncommon by 1762. Ostenaco, who was over sixty years old, also met the poet Oliver Goldsmith.[7] The Cherokee chief Attakullakulla, also known as Little Carpenter, had been on a

Atlantic Traveler: Portrait of Benjamin Franklin by Mason Chamberlin, 1762. Philadelphia Museum of Art. Gift of Mr. and Mrs. Wharton Sinkler, 1956.

similar delegation in the 1730s and was anxious to go again. "Every time I saw Attacullaculla," during the Augusta conference in 1763, said British Indian superintendent John Stuart, "he renewed his Applications" to go to England.[8]

Separated by time and distance, American communities in 1763 were nevertheless neither immune from change nor isolated from the outside world. When Thomas Morris traveled to the Wabash River on a peace mission in 1764, he was able to read "Anthony and Cleopatra" because an Indian gave him a volume of Shakespeare's plays in exchange for some gunpowder![9] Eastern cities were tied to Europe; Indian communities were linked to eastern cities. Gentlemen in Paris and London wore hats made of beaver pelts from the lands beyond Hudson Bay; Indians on the northern Plains carried guns from Birmingham. Slaves from West Africa labored in fields in West Florida wearing textiles from West Yorkshire. Products and profits, people and plagues, news and fashions traveled the shipping lanes and the traders' paths.

The people living in America in 1763 were a diverse lot. Even in the British colonies, English, Scots-Irish, Irish, Highland Scots, and Welsh settlers mingled with Palatine Germans, Dutch, Swedes, Finns, French Huguenots, and Jews as well as Indians, Africans, and British soldiers. Farther west, Spaniards and French mixed with numerous Indian tribes, many of whom British North Americans had never even heard of. Off the coasts of Alaska, Russians had begun trading with Aleutian Natives.

The population was tiny by modern standards. The number of people in the British colonies was growing dramatically—doubling every twenty-five years in fact—but it still stood at less than two million in 1763. Virginia, the largest colony, had almost 350,000 people; the capital at Williamsburg no more than 2,000 residents. Pennsylvania had about 300,000; Massachusetts about 250,000; New York about 100,000; Connecticut 145,000; Maryland about 164,000; New Hampshire perhaps 45,000; Georgia only about 11,300, 4,500 of whom were black slaves. The total number of Frenchmen scattered across the continent was about 80,000, the vast majority settled in the St. Lawrence Valley.[10] Indian populations were falling almost everywhere: European diseases and European disruptions did deadly work, and a population estimated at 4 or 5 million before 1492 was tumbling toward half a million by the end of the eighteenth century.[11]

Nevertheless, many Indian communities were as large as most non-Indian communities in North America.

America in 1763 looked very different to different people. The Peace made in Paris registered lightly at first in the daily lives of most Americans, but almost all were affected by it. Some individuals felt at once the impact of peace. For Robert Stewart, it was a disaster. He had been waiting in New York for a passage to England where he hoped to advance his case for military preferment "when the dire accots of the Cassation Thunder'd on my disconcerted Mind and at once annihilated my Plann and Blasted my well grounded hopes." Out of funds, he asked his friend George Washington to lend him £400, but Washington had troubles of his own and could not help him. Stewart's luck did not improve: "Fortune is not yet tir'd of persecuting me," he later whined to Washington.[12] Others took a broader, though not necessarily less self-interested, view of things. For instance, British commander-in-chief Sir Jeffery Amherst, British Indian superintendent Sir William Johnson, George Washington, the Delaware chief Teedyscung, the Ottawa war chief Pontiac, and Governor Jean-Jacques Blaise d'Abbadie of French Louisiana all understood what the Peace meant, might mean, or might be made to mean. But none of these individuals could have imagined how it would it all play out, and the events of 1763 affected each of them differently.

At the beginning of the year, General Jeffery Amherst was riding high on his victories as the conqueror of Canada but he was thinking of England. Amherst had entered the army in 1735, when he was eighteen, and had served in European campaigns in the 1740s. He commanded the army that captured Louisbourg in 1758; two years later he took Montreal. He was made a Knight of the Bath and feted as Britain's greatest general since Marlborough. The town of Amherst, Massachusetts, was named for him even before he became a lord. With France thoroughly defeated in North America, Amherst's work as commander-in-chief was largely administrative.[13] He was anxious to return home. Before the year was out he got his wish, but by the time he sailed for England Pontiac's warriors had tarnished his military record.

In the Mohawk Valley, the future looked good to Sir William Johnson in 1763. Having made his start as a trader, the Irishman had earned a baronetcy from a grateful king after his role in the victory over the French at the Battle of Lake George in 1744. His first wife,

Jeffery, First Lord Amherst (1717–1797). Engraving by J. Scott after Thomas
Gainsborough. Library and Archives Canada, E-002139935. Peter Winkworth
Collection of Canadiana.

his German housekeeper Catherine Weisenberg who had borne him
three children, had died in 1759, but Johnson barely mentioned her in
his extensive correspondence. He promptly took up with Molly Brant,
a Mohawk, and used his relations with Indian women to build connections in matrilineal Iroquois society.[14] Johnson lived like a marcher
lord where the British and Iroquois worlds met and merged, and he
played a pivotal role in British-Iroquois diplomacy. He dressed in the
style of a baronet when the occasion demanded; on other occasions he
dressed like a Mohawk, painted himself like a Mohawk warrior, danced
the war dance, and sang Indian war songs. The Mohawks called him
Warraghiyagey, "Doer of Great Things." According to governor of
New York Cadwallader Colden, "something in [Johnson's] natural
temper suited him to the Indian humour."[15] Johnson was constantly

surrounded by Indians but he was not becoming an Indian: aged forty-eight, he had his portrait painted in 1763 in the formal clothing and pose of a baronet. Confident of increased business and continued good fortune now that Britain was paramount in North America, he also set about building himself a grand new mansion.

George Washington on the other hand was struggling to make ends meet as a gentleman planter, growing tobacco in the depleted soils of his Mount Vernon plantation in Virginia. Like Amherst and Johnson, Washington too looked east and west, to London and to the backcountry. Having begun his career as a surveyor at seventeen, Washington knew good lands when he saw them, and he had seen them during his expeditions beyond the Appalachians. He escaped unharmed from the disastrous defeat of Braddock's army in 1755, and

Sir William Johnson (1715–1774) by Edward L. Mooney, 1838, after a lost portrait by Thomas McIlworth that was painted in 1763 to hang in Johnson Hall. Collection of the New-York Historical Society.

after resigning his commission in the Virginia militia, he had married a wealthy widow, Martha Dandridge Custis in 1759. Martha brought him land, property, and some 300 slaves (including a household servant called Ann Dandridge, who was Martha's half sister, the daughter of Martha's father and a part African, part Cherokee slave woman—such familial slavery was not uncommon in the slaveholding South). Martha also brought George two children (two others had died in infancy). Washington inherited one third of Daniel Parke Custis's rich estate and controlled the other two thirds as guardian of the children. But his wife could not provide him with the business acumen necessary to do well in Virginia's precarious tobacco economy. Tobacco was the colony's sole cash crop, and when prices collapsed after the war, Washington and other Chesapeake planters plunged into debt. Explaining to friend-in-need Robert Stewart in April why he could not lend him £400, Washington said he had found his estate in "terrible circumstances" when he returned from the war. He had had to buy provisions and stock, build buildings, and purchase additional land and slaves, all of which "swallowed up before I knew where I was, all the money I got by the Marriage, nay more, brought me in Debt." In fact, Washington was in debt to his London creditors to the tune of almost £2,000 in 1763. The Peace of Paris in February brought hopes for a change of fortune. The growing population of the colonies needed land in the West. Washington had his eyes on the rich lands of the Ohio Valley and the "the profits to be made from buying good land cheap."[16] Unfortunately, the Indians and the British government would both have something to say about that.

In Indian country, tribal leaders looked east with growing concern that the western ambitions of men like Washington might be realized. Teedyuscung, chief of the eastern Delawares, was a spent force by 1763. His wife had died the year before in an epidemic. All his life, it seemed, he had struggled to preserve Delaware lands and independence. He had protested against the infamous Walking Purchase in 1737 when Pennsylvania stripped his people of their lands in the Lehigh Valley; he had argued against Iroquois claims to speak for the Delawares in dealings with the British. He had a reputation for hard drinking and astute diplomacy. He had fought with the French in the early years of the war but had since made his peace with the British. Now he protested against the invasion of Delaware lands in the Wyoming Valley by settlers from Connecticut. It would be his last fight. But another Delaware, a prophet called Neolin, was preaching a vision of revitalization that required purging Indian country of white men and their ways.

Farther west, an Ottawa war chief named Pontiac would pick up Neolin's message and emerge as the man of the year, at least in the minds of many British officers and later historians. They gave his name to a conflict that was really a war of independence in which Indian peoples resisted the British Empire a dozen years before American colonists did.[17] Pontiac was clearly a remarkable man. Some sources portray him as "proud, vindictive, war-like, and easily offended."[18] Francis Parkman described him in language that revealed more about Parkman than Pontiac: "hideous in his war paint," "artful and treacherous, bold, fierce, ambitious, and revengeful," Pontiac was "the Satan of this forest." "He possessed commanding energy and force of mind, and in subtlety and craft could match the best of his wily race. But, though capable of acts of lofty magnanimity, he was a thorough savage, with a wider range of intellect than those around him, but sharing all of their passions and prejudices, their fierceness and treachery."[19] Irish trader and Indian agent George Croghan, who wasted few kind words on Indians, actually met Pontiac and left a more balanced description of him as "a shrewd sensible Indian of few words, & commands more respect amongst those Nations than any Indian I ever saw could do amongst his own Tribe." Lieutenant Alexander Fraser thought he was "the most sensible man among all the Nations and the most humane Indian I ever saw." An officer in the Black Watch described him as a genius, "a Man of uncommon Spirit, parts and Abilities," who led his people in a war for freedom.[20] General Thomas Gage despised Pontiac as a savage foe but grudgingly reported the assessment made by Governor d'Abbadie of Louisiana that he was "a person of extraordinary abilities." Pontiac kept two secretaries, "one to write for him, and the other to read the letters he receives; and he manages to keep each of them ignorant of what is translated by the other."[21]

Thirty-seven-year-old Jean-Jacques Blaise d'Abbadie arrived in Louisiana in June 1763 after several delays. He had been appointed to administer the colony eighteen months before but a British fleet had intercepted the convoy transporting him across the Atlantic and D'Abaddie and several other officers were detained in Barbados. (D'Abbadie must have thought this was becoming a habit: he had been taken prisoner by the British once before, in 1746, when the British navy captured the warship on which he was serving.) After his release, he returned to France and prepared for a second departure, only to be delayed again until the final Peace of Paris was signed in February 1763. When D'Abbadie finally arrived in Louisiana, as director-general, with broad powers as governor and chief administrator, his colony had already been ceded to Spain. He brought with him his wife and family (another son was born in spring 1764), and a personal library of more than three hundred books, which reflected his interests in history, natural history, geography, politics, philosophy, military science, geology, law, medicine, and folklore and included works by Rousseau, Montesquieu, Virgil, and Voltaire.[22]

Not all the people who looked east from Indian country in 1763 were Indians—captives, traders, and runaways sometimes found new lives in Indian communities—and not all Indians lived in Indian country. Indian people resided in colonial towns and seaports, worked in colonial households as indentured servants, and studied in colonial schools like the College of William and Mary in Williamsburg, Virginia, and Eleazar Wheelock's Indian School in Lebanon, Connecticut. European and colonial armies rarely brought back captives from their campaigns in Indian country—the lack of references to Indian prisoners in military reports is glaring—but some of the students in these colonial schools must have felt themselves captives just as much as did white captives in Indian country and ached to bolt for home. Some, like the Mohegan preacher Samson Occom, were embarking on a new life path dedicated to teaching and preaching to fellow Indians, but others balked. Jacob Woolley, a Delaware, signed a confession that summer, probably dictated by Wheelock, that he had "been scandalously guilty of several gross Breaches of the Law of God," particularly getting drunk, giving vent to fits of anger, and using "very vile & prophane Language, daring God Almighty to damn me." Jacob's cousin, eighteen- or nineteen-year-old Joseph Woolley, had struggled against a young man's temptations that spring. Had it not been for divine assistance, he wrote to Wheelock, "the Carnal effections, rising in my Heart were so strong, they almost overcome me." When a teenage Indian girl named Hannah Garret arrived at the school, Joseph began to court her; evidently unwilling to rely solely on divine assistance in such matters, Wheelock promptly dispatched Joseph to upstate New York to teach Mohawk children. Although Joseph proposed marriage, the couple never saw each other again; Joseph died of consumption a year later. Hannah subsequently married a Montauk student named David Fowler, although he was about fourteen years her senior. Mary Secutor, a Narragansett, arrived at Wheelock's school in December 1763. Like Hannah, she was thirteen or fourteen years old.[23]

Other Indian people lived and worked in colonial households. Margaret Van Cealan, "Daughter of Jannitye an Indian Squaw of full age" was an indentured servant in 1763. For "Sundry Good Causes & valuable Considerations" and "of her own free will & Accord," she "put herself Servant" to Abraham Wendell of Albany "To serve him His Exers. Administrators and Assigns all the Days of Her Natural Life." In the event she had any children, they too would serve Wendell "all the Days of Their Natural Life." In return, Wendell provided "Sufficient Meat Drink Washing Clothing, Lodging." Three years later, Wendell signed over the contract, and Margaret, to Sir William Johnson.[24]

Such experiences were common. When Samuel Moho, a Punkapoag Indian from Stoughton, Massachusetts, died, he left eleven children. Seven of them were small and "unable to provide for themselves," and all were "in a suffering Condition." The Massachusetts Legislature granted the tribe's guardians permission "to bind out to Service, all such Orphan Children, until they arrive at the Age of Twenty-one Years, as in the Case of poor white Children."[25] Indian slaves and servants were common in French and Spanish as well as British colonial settlements. Thousands of white people too were bound to servitude, particularly in the mid-Atlantic region.

Few people questioned such inequalities in the social order. "It was," as historian Jean Lee notes, "the only order they had ever known."[26] And of course there was slavery everywhere. "British America was the land of the unfree rather than of the free," writes historian Philip D. Morgan. The events of 1763 rippled through the lives of countless Americans but the lives of America's slaves went on as before. African slavery dwarfed other forms of servitude and was growing. One out of every five people in the British colonies was a slave, in an African population that was as ethnically mixed as that of the Europeans and the Indians, and was also divided between Creoles and people newly arrived from Africa.

They came primarily from the west coast of Africa—Senegambia, Sierra Leone, the Gold Coast, the Windward Coast, the Bight of Biafra, and Angola—although some came from as far away as Mozambique and Madagascar. Massachusetts held over 5,000 slaves; New York close to 15,000; South Carolina about 70,000 (where they constituted about 60 percent of the population), and Virginia a whopping 170,000. In the North, whether in towns or on farms, slaves tended to work alongside whites in a variety of tasks. In the Chesapeake region slaves worked in tobacco fields under the close supervision of white planters and in close proximity to the white population. In the Georgia and South Carolina low country, where they worked in gangs cultivating and harvesting rice, the growth of plantation slavery increasingly separated blacks and whites. African slaves constituted almost a third of the population of the French villages in the Illinois country in 1763; in French Louisiana, in the area from the mouth of the Mississippi to Pointe Coupe, there were 4,598 slaves and 3,654 free people. "Most eighteenth-century Americans did not find it an embarrassment or an evil," notes Morgan. "Rather, slavery was a fundamental, acceptable, thoroughly American institution." And, of course, it was an institution in which the bonds of common humanity were submerged by inhumanity.[27] "[Do] with the Wench the best you can," New York merchant John Watts wrote to a business associate in Virginia. "She is not as the New England Men say dreadful handsome, nor very young, yet I would be content to give for just such another harmless, stupid Being, that possesd only the quality she does of Cooking, a hundred pounds with great readiness."[28]

Slaves were bought and sold like cattle. August 25, 1763, was a special day for South Carolina merchant Henry Laurens: his son was born. But Laurens's correspondence that day was all business, more concerned with the cost of human labor than with the miracle of human birth. African slaves were bringing good prices in Charles Town, he wrote. "A Cargo of Angola's lately averaged £32 Sterling round & 50 prime Gold Coast Negroes bought in Antigua at £34 per head sold in one lot at £300 round." In fact, he wrote in the fall, "The Sale of Negroes has been beyond all former Years."[29] Laurens's correspondence reveals his attitudes toward and treatment of these people. One of the men, George, was "a Cunning, Quarelsome [*sic*], Young fellow," said Laurens. "You must be watchful & take him down early but dont drive him away." Another slave, "Rinah a Negro Wench big with child," was "a sullen Slut but easily kept down if you exert your Authority."[30]

Slave women had little or no protection against their white masters. White men who raped black women were rarely punished, unless a slave's owner sought damages against his property. But black men who forced themselves on white women unleashed deep-seated anxieties and attitudes about interracial sex, violence, and power, and could expect to be castrated or killed. A black slave who attempted to rape a white girl was hanged in New York in late 1763. The crowd that had gathered to watch the execution cut down the body and dragged it through the streets. The corpse was finally turned over to medical students of anatomy to be dismembered, fitting treatment, most people believed, for a black rapist.[31]

Most slaves suffered their lot most of the time, but others exploded in acts of violence, resisted in countless small ways, and, of course, ran away, sometimes more than once. Neptune, an African slave, spent much of 1763 on the run. When he ran away in March, his master, John Moody of Newmarket, New Hampshire, placed an advertisement for his return in the *New Hampshire Gazette*. New Hampshire was one of the few places where slavery was not on the increase and the *Gazette* carried nothing like the volume of runaway notices found in newspapers in Virginia, Carolina, and Pennsylvania; nevertheless, it published regular notices of runaway slaves alongside those for stolen horses, strayed pigs, and sales of land and livestock. Neptune, who could be identified by his broken jaw and a missing big toe (slaveholders sometimes amputated toes to discourage runaways from repeating escape attempts), evidently was caught, because he ran away again in May.[32]

Publications like the *Pennsylvania Gazette* carried regular advertisements for the capture and return of runaways. In June, John Waterman offered £5 for Joe, a twenty-eight-year-old slave "branded on the Right Breast I, and on the Left F." In September, Samuel Read offered 40 shillings for "a likely Negroe Man, named Peter, who ran away wearing a grey jacket, old coarse Trowsers, soaked with Apple-juice," and old shoes. "He is much given to laughing," the advertisement noted, "and has some Marks on his Back and Belly with the Horse-whip." Joe, a mulatto slave who ran away in November, was thought to be heading across the mountains to join the Indians.[33] Slaves who joined Indian communities—and there were many—raised the specter of united racial resistance to white domination. A Shenandoah Valley slave owner feared that Pontiac's War might produce a general insurrection because the Indians were "saving and Carressing" all the slaves they captured.[34] If so, it was one of the few occasions where groups came together in 1763; for the most part, events that year separated and divided people.

AMERICA IN 1763 was not a world of cities, but cities existed. Some colonial towns were expanding at a remarkable rate but American cities were "overgrown villages compared to the great urban centers of Europe, the middle East, and China," writes historian Gary Nash. In North America less than one person in twenty lived in a city (today, only about one in four do not). Colonial armies sometimes contained more people than colonial

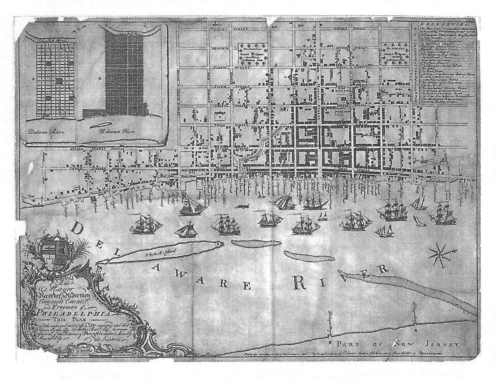

Plan of Philadelphia (of the improved part of the City...). Print map, 1762, surveyed and laid down by Nicholas Scull. Plan of Philadelphia, map #360, MG-11 Map Collection, Pennsylvania State Archives.

capitals. Nevertheless, cities were on the cutting edge of social, economic, and political change and "predicted the future" in their organization of work, time, and capital.[35]

The largest city north of Mexico in 1763 was Philadelphia. Described by a visitor as "one of the wonders of the world," it had about 23,000 people. New York was second with 18,000 or so (it caught up by 1775); Boston was third with around 16,000.[36] (By contrast, the Spanish silver mining town of Potosi in southern Bolivia had reached 150,000 in 1600, its numbers declining rapidly thereafter.)[37] While people concentrated in growing numbers in urban areas, they also gravitated to new geographic areas. Philadelphia had surpassed Boston because it looked west as well as east; it grew as people and goods moved through on their way to and from the growing settlements in the West.

Quebec, founded by Samuel de Champlain in 1608 at the mouth of the St. Lawrence (on the site of the Iroquoian town of Stadaconna), had been the French gateway to the continent. Wolfe's artillery had bombarded the city into ruins during the siege in 1759 and it was undergoing extensive reconstruction under British military rule in 1763. Its population, which had grown to 4,750 by 1744, slowed after the British capture. Not counting British soldiers, about 3,500 people lived in Quebec.[38]

Onondaga, the central council fire for the Six Nations of the Iroquois (the Mohawks, Oneidas, Onondagas, Cayugas, Senecas, and Tuscaroras) near present-day Syracuse in upper New York, had an estimated population of "150 men" in 1763, indicating a total population of perhaps 600–750 people. The Senecas at the western door of the Iroquois league, closer to Niagara, were far more numerous, with more than 1,000 men, perhaps 4,000 people, in about 20 villages, two of which were particularly anti-British. But Onondaga was the political nerve center of the Six Nations, "the place of congress for the Confederates," where delegates met to debate and reach consensus on confederacy business, and where the wampum belts, the records of the confederacy's diplomatic dealings with colonial powers and Indian nations, were kept. Like all Native peoples, the Iroquois had suffered catastrophic losses in the last hundred years: in 1763, the British estimated, the Six Nations could muster 2,230 men, suggesting that a total population of about 9,000 people inhabited its longhouses, but William Johnson said they were "vastly inferior in Number to what they were 50 Years ago." Yet they remained a potent force in the Northeast, and Onondaga's influence was felt from Canada to the Carolinas and from the Ohio Valley to London.[39]

The largest city in the southern colonies was Charles Town, South Carolina, a postwar boomtown. A visiting officer described it as a very pleasant place. "The Streets are Straight, broad and Airy, the Churches are handsome.... There is a Law against building houses of Wood, which like other Laws in other Countries no body observes." He estimated there were about 1,500 houses, but said they "increase annually in a very surprising manner." The streets were not paved (not until 1800): sand was more suitable for drainage and cleaning. In 1765 the population of Charles Town still numbered only about 5,000 whites, outnumbered by "great multitudes" of black slaves at a ratio of four to one, similar to the ratio throughout the colony. It was the major port of the South for shipping out cargoes of rice and indigo and Indian slaves bound for the Caribbean, and for shipping in cargoes of African slaves.[40]

Key to Charles Town's prosperity was the deerskin trade with the Indians of the Southeast, especially the Creeks and Cherokees. The Creeks of what is now Georgia and Alabama lived in more than fifty towns, divided into two geographical divisions, Upper and Lower Creeks. Towns were the centers of Creek life and exercised considerable autonomy, and the British dealt with town headmen, not with "tribal chiefs." The trading path that ran from Charles Town via Augusta entered Upper Creek country at Okfuskee on the Tallapoosa River, one of the largest and most important towns, with a population of 1,500 in 1763.[41] Cherokee population was falling in the 1760s, as it had throughout the century. (Smallpox was reported to have killed half the Cherokees in 1738, and it struck them again in the 1750s and 1760.)[42] Cherokee towns were declining in number, and relationships between towns were changing under the impact of British colonial contact. Chota, the capital of the Overhill Cherokees in the Little Tennessee and Tellico valleys, had grown to prominence in mid-century. Located at the terminus of a trade route from Charles Town and Savannah, it was well situated in the deerskin trade that was as crucial to the Cherokees as to the South Carolinians and it emerged as the political and diplomatic center in dealings with the colonists. It was also a ceremonial center, a "beloved town," where no blood was shed, and where emissaries came and went in peace. A map sketched by Lieutenant Henry Timberlake in 1762 credited Chota with 175 warriors, but his data may not have reflected recent losses occasioned by war and disease (Cherokee villages were burned by British troops in 1761 and raided by Indians from the north in 1763). British Indian Superintendent John Stuart said Chota had 100 warriors in 1764. The figures from Timberlake and Stuart suggest a population of somewhere between 400 and 700 in 1763. Cherokee population was clearly in serious decline: "Our women are breeding Children night and Day to increase our People," said Ostenaco in 1763.[43]

Britain's North American colonies were geographically dwarfed by Spain's American empire, which stretched from Tierra del Fuego to Florida. Founded in the 1560s, St. Augustine in Florida was the oldest European town in North America. At the beginning of 1763, about 3,000 Spaniards inhabited Florida, "and these were all such as were in the pay of the King of Spain, their wives, children and servants." Most lived in or around St. Augustine, in the shadow of the fortress of San Marcos, which dominated the town, and confined by the water, swamps, and Indians around it. According to one British officer, the town "has several good houses in it, the Streets are not ill laid out, but too narrow (a Spanish Mode)."[44]

More than a century and a half after the founding of Jamestown in Virginia, British settlement in North America remained confined east of the Appalachian Mountains. People referred to the interior of North America as the "backcountry," implying that they faced east to an Atlantic world, linked to Britain by trade, communication, and sentiment. "Backcountry" would not immediately give place to "frontier" but things would change in 1763, as more individuals looked west for their fortunes and futures, only to be held back by the government in London. Much of interior America was still "unknown" to Europeans. But Europeans were not unknown in much of interior America. The peoples living there felt the impact of their diseases, their animals, their religions, their wars, their alcohol, their trade goods, their ambitions, and their ideas.

The European communities that existed west of the Appalachians were French or Spanish, not British. Detroit had been transferred to Britain in 1760 when Major Robert Rogers took possession, and it was the center of British interests in the Great

Plan of Detroit by Lieutenant John Montresor in the fall of 1763. The plan shows the stockaded town, protected by outposts built the previous summer, and neighboring Indian villages. The farms of French *habitans* border the river. William L. Clements Library, University of Michigan.

Lakes and the Ohio Valley; but it was still essentially a French community. In the nineteenth century Detroit would be transformed into an industrial giant, but in 1763 it was still a fortified village. When Antoine de la Motte Cadillac founded Detroit in 1701, he had envisioned it as the Paris of the West, the center of a grand French empire built on Indian trade. Located on the water corridor connecting Lake Erie with lakes Huron and Michigan, it lay close to the Maumee-Wabash river system and the Indian peoples of Ohio, Michigan, and Indiana. It contained a garrison and a resident population of colonists, but like most French outposts in the West, depended for its defense on Indian allies outside its palisades rather than on the firepower within. By mid-century, Fort Detroit had a population of between 200 (in the winter) and 400 (in the summer), with another 500 people of French background living outside the fort.[45] In 1763, there were some seventy or eighty houses within the fort, arranged in regular streets. Outside the fort, the larger community was laid out in a pattern similar to that of French settlements along the St. Lawrence: individual cabins along the river, with "longlot" plots of farmland stretching back from the riverbanks. French-Canadian cottages dotted both sides of the river for about ten miles.[46]

There were several Indian villages in the vicinity. Across the river was a community of Hurons or Wyandots who, according to British records, had 250 men—more than 1,000 people in all. There was a Potawatomi village on the western shore, about a mile below the fort, and an Ottawa village a couple of miles higher up from the Wyandot village. The Ojibwas, Ottawas, and Potawatomis, loosely joined in the Three Fires confederacy, represented one of the heaviest concentrations of Indian population in the Great Lakes; the British placed their warrior count in the Detroit region in 1763 at 150 Potawatomis, 300 Ottawas, and 320 Ojibwas, indicating a total population of more than 3,000 people. The settlers lived on good terms with the Indians and many of the population were métis.[47]

St. Louis did not yet exist. There was no city at the junction of the Ohio, Missouri, and Illinois rivers. Only mounds and memories remained of the great Indian city that had flourished at Cahokia hundreds of years before. But if St. Louis was not yet born, it was, to use Jay Gitlin's phrase, conceived in 1763.[48] The trading post that was built there would grow into a fur mart that, like Cahokia, would become a major trade city in the heart of the continent.

Founded in 1718, New Orleans had been the southwestern portal of France's North American empire, as Quebec had been its northeastern portal, and like Quebec it commanded a key strategic location. The French engineer Adrien de Pauger had laid the city out in a classic eighteenth-century gridiron pattern, with a central square, church, and walls, but most of the buildings initially were simple wooden structures and the city hardly yet matched his vision. In 1763, the colonial population of the Lower Mississippi Valley numbered about 4,000 whites, 5,000 black slaves, and a few hundred Indian and mulatto slaves and free people of color, and the new colonial authorities in 1763 were anxious to encourage the immigration of settlers and slaves into the area. Meanwhile, the colonial populace lived alongside and traded with the many "petites nations," small tribes of Indian people who inhabited the region.[49]

Santa Fe had been founded in 1610, within a few years of Jamestown and Quebec. In 1680, in an unprecedented display of united tribal

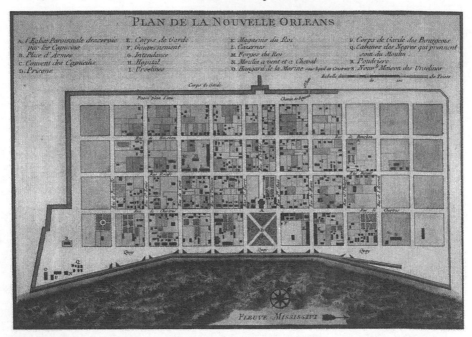

Plan de la Nouvelle Orleans (1764) by Jacques Nicolas Bellin. Courtesy of the Louisiana State Museum.

power, the Pueblo peoples of the Rio Grande Valley had besieged the town and expelled the Spaniards from New Mexico for a dozen years. Spain retook New Mexico in the 1690s, and since then Spaniards and Pueblos had favored coexistence over conflict, sometimes uniting against common threats from Apaches and growing Comanche power on the southern Great Plains. Visitors to modern-day Santa Fe are often attracted to its romantic heritage as the heart of the Spanish Southwest, but eighteenth-century visitors were not impressed by the appearance of the town, its location, or its garrison. Then, it was a remote northern outpost, separated from the power bases of Spain's American empire, which lay many miles and many months to the south. Santa Fe was the Spanish administrative capital in New Mexico, but the edicts of its governors carried little weight among the Apaches and Comanches, who held real power across much of the Southwest.

Two of the most important places in 1763 often do not feature on maps of the American colonies. Louisbourg on Cape Breton Island dominated the northern approach to North America. It overlooked the straits between Cape Breton Island and Newfoundland and commanded access to the offshore banks that teemed with codfish, a resource as valuable as any in America except the silver mines of Mexico. Havana dominated the southern approach to North America. Founded in 1519, Havana was "the Queen of the Indies." By the mid-eighteenth century, it was the third largest city in the Western hemisphere, the key to Spanish power in the Gulf of Mexico, and the central rendezvous for Spain's American fleets before they sailed across the Atlantic. Louisbourg and Havana both looked over important sea routes between Europe and America, afforded protection or access to the mainland, and were entrepôts for the exchange of resources. At the beginning of 1763 both were in British hands— Louisbourg captured in 1758, Havana in August 1762. But Spain dared not leave Havana in British hands and gave up Florida to get it back at the Peace of Paris.[50]

A map that pinpoints colonial towns obscures and distorts much of the reality and movement of America in 1763. Activity pulsed along trade networks as well as in towns and cities, and trade networks reached across Indian country as well as across the Atlantic. Philadelphia and Charles Town thrived because of wagon roads and trading paths to the hinterland as well as sea lanes across the Atlantic. Standing in Santa Fe or reading the records written there, one might see Comanches come and go but miss the action out on the southern plains, where Comanches operated a flourishing pastoral economy and long-distance trade network based on horses and buffalos. On the upper Missouri River, the Mandan villages sometimes bustled like Boston. When Lewis and Clark wintered there in 1804–05, about 4,500 Mandans inhabited a couple of villages. In 1763, before they had been depleted by epidemics and the attacks of westward-moving Sioux, they were far more numerous and lived in more villages. To Europeans, the Mandan villages represented the limit of exploration and knowledge; but they were central not remote, a trade rendezvous where people from the Plains came to exchange horses, buffalo robes, and meat for corn, beans, squash, and, increasingly as the century wore on, firearms. The pivotal location of their villages placed the Mandans in the direct path of the epidemics that coursed through Indian country.[51]

WITHIN NORTH AMERICA's Indian and European villages, people saw the world through different eyes, explained it in different ways, and performed different rituals to keep it in balance. But they shared common concerns. Family was more important than empire, prayer more important than political power, weather more important than world news. People worried about crops and children, animals and food, and always, about sickness and health. "My dear child continues to recover," Colonel James Gordon wrote in his journal. It was January 1, 1763, a Saturday. "As we begin the New Year, O Lord, enable us to begin new lives so that all we do may be to the glory of God & the good of mankind." Gordon had good reason to be thankful for his daughter Nancy's recovery; another daughter, Sally, had become ill and died in the summer—"our dear child left us," read the journal entry. Gordon was a wealthy merchant and slave owner in Lancaster County, Virginia. He kept a daily journal in which he recorded domestic concerns, business affairs, goings-on at church and sermons, and noteworthy events in the neighborhood (such as when a neighbor "ran away last week, & took a young woman with him, & left his wife"). But no subject received more attention in Gordon's journal than sickness and health, and death. Gordon grieved for lost children, worried about his wife's health, his family's health, his own health, and his slaves' health. He prayed for friends and neighbors in sickness, and his wife visited and sat with the afflicted. When they died, he asked God for strength in meeting his own death; when they recovered he gave thanks: "Blessed be the Lord," he wrote when Scipio, a slave, pulled out of danger in March.[52] Fellow Virginia planter Landon Carter ended the year complaining in his diary about his health: a severe cough and excruciating rheumatic pain reduced him to a walking corpse, he said.[53]

To an extent almost impossible to imagine today, Americans in 1763 lived always in the shadow and presence of death. Death was not yet romanticized as it would be in the nineteenth century, nor sanitized as it would be in the twentieth century. It occurred often in public, surrounded by family and friends, and accompanied by communal rituals of grief, but it often received terse mention in private journals and correspondence. Parents frequently recorded the death of a child—a routine tragedy in the eighteenth century—but rarely did they record how they coped with the nightmare. They looked to their religion for strength.[54]

In the same month the Peace was signed in Paris, Sarah Gilman lay awake one Sabbath night, listening to her mother cough so hard she seemed likely to choke to death. It was a night of terror but, Sarah wrote in her diary, "God was Gracious and saved her from Sudden Death."[55] The brief and sporadic entries in the diary of Mary Holyoke of Salem, Massachusetts, record visiting and drinking tea with friends and relatives, sowing and preparing vegetables as well as events of local interest and news of births, marriages, and deaths. Consecutive entries in the fall of 1763 mention a child sick with the mumps, a marriage, a fatal shooting, and the purchase of a pair of new shoes. Sickness and death were never far away. Mary's two-year-old daughter Polly went to school in April and first went to meeting in May, but the next January, the following is recorded in the diary:

9. My Daughter Polly first confined with the quincy. Took a vomit....
13. My Dear Polly Died. Sister Prissy came.
14. Buried.
17. Small Pox began to spread at Boston.[56]

In August 1763, Sarah Ogden sat down to write a short letter, filled with the kind of news most families were anxious to hear:

Dear Uncle and Aunt
By reason of your long absence from us, I have undertaken to write to you, to let you know that we are in a state of health at present, though we have had sickness and misfortune in our family. Last March, *Brother Jonathan* had his thigh broken, and it was not set right and he is something lame. In April *Sister Phoebe* was brought near death but through the goodness of God to us she recovered. *Uncle Jonathan's* and *Uncle Elishelets* [?] families are in health at present, *Uncle Brown* was seized with the numb palsy and hath had five or six fits but keeps about house. *Aunt* is better this summer than she was last. *Grandfather* is worse this summer and we don't expect his continuance long, he is confined to his bed and hath a fever.
Dear Uncle and Aunt I desire to be excused for not writing a better hand, I add no more,

But remain your Affectionate Cousin
Sarah Ogden[57]

Standards of hygiene, knowledge of diseases, and precautions against infection were limited. To illustrate the state of medical knowledge, there were no medical schools in North America in 1763: the College of Philadelphia (later the University of Pennsylvania) opened the first one two years later. Diseases spread virtually unchecked, as traders, settlers, soldiers, and Indians moved through the country, and sailors, slaves, and emigrants moved across the Atlantic. Philadelphia, a major port of entry for immigrants, was a hazardous place to live. The city suffered a large-scale epidemic of throat distemper—diphtheria or scarlet fever—in 1763, the first major outbreak since before the war. The eminent physician Benjamin Rush said it carried off many children that winter. Smallpox hit Philadelphia as it did other places in 1763. At least 1,095 people died in Philadelphia in that year, about 5 percent of the population. Yet even in a year of high mortality like 1763, birth rates exceeded death rates in Philadelphia.[58]

In North America, 1763 was a smallpox year. There were cases in Charles Town at the beginning of the year, causing some people to flee from the city and others to avoid coming to it. One of Henry Laurens's slaves was infected "to the great danger of my own Interest & the terrour of all the neighbourhood."[59] The presence of smallpox at Charles Town explained in part why the meeting leading to the treaty with the Southern Indian nations in 1763 was held instead at Augusta, Georgia, "a Country Village 150 Miles from Savannah."[60] Georgia moved quickly to impose quarantines on "Ships and other Vessels coming from Places infected with Epidemical Distempers," especially from South Carolina.[61] In February, twenty-year-old Thomas Jefferson postponed a trip to Williamsburg because the smallpox was in town. (Jefferson had enrolled in the College of William and Mary in 1760 and was now studying for the bar. His father had died six years before, leaving him 5,000 acres and the slaves to work them.)[62]

The Marquis de Frémeur, commander of all Louisiana troops and militia and a member of the Superior Council, "was attacked by the most acute and the most dangerous smallpox" in October, just three days before he was due to leave the province. "He is in the most critical condition at the present time," wrote Governor Louis Belouart de Kerlérec, "and if he recovers from it, there is every reason to fear that he will lose the sight of one eye, which is in the most deplorable condition."[63] In November, smallpox had spread to Fort Augusta in Pennsylvania. Colonel James Burd reported that many of his garrison had never had the disease, "so I expect they will be infected." He had no medicine, and even though the Pennsylvania commissioners agreed to send up medicines and blankets, he doubted they would arrive before winter closed the river. "[T]herefore," concluded Burd, "Nature must do the Whole."[64] There was little to do but pray. Elsewhere, Mary Cross lost her father in December: "he was taken Saturday morning the 10TH of this month with a vomiting and fever following, and died the 12TH. Sudden and awful is the change, God grant that it may be a warning to us all, to be ready to meet death with the same composure as he did." The family feared it was smallpox, "for the day he died he broke out in spots all over of a purple color, but never above the skin, but we cannot be certain till the time expires which we shall all have it." Mary asked her uncle to pray for them "that we may be supported under this severe trial and fitted for what event is before us."[65]

Smallpox arrived in Boston in December, evidently on board a ship from Newfoundland that had lost one of its crew to the disease en route. One hundred seventy people died in Boston. The outbreak revived the debate about inoculation but by the turn of the year, Bostonians were being inoculated. In January, the legislature, the General Court of Massachusetts, moved across the Charles River to Cambridge for safety. They had been sitting in Harvard Hall for less than a week when it burned down in the middle of a nocturnal snowstorm.[66]

The smallpox epidemic spread to Indian country, whether by accident or design. It was a regular visitor there. Since the Native Americans' first contacts with European diseases, Old World epidemics had torn through Indian populations that lacked the levels of immunity Europeans had built up over generations of familiarity with the diseases. The 1763 smallpox outbreak in Indian country does not appear to have reached the pandemic proportions of some earlier and later epidemics, but diseases were nonetheless commonplace and widespread. The movement of troops during the Seven Years' War and of refugees after the war provided prime conditions for contagion. In the Great Lakes and the Ohio Valley, Indian peoples died of influenza in 1761, typhus in 1762, smallpox in 1763–64, and another, unidentified disease in 1764. In August 1763, an Indian woman on the island of Nantucket fell ill after washing the clothes of some sick sailors. She suffered "much pain, a high fever & then soon appear[ed] yellow" and died in a few days. The disease, likely yellow fever, killed 222 people (62 percent of the island's Indian population) in six months.[67]

The presence of the British army introduced "a new disease factor" into Indian country as soldiers recruited from the crowded slums of Britain—or transferred from service in the Caribbean—brought a variety of deadly diseases. Those regiments unfortunate enough to be posted to Cuba were especially hard-hit. No sooner had the British captured Havana than yellow fever broke out. Of the 5,366 British soldiers who died at Havana, 4,708 died of disease. Among the British sailors, only 68 died in combat, but more than 1,200 died of disease, and another 3,300 fell ill. "May my country never be cursed with such another conquest," wrote Dr. Johnson.[68] In retrospect, he might have said as much about Britain's victory in North America.

CHAPTER 2

Contested Lands

*W*HEN GEORGE III AND HIS MINISTERS surveyed what they had won in North America, the possibilities for expansion and commerce seemed limitless. The fur trade, formerly almost entirely in French hands except in the territories draining into Hudson Bay, was now almost entirely British, as were the rich fisheries of the Gulf of the St. Lawrence.

> Another Advantage attending the late Treaty is the secure settling of the whole Coast of North America, as it's [*sic*] produce may invite, or Convenience for Settlement may offer, from the Mouth of the Mississippi to the Boundaries of the Hudson's Bay Settlements, with the whole Variety of Produce which is capable of being raised in that immense tract of Sea Coast, either by the Industry of Emigrants from Europe, or from the Overflowing of Your Majesty's ancient Colonies.

There would be vast supplies of timber to furnish the Royal Navy with masts and stores; cotton and indigo from Georgia and the Floridas; rum, sugar, and coffee from the newly acquired islands in the West Indies, and unprecedented opportunities for commerce, navigation, prosperity, and power.[1] Hemmed in for decades by the threat of French and Indian dominance in the West, Anglo-Americans looked forward to seizing the fruits of their victory. Unfortunately, the end of the Anglo-French contest for North American dominion did not end the contest for North American land. In fact, it intensified the competition. As the year began, Indian peoples complained about the presence of British garrisons and braced for an invasion of their homelands, settlers pushed into Indian country, and speculators rubbed their hands in anticipation of the profits to be made from buying and selling Indian lands. The British government had plans to regulate and limit contests for lands but the scope and intensity of the contests defied regulation.

LAND AND FREEDOM IN INDIAN COUNTRY

For Indians the so-called French and Indian War was about Indian lands. "They have repeatedly said at several conferences in my presence," Sir William Johnson wrote to the Lords of Trade in November 1763, "that 'they were amused by both parties with stories of their upright intentions, and that they made War for the protection of the Indians rights, but that they plainly found, it was carried on, to see who would become masters of what was the property of neither the one nor the other.'"[2]

Indian communities had felt the reverberations of the global conflict between France and England. People debated the war in Onondaga and Chota as well as in Paris and London. Wampum belts and speeches circulated throughout Indian country, summoning warriors to come to the aid of their French or English father, warning chiefs not to trust French or English emissaries who would lead them to destruction, and promising good or hard times in the event of a French or English victory. Europeans gave war chiefs medals and support, undermining traditional systems of shared power and consensus politics. Warriors traveled hundreds of miles to fight alongside and against European regulars and colonial militia, and clashed with other Indians. Colonial armies trudged through Indian country, fought battles there, built and besieged forts there, and destroyed Indian villages. Indian communities lived on a war footing. As war disrupted normal economic patterns, Indian communities relied on allies to provide them with food, clothing, and gunpowder; then Europeans cut back on supplies when Indian allies were no longer needed. In 1763, Indians who had been accustomed to receiving goods and gifts from the French now had to look to the British, but cost-conscious British officials and profit-minded British traders were not in a generous mood.

Indians who fought in the war had sided mainly with the French, sometimes with the British, sometimes with one then the other. Hundreds of Indians from the Great Lakes—Ottawas, Menominees,

Ojibwas, Missisaugas, Potawatomis, Winnebagos, Sauks and Foxes—
fought alongside the French, who also drew recruits from mission
communities in eastern Canada—Iroquois, Hurons, Algonkins,
Nipissings, Abenakis.[3] Western Delawares, Shawnees, and others in
the Ohio country sided with France as the best hope of preserving
their lands from English invasion, although eastern Delawares and
other Indians along the Susquehanna Valley tried to remain neutral.
Mohawks from eastern New York and Mohegans and Mahicans from
New England fought with the British.

Despite their council fire rhetoric of kinship and affection for their
European "fathers" and "brothers," Indians fought not out of love for
the French or the British but in a consistent effort to keep their
country independent of either. Tanaghrisson, the Seneca "half king"
(a delegate from Onondaga to the tribes in the Ohio country), told the
French at the start of the war: "Fathers, both you and the English
are white, we live in a Country between; therefore the Land belongs
to neither one nor t'other: But the Great Being above allow'd it to be
a Place of Residence for us; . . . I am not afraid to discharge you off this
Land."[4] The "country between" was Indian land, off limits to English

A Great Lakes Indian family in the 1760s. This engraving of "A Man and Woman of the
Ottigaumies" appeared in Jonathan Carver, *Travels through the Interior Parts of North-
America in the years 1766, 1767, and 1768* (London, 1788). The Ottigaumies were the
Mesquakie or Fox Indians. Dartmouth College Library, Rauner Special Collections.

and French alike, except for purposes of trade. Many of the Indian people inhabiting the Ohio Valley had already lost homelands; they were not about to let it happen again. They attempted to "hold the scales & direct the Ballance" between competing French and English power, and backed the ally most likely to help them secure their goal.[5]

Indians, explained New York's Indian secretary, Peter Wraxall, saw the Anglo-French struggle as "selfish Ambition in us both" and feared "that which ever Nation gains their Point will become their Masters not their deliverers." Dr. Samuel Johnson likened the contest for America to "the quarrel of two robbers for the spoils of a passenger, ... each is endeavoring the destruction of the other with the help of the Indians, whose interest is that both should be destroyed."[6] Captain Pierre Pouchot, the French commander at Fort Niagara, said Indians thought it "very strange that others should fight for a country where the author of life has, in their view, created them, where they have always lived & of which the bones of their ancestors have had possession from the beginning of time. They are unwilling to recognize any foreigner as their master, just as they have none among themselves."[7]

Indians wanted to see neither European power victorious if the victors intended to stay. "Why don't you & the French fight in the old country and on the sea?" Delawares asked Christian Frederick Post. "Why do you come to fight on our land? This makes everybody believe you want only to take & settle the Land." They believed the English and French had "contrived the war" and intended "to kill all the Indians and then divide the land among themselves."[8]

Even before the war ended, many Indians resented the increase in British power and the decline of French support. Sir William Johnson believed they would have "protracted it in order to preserve the balance of power."[9] Johnson's deputy, George Croghan, said much the same thing: The Indians used to regard the British as "a Counterpoize" to the power of the French, but since the conquest of Canada "they consider us in a very different and less favorable light, as they are now become exceeding jealous of our growing power in that Country." Indians had "the highest notions of Liberty of any people on Earth" and "will never Consider Consequences when they think their Liberty likely to be invaded, tho' it may End in their Ruin."[10]

Nevertheless, Indian people had to learn to deal with the British empire. After debilitating wars and recurrent bouts of disease had sent

Iroquois numbers plummeting at the end of the seventeenth century, confederacy leaders had charted a new course: in 1701 they made peace with the French and their Indian allies and adopted a position of formal neutrality in the Anglo-French wars for North America. Neutrality was never total—Mohawks generally supported the British and Senecas sometimes sided with the French—but the strategy allowed the Iroquois to recoup some of their population and to hold the balance of power in the Northeast.[11] Now, with the French gone, the Iroquois could no longer play imperial rivals against each other. As events spiraled out of their control in 1763, they also struggled to exert their influence with the western Indians, and many Senecas followed a separate course from the rest of the confederacy.

Abenakis in southern Quebec and northern New England found that once-effective strategies of survival now worked against them. As English pressures on their homelands increased in the first half of the century, Abenakis had responded with strategies of calculated withdrawal, following traditional patterns of seasonal movement and serial exploitation of resources. Accustomed to vacating their villages during spring fishing and fall hunting, they found it a relatively simple matter to evacuate when English troops threatened and to return and rebuild their burned lodges once the enemy had departed. After the war, Abenakis filtered back to their homelands as usual, but now they encountered English families farming their lands, not English soldiers leaving them. The newcomers were here to stay, and they kept coming. They occupied the best land, claimed ownership according to English notions of property, felled trees and inflicted extensive environmental degradation. British authorities became alarmed that deforestation in Abenaki country posed a threat to the Royal Navy's timber supplies for masts. Many Abenaki people recoiled from the new settlements in their river valleys and moved to the margins of their homelands. At Odanak, or St. Francis, in Quebec, Abenakis who had regularly furnished warriors for French raiding parties against New England (and whose village Robert Rogers's Rangers had burned in 1759) now had to deal with British authority and British soldiers.[12]

In Nova Scotia, Mi'kmaq Indians who had experienced violent encounters with the English throughout the eighteenth century made peace with the British by 1762. But after St. Pierre and Miquelon were restored to France in 1763 some migrated eastward to the islands where they could retain contact with French-speaking colonists.

Hundreds more migrated to the coast of Newfoundland, where they could live independent of British colonial control and distant from British settlements.[13]

Almost everywhere, it seemed, peace brought British soldiers, settlers, and domesticated animals onto Indian lands: "they are greatly disgusted at the great Thirst which we all seem to shew for their Lands," said Sir William Johnson in October 1762, and things got worse in 1763.[14] Indians struggled to protect their autonomy and their lands in peacetime as much as they had in wartime.

On the east coast, Indian communities that had contended with colonial encroachment for generations raised their voices in renewed protest in 1763. Indians from the mission town of Stockbridge in Massachusetts, whose young men had served the British in war, complained to Sir William Johnson and to the General Court in Boston as their colonial neighbors nibbled away at their land.[15] Indians on Long Island petitioned Cadwallader Colden, lieutenant governor of New York, requesting that lands around Indian Neck and Southeast Harbor in Southhold be restored to them, based on a land grant dating back to 1685. Colden and his council determined the Indians had a valid claim and instructed the attorney general in Southold to commence suit for the recovery of lands in question, but the towns-people disputed the claim. The attorney general dragged his feet, offered counterarguments, and replied that the decision was too diffi-cult to enforce.[16]

The Wampanoag community at Mashpee on Cape Cod, about 250 people living in "about 60 wigwams and 6 houses," on the other hand, won a victory in 1763. It culminated a long struggle against the system of overseers Massachusetts had established in 1746, whereby appointed guardians had the authority to lease the Indians' lands. After protesting in vain to the General Court of Massachusetts, the Mashpees appealed directly to the King of England. In 1760 they sent Reuben Cognehew, their schoolmaster, to London. Cognehew had quite a journey. The master of the ship he boarded pretended to be sailing for England but headed instead for the West Indies, intending to sell Cognehew into slavery. Fortunately, said Cognehew, the "Almighty was pleased to frustrate his wicked designs" and caused the vessel to be shipwrecked. Rescued by a British man-of-war, Cognehew and the crew were impressed into service in the Royal Navy at Jamaica. But Cognehew somehow persuaded the admiral of the fleet to provide him with passage to England. After such an odyssey, Cognehew must have found it a piece of cake to plead the Mashpee case to a government that was already leaning toward tightening control over its colonies. The Crown ordered an investigation and in June 1763 Massachusetts incorporated Mashpee as a self-governing district. The Indians of Mashpee were able to manage their own resources, hold annual meetings, and elect some of their officers. Massachusetts repealed the law and restored the guardian system after the Revolution, but the Mashpees were not finished. In 1833 they staged a bloodless little revolt of their own and won back a measure of self-government.[17]

Land sales were peculiarly divisive among the Narragansetts of Rhode Island in 1763. Four years earlier their sachem, Thomas Ninigret, had persuaded the Rhode Island General Assembly to repeal all laws limiting the sale of reservation lands and proceeded to sell lands to pay his personal debts, which were substantial. Other Narragansetts petitioned the assembly to prevent Ninigret from selling any more land without the joint consent of both the tribe and the assembly. In 1763, in an attempt to reach a compromise between the opposing factions, the General Assembly appointed a committee to determine which areas of land were used by the sachem and which areas by the tribe as a whole, and to issue deeds to tribal members for the land they claimed. But the committee was unable to complete its task. The frustrated Narragansetts retained a lawyer and sent delegates to Sir William Johnson, superintendent of Indian Affairs, asking for justice. Johnson ducked the issue, saying the Narragansetts fell under the authority of a colonial government, and the government of Rhode Island refused to curb Ninigret's land sales. After Ninigret's opponents tried and failed to depose him in 1766, two Narragansetts, Tobias and John Shattuck, Jr., followed Cognehew's example and sailed to England, in the hope of enlisting the sympathy and support of the King. Their voyage was less eventful than Cognehew's but also less successful. Tobias died of smallpox in Edinburgh in 1768 and no one intervened on behalf of the Narragansetts. After Ninigret died in 1769 the Rhode Island General Assembly continued to sell Narragansett property until all his debts were paid.[18]

Iroquois and Delawares watched with growing alarm as settlers from Connecticut pushed into the Susquehanna Valley. The Susquehanna Company, a joint-stock company formed in 1753 by Connecticut land speculators, believed that Connecticut's colonial charter, which granted sea-to-sea land rights, entitled the province to the Susquehanna Valley (a position that produced controversy with Pennsylvania). The eastern Delaware chief, Teedyuscung, had led attacks on English settlers in the Wyoming Valley along the Susquehanna in the early years of the war. After coming to terms with the British, he tried to protect the Wyoming Valley from his new allies. He declared "that he did not unders[tan]d what the White People meant by settling in their Country unless they intended to steal it from them." In November 1762 he traveled to Philadelphia to complain in person to the governor, and he also warned off settlers and speculators whom he found on the land. In January 1763, Lord Egremont informed the governor of Connecticut of the king's concern that the settlers seemed intent on proceeding with a project which was likely to provoke "all the horrors and Calamities of an Indian war," the very thing His Majesty was trying to prevent. Governor Fitch and General Amherst issued orders to desist but the Susquehanna Company "were Determined to Settle Immediately on the Land, to the Amount of a Thousand families and Upwards." In April, the Iroquois met in general council at Onondaga, "much alarmed at the proposed settlement." William Johnson warned it would have "fatal consequences" if it went ahead.[19] He was right.

On April 19, as Teedyuscung lay sleeping in the town of Wyoming on the north branch of the Susquehanna (near present-day Wilkes-Barre), someone set his log cabin on fire. The sixty-three-year-old chief, veteran of many battles and treaties, burned to death. Some say he was in a drunken sleep—Teedyuscung was known for his hard drinking—and some tried to pin the blame on the Iroquois, although they had little reason to rid themselves of an ally in the struggle to preserve the Susquehanna. The culprits were more likely agents of the Susquehanna Company. The whole town, about twenty homes, burned. Its inhabitants, many of them refugees from broken communities elsewhere, became refugees again. Within weeks, settlers from New England, most of them people Teedyuscung had chased away the previous fall, were building cabins and planting fields in the Wyoming Valley. Teedyuscung's son, Captain Bull, went to Philadelphia to protest. Six Nations delegates took their complaints to Hartford, where they addressed the Connecticut Assembly with "all the Dignity of Indian oratory," according to Ezra Siles. "Brothers, We have heard very grevious News this Winter," they said; "that you were about to come with Three hundred families to settle on our Lands, which was very astonishing to Us." They knew nothing of having sold land and they had no intention of doing so. How would you like it, they asked, to have your lands stolen from you? The assembly gave them reassurances but could not speak for the Susquehanna Company. Then, late in the summer, drunken Pennsylvania militiamen murdered Captain Bull's cousin, a baptized Delaware named Zacharias, together with his wife and child. Six months after Teedyuscung's death, Captain Bull led a Delaware war party against the Wyoming settlers, killing twenty-six people and exacting grisly revenge for his father's murder.[20]

British forts on Indian lands were a source of particular anger. These forts, most of them constructed by the French, were occupied by British troops before peace was made in 1763. Between 1759 and 1761 the British erected a fortress on the site where Fort Duquesne had stood and named it Fort Pitt after their wartime prime minister. Even though a flood caused part of the ramparts to fall into the ditch, Fort Pitt was far more formidable than Fort Duquesne had been, an imposing symbol of imperial presence and a threat to Indian independence.[21] Fort Pitt and Fort Augusta at Shamokin (later Sunbury, Pennsylvania) were "the greatest Eye sore to all the Inds. in them parts."[22] The British army built or reoccupied a dozen more forts. Now that the war was over, Indians wondered what was the purpose of the forts? The Six Nations had given permission for small forts to be erected in their country on condition that they be demolished at the war's end. That had not happened. "[I]nstead of restoring to us our lands, we See You in possession of them, & building more Forts in many parts of our Country, notwithstanding the French are dead," Indians complained. They saw "in every little garrison the germ of a future colony."[23] The British did not yet appreciate what the French had long understood: that small outposts were untenable unless their garrisons were on good terms with the surrounding Indians.

Three days after Fort Duquesne fell in 1758, the Delaware chief Tamaqua (Beaver) had advised General Forbes "in a most soft, loving and friendly manner, to go back over the mountains and stay there." Another was more blunt and warned that if the British settled west of the mountains, "all the nations would be against them." It would, he said "be a great war, and never come to peace again."[24] Almost with his dying breath, Forbes had warned Amherst that preserving the West depended on preserving the Indians' allegiance: "I beg ... that you will not think trifflingly [*sic*] of the Indians or their friendship," he wrote.[25] But preserving Indian friendship required safeguarding Indian lands, and the road Forbes cut to Fort Duquesne opened the Ohio country to British settlement. British assurances that they had no designs on Indian lands rang hollow in Indian ears. Six Nations, Shawnees, and Delawares regarded British occupation of forts as a tactic to take their lands and reduce them to slavery.[26]

Indians used the language of slavery regularly to describe the prospect of life under British domination. It was a condition they could not accept. In the spring of 1763 Major Henry Gladwin at Detroit tried an Indian slave woman as an accomplice in the murder of an English trader, and found her guilty. He had her hanged "in the most publick manner," an act that, historian Gregory Dowd points out, stood as a stark image of what British domination could mean for Indian people. If the execution was intended to deter Indians from further violence, it seems to have had the opposite effect. Gladwin feared the lifeless body hanging from his gibbet affected "the Temper of the Indians."[27] Indians around Detroit said "they had better Attempt Something now, to Recover their Liberty, than Wait til We were better Established."[28] Two weeks after the hanging, Indian warriors attacked Detroit.

EMIGRANTS AND SETTLERS

"The back parts of this province will soon be better settled than ever," announced a South Carolina newspaper in January 1763; an "abundance of people" was "coming daily from the Northward" and they intended to apply for land grants and settle there.[29] Up until the end of the seventeenth century, the British had feared for the survival of their infant American colonies. In the eighteenth century, that fear had given way to confidence in the colonies' growth. But by 1763, there was new cause for alarm. Now the growth would be geographic as well as demographic, as people pushed west in unprecedented numbers into lands they felt they had "won" from the French and Indians. Benjamin Franklin still viewed the growth of population in the colonies as a positive development that would strengthen British North America, as did speculators who hoped to provide the growing population with land. But many Britons feared that the increase in population and size might lead to separation from Britain. The question was how to keep the expanding colonies under British control.[30] The answer moved them further toward separation.

Settlers who moved west stretched and sometimes tested their ties with the East. Provincial officials who claimed jurisdiction over them fretted about backcountry settlers and feared that the farther west they pushed, the less responsive they would be to law and authority. This was nothing new. But in 1763 the scale of the problem was new: emigrants were coming to America in unprecedented numbers; settlers were on the move like never before and over territory of a geographic scope previously unimaginable.

Immigration from Europe tripled in the postwar years.[31] Thousands of German-speaking immigrants, lured by promises of free land, low taxes, and religious toleration, came to America in the eighteenth century. Although their immigration peaked in the five years or so before the Seven Years' War, they made up almost 10 percent of the population in Britain's mainland colonies and about a third of the population in Pennsylvania, where Benjamin Franklin worried they would "swarm into our settlements, and by herding together, establish their language and manners, to the exclusion of ours."[32] Emigration from the British Isles increased dramatically, bringing about 125,000 people to America by the time of the Revolution. Migrants from Ulster continued to come in thousands, as they had since the 1720s. James I had transplanted groups of predominantly Lowland Scots to northern Ireland in the early seventeenth century to act as a buffer against the "wild Irish." In America, their descendents, known as Scots-Irish or Scotch-Irish, pushed downward from the Appalachian Mountains into southwestern Virginia and the Carolinas, where they often acted as a buffer against the "wild Indians."[33] In addition, more than 20,000 Scots (some estimates say twice that number) crossed the Atlantic in the dozen years after 1763. Emigration from Scotland was not a new phenomenon—Scottish soldiers and traders appeared in Poland and Denmark in the sixteenth and seventeenth centuries and there were Scottish communities in Rotterdam and Danzig. But even allowing for the exiles after the failure of the 1745 Jacobite Rebellion, Scottish emigration to America was relatively small before 1763. After 1763, it reached epidemic proportions, a social movement that has been chronicled from James Boswell to Bernard Bailyn. Pushed by the need to escape wrenching economic change at home and attracted by the prospect of betterment in America, Scottish migrants worried landlords and government authorities in Britain, who feared a population drain, and provincial authorities in America, who saw them flooding into the backcountry. Scots moved to the perimeters of the empire in unprecedented numbers, settling in Georgia, the Carolinas, upper New York, and Pennsylvania as well as Canada.[34] The British government provided land grants for veterans, and many disbanded Scottish soldiers stayed in America after the war; for example, men from Fraser's Highlanders, enticed by land grants "and knowing that there was not much for them at home," settled in Prince Edward Island and along the St. Lawrence Valley. Some men enlisted for service in America as a means of acquiring free passage and acquiring land. The reports these veterans sent home no doubt stimulated some of the postwar emigration.[35]

The acquisition of Canada opened up a new world for Scots and they exerted enduring influence in the development of the Canadian nation. Access to England's overseas empire had been a key motive in the Act of Union in 1707, when Scotland amalgamated its parliament with that of England. Now Scottish merchants moved quickly to take advantage of the opportunities the vast new empire offered. Soon after 1763, merchants in the port towns of Glasgow, Greenock, Kilmarnock, and Leith established Canadian agencies, beginning a long and extensive Scottish involvement in transatlantic trade, especially the fur trade.[36]

The expansion of Britain's mainland colonies began with family and community groups searching for new locations along a thousand mile perimeter and grew to a flood pouring north, west, and south.[37] In New England, population bulged west from the coast of Maine, north up the Connecticut Valley into New Hampshire and what would become Vermont, and up the Hudson Valley. New Englanders founded an average of six towns a year prior to 1760; after 1760 the annual average rose to eighteen: a total of 283 new towns between 1760 and 1776. In what became Vermont, six towns were founded in 1763, seven more in 1764. New Englanders from Connecticut pushed into the Susquehanna Valley and others flooded into Nova Scotia, replacing the Acadian population deported during the war years.[38] Nantucket whalers entered the Gulf of St. Lawrence and "met with extraordinary success there in that Fishery." In 1763, they submitted a petition to Jeffery Amherst requesting a grant of land for settlement on the Island of St. John in the Gulf, "their own

Island being too full." Benjamin Franklin penned their petition for them, as they were "mostly my Relations."[39]

In New York, settlers migrated west from the Hudson along the Mohawk Valley. In Pennsylvania, the European population in 1760 was confined to the fertile southeastern corner of the colony, held back by the Appalachian Mountains. Now Fort Pitt became a major hub as migrants pushed west. Pennsylvania's population rose 40 percent from 1760 to 1776; by 1771, 10,000 families were living on Pennsylvania's Appalachian frontier.[40] Many more pushed southwest out of Pennsylvania, through the Cumberland Valley. Most followed the Great Wagon Road, past York and Lancaster, through the Shenandoah Valley and southern Virginia, North and South Carolina, and on into Georgia and the backcountry. In 1763, Benjamin Franklin guessed that in the three previous years 10,000 families had migrated to North Carolina just from Pennsylvania. Georgia's population more than tripled between 1760 and 1773 (its slave population almost quintupled), as migrants from the Great Wagon Road were joined by Germans, Scots, Scots-Irish, and other immigrants from Europe.[41]

Backcountry settlers established borderland societies, distant from provincial control. Many of these backcountry settlers brought with them characteristics, speech patterns, family ways, folkways, clan loyalties and clan rivalries, gender relations, sexual practices, and a combativeness derived from generations of hard life in the borderlands of northern Britain. Colonial travelers from the eastern seaboard regularly commented on the unruly nature of backcountry societies, whose inhabitants, it seemed to them, looked and lived more "like Indians" than civilized white folks. They lived close to Indian country and communities, but they rarely made good neighbors. Scots, Scots-Irish, and German-speaking "fighting farmers" were often the shock troops in the invasion of Indian country. And they were often the first victims of Indian retaliation.[42]

The territorial and demographic expansion of the colonies strained relations with seaboard societies and with the mother country. In Bailyn's words, "this massive *Völkerwanderwung*, this surge of innumerable farming families from all over North America and from western Europe, could not be contained within the margins of the existing colonies, or even within the newly extended boundaries of permissable white settlement outside the established provinces. Settlers defied all legal constraints." It was a social force that Britain could barely control.[43]

SPECULATORS

The movement of people looking for land gave those with lands to sell a rich opportunity. British victory removed the "French and Indian menace" that Anglo-Americans had long-regarded as their only barrier to settlement in the West. Beginning in 1745, "the gentry-dominated Executive Council of Virginia gave gentry-owned land companies preliminary grants to millions of acres west of the Appalachians," but the war had prevented the companies from acquiring and selling the land.[44] The Susquehanna Company claimed to have bought lands in northern Pennsylvania from Iroquois delegates at the Albany conference in 1754. The Iroquois claimed the deed was fraudulent and the war had prevented settlement of the lands, but in 1762 the company sent settlers to the Wyoming Valley.[45] Land speculation reached dizzying heights. Governor Benning Wentworth of New Hampshire grew rich opening the upper Connecticut Valley to settlement. Land companies dispatched delegates to London with petitions for grants in the new territories. The Ohio Company, dormant since French fort-building curtailed its efforts in 1754, resumed its activities and sent George Mercer as its agent to London in 1763. "A body of Adventurers" from Virginia and Maryland organized the Mississippi Land Company in 1763 "with a View to explore and settle some Tracts of Land upon the Mississippi and its Waters." They sent a memorial to the king in September. They hoped that "by a Union of their Councils and fortunes they may in the most prudent and proper manner explore and as quickly as possible settle that part of the Country hereafter mentioned." They requested a grant of two and one half million acres at the confluence of the Ohio and Mississippi rivers. The signatories included Thomas Ludwell Lee, Francis Lightfoot Lee, Richard Henry Lee, William Lee, William and Henry Fitzhugh, Thomas Bullitt, and George Washington.[46]

Washington needed the money that selling or leasing western lands could bring, if only the government would permit it. Washington's correspondence with the firm of Robert Carey and Company in London reveals much about his aspirations and frustrations as a Virginia tobacco planter and slave owner tied to the colonial economy of Great Britain. Some planters preferred to take fewer risks, and to accept lower profits, by selling their tobacco on this side of the Atlantic to Scottish merchants who assumed the costs and risks of shipping it across the ocean and the higher profits to be made selling it in Britain.[47] But like most other gentry Washington used a "factor" in London. The factor purchased goods for his colonial client and paid for them with earnings from the sale of his client's crops. Carey and Company had managed affairs for Martha Washington's first husband, and George W. took them on when he married. A sample invoice, this one from April 1763, lists the kinds of items Virginia planters relied upon their factors to procure: linen, woolens, raisins, currants, almonds, ginger, pearl barley, lead shot, pipes, pickles, walnuts, anchovies, capers, olives, wood, cordage, medicines, hair powder, ribbons, tin boxes, tableware, kitchenware, ironware, wine, shoes, and more, to a total of £298. The factor determined the prices at which he bought the goods and sold the tobacco. Not surprisingly, planters like Washington complained that their goods cost too much and their tobacco sold too low. "My debt is greater than I expected to have found it, owing in some measure to the short prices of my Tobacco," Washington wrote to Carey that same month, nonplussed that his neighbor Colonel Fairfax's tobacco that was "no more than leaf" should fetch higher prices than his own. "I am at a loss to conceive how my balance can possibly be so much as £1811.11 in your favour," he complained a year later; "had my Tobacco sold as I expected and the Bills been paid according to promise I was in hopes to have fallen very little in Arrears." He had been unlucky, he said, with three years of bad seasons; "Mischances rather than Misconduct" explained his financial situation.[48]

But Washington's predicament was not entirely due to bad luck. Despite his debts, Washington drank and dressed well, as befitted a gentleman of his station. No sooner had he written one letter explaining his financial straits to Carey and Co., than he would pen a note ordering "a Pipe of the best Madeira Wine," to be drawn on account with Carey and Co. The same day he complained to Carey about the price his tobacco brought, he ordered "a cargo" of shoes from London for himself and his family, with instructions to charge them to Robert Carey.[49]

Planters in general and Washington in particular complained about the quality and prices of the goods they received from London. Items that had been ordered did not come, things went missing, goods were of inferior quality, clothes and shoes did not fit well. At well over six feet in height, George Washington encountered particular problems with his clothes, although his order to his London tailor (again, written the same day he expressed shock to Robert Carey at the size of his debt) may not have helped matters:

> Be pleased to send me a genteel suit of Cloaths made of superfine broad Cloath handsomely chosen. I should have Inclosed you my Measure, but in a general way they are so badly taken here that I am convinced it would be of very little Service. I would have you therefore take measure of a Gentleman who Wares well made Cloaths of the following size: to wit, 6 feet high and proportionately made; if any thing rather slender than thick for a person of that highth with pretty long Arms and thighs. You will take care to make the Breeches longer than those you sent me last.

He asked his tailor to keep the measurements he made for this suit of clothes so that alterations could be more easily made on the next suit. "Mr. Carey will pay your Bill," he ended. The next summer, Washington threatened to stop doing business with his tailor "unless I am to experience some alteration for the better." He was referring to prices, not fittings. As his costs and his clothes continued to pinch, Washington found his tailor's charges "exorbitantly high."[50]

Groups such as the Mississippi Land Company formed in anticipation of western lands opening up as a result of Britain's victory over the French. The British government's decision in 1763 to restrict and regulate rather than permit and promote expansion onto Indian lands disappointed Washington and his fellow speculators, but they would not be deterred. George Washington led the expansion of Virginia into the Ohio Valley,[51] and he aimed to do it with or without the blessing of the British government.

Another seasoned land speculator was busy with plans in the Mohawk Valley in 1763. Visiting Iroquois delegates who came early in the year presented Sir William Johnson with wampum belts of condolence to ease his grief following the death of his father.[52] But Johnson had plenty of projects to keep his mind occupied. He was building a new home, Johnson Hall, at present-day Johnstown, New York. Fort Johnson, his base of operations during the war, was "a thoroughly utilitarian complex," with "stout, defensible living quarters"; now the war was won, Sir William was intent on building himself an elegant Georgian mansion.[53] In February, he wrote to a friend that he was "swallowed up to the Head & ears in Mortar Stone and Timber" which had been delivered by sleds—as many as thirty and forty a day—during the past month, in preparation for construction in the summer.[54] His situation is reminiscent of Thomas Jefferson in building Monticello, but Jefferson lived permanently amid construction and never finished rebuilding; Johnson knew exactly what he wanted and got the job done. He hired Samuel Fuller of Schenectady to build it, at 8 shillings a day, New York currency, plus food and lodging. He refused to pay any of Fuller's workmen more than 5 shillings a day.[55] He sent Fuller clear plans, which are worth quoting from a time when house construction was a simpler affair than it is today:

> The House is to be 55 feet long from outside to Outside, four rooms on a floor of abt. 18 feet Square, with a Hall in the Middle of the House 18 feet Wide thro the House, with a good Staircase at the end thereof on one side of the Back Door, as many Windows in the rear as in the Front of the House, the first story to be 12 feet high from Beam to Beam. The next as it will not be a full Story to be 8 feet from the floor to the Ceiling—A large Cellar under the whole House with 2 Fire places."[56]

Made of wood to look like stone, the house was finished before Christmas and Johnson enjoyed "the happy riddance of the cursed hammers."[57]

Johnson Hall became a pivotal place in the conduct of British-Indian relations. It was a meeting ground of cultures. Johnson employed Dutch, German, and Irish workers on his estate and owned some African American slaves.[58] He also attracted emigrant Highland Scots to settle as tenants on his lands. Delegations from dozens of tribes made their way to Johnson Hall, as did soldiers and travelers. Even before the house was finished, Johnson held meetings there with Iroquois and other delegates, to divide the Indian confederacy and isolate Pontiac. In the next eleven years, the Irish baronet presided over countless councils at Johnson Hall, while servants worked to feed the assembled delegates and interpreters worked to communicate the conversations across multiple languages. Johnson's efforts matched those of the French in cultivating good relations with Indian people and entailed great expense

Johnson Hall (Sir William Johnson Presenting Medals to the Indian Chiefs of the Six Nations at Johnstown, N.Y., 1772.) Edward Lamson Henry (1841–1919), 1903. Oil on canvas. Albany Institute of History & Art Purchase. 1993.44.

and tireless politicking. The relationship seems to have been mutually beneficial: the Mohawks elevated their status as much important confederacy business was now conducted in Mohawk country rather than at Onondaga; Johnson diverted much of the management of Indian affairs and Indian trade from Albany to Johnson Hall.[59] He complained regularly that every room and corner of his house was "Continually full of Indians of all Nations," "each individual of whom has a thousand things to say, & ask and any person who chuses to engage their affections or obtain ascendancy over them must be the greatest Slave living & listen to them all at any hour."[60]

But he didn't have much to complain about. He was both friend and exploiter of the Iroquois, an agent of empire and an independent entrepreneur pursuing his own goals. He built himself a personal empire as marcher lord on Indian lands. By the time of his death in 1774, he was the largest landowner in the Mohawk valley. Major Robert Rogers, who shared Amherst's distrust of Sir William, may well have had the baronet in mind when he wrote his play, *Ponteach, or the Savages of America*, in which an unscrupulous trader kept a foot on the weighing scales when buying furs from Indians:

By this old Ogden built his stately House,
Purchas'd Estates, and grew a little King.[61]

The year 1763 was a good one for Sir William. Formerly he had had one deputy; now he had three. Britain's huge North American empire brought new contacts with a vast array of Indian nations. George Croghan was responsible for the Ohio region; Daniel Claus for Canada; Guy Johnson dealt with the Six Nations, and Sir William oversaw it all.[62] In historian Francis Jennings's words, Johnson came out of Pontiac's war "a clear winner by any standard." Parliament voted him £1,000 and the king bestowed on him the order of the garter and knighted his son, John.[63] His handsome new mansion would serve to promote settlement in the Mohawk Valley and increase the value of his lands. His dynasty must have seemed secure in their dominance in the valley for generations to come. But even before Johnson died, the world he had built was beginning to crumble. When the revolution broke out, John Johnson remained loyal to the crown and fled to Canada. American troops occupied Johnson Hall (and hacked chunks out of the banister of the staircase) and New York confiscated it in 1779, later selling it off at auction. During and after the Revolution, the Indian Department Johnson had directed made common cause with the Indians in resisting settlers and speculators. By then, those settlers and speculators were Americans, and they sought to build not just private fortunes, but a new nation on the lands they took from Indians.

Indians, settlers, and speculators like Washington and Johnson expected different things to emerge from the peace and had different visions of what America should look like after 1763. Each vision depended on acquiring or retaining land that other people occupied or wanted. In attempting to manage its new empire the British government had to deal with competing groups, incompatible goals, and increasingly vicious contests over the spoils of victory, and it sometimes found itself in the middle. But its first crisis was an Indian storm out of the West that threatened to sweep away much of what Britain had won, and to put out of reach the coveted lands beyond the Appalachians.

CHAPTER 3

The First War of Independence

THE DELAWARE CHIEF, NETAWATWEES or Newcomer, was "Struck dumb for a considerable time" when he heard the terms of the Peace of Paris. He said the English "was grown too powerfull & seemd as if they would be too Strong for God himself." Englishmen celebrated 1763 as a victory for liberty, but Indians saw Britain's victory as a threat to freedom. Most of the territory that changed hands at the Peace of Paris was Indian land. Indians were stunned by the news that France had handed over their lands to Britain without even consulting them: they were undefeated and the French had no right to give up their country to anyone.[1] Having fought for their sovereignty and autonomy in the war, Indians were not likely to acquiesce in a peace that subjected their lands and lives to British imperial authority.

Indians had never regarded the French presence and alliance as constituting any kind of dominion over them. Minavana, an Ojibwa chief also known as Le Grand Sauteur, told trader Alexander Henry in 1761 that "although you have conquered the French, you have not yet conquered us! We are not your slaves." "The Indians were not governed by the French," a Huron chief reminded a British colonist in 1763, "but were free all over the world." Sir William Johnson told the Lords of Trade that the Iroquois and the western Indians "having never been conquered, Either by the English or French, nor subject to the Laws, consider themselves as a free people."[2] For Indian people, a peace that threatened their freedom was no peace at all. Indian country belonged to Indians, no matter what the Peace of Paris said.

British disregard for the strength of these Indian sentiments produced a struggle for independence a dozen years before Lexington and Concord and a war that rocked the empire back on its heels.[3]

PONTIAC'S WAR

Despite the recurrent protests about encroachments on Indian lands, Pontiac's War, as Gregory Dowd points out, first exploded in areas where land was not the immediate issue.[4] When Benjamin Franklin heard the first reports of Indian hostilities in 1763, he wrote: "I do not hear of any Offence given them, and suppose it occasion'd by the mere Relish they acquir'd in the last War for plunder." In fact, Franklin had put his finger on a root cause of the conflict three months earlier when he urged Britain to return to the practice of giving gifts when dealing with Indians. "The Indians think us so wealthy," he explained, "and we have such Plenty of everything valuable to them, that if we omit so essential and so establish'd a Ceremony, it must proceed from Contempt."[5] Indians expected the British to lubricate their diplomacy with gifts, as the French had done, but Britain, on the brink of financial ruin at the end of the most expensive war it had ever fought, cut back on expensive gift giving.

Concerned about the intrusions of settlers and the presence of redcoat garrisons on their land, Indians looked to the British to build the kind of relationships that had constituted the core of the French-Indian alliance. By giving gifts, the British could appease the spirits of warriors who had fallen in the war, demonstrate that they spoke from the heart when they assured Indians of their good intentions, and show that they were prepared to fulfill the role of a benevolent father, as that term was understood in Indian country. Giving and receiving gifts could restore relationships and turn enemies into friends. Withholding gifts and sending in troops sent a clear message, reinforced by the language of British officers: Britain intended to "reduce" the Indians to submission and take over their land. Shawnees, Senecas, and Delawares told agent George Croghan that "they never Intended to make War on the English, but Say it's full time for them to prepare to defend themselves & their Country from Us." They were convinced the redcoats intended to wage war on them—why else would they stop selling them powder and lead? The Indians interpreted Amherst's postwar

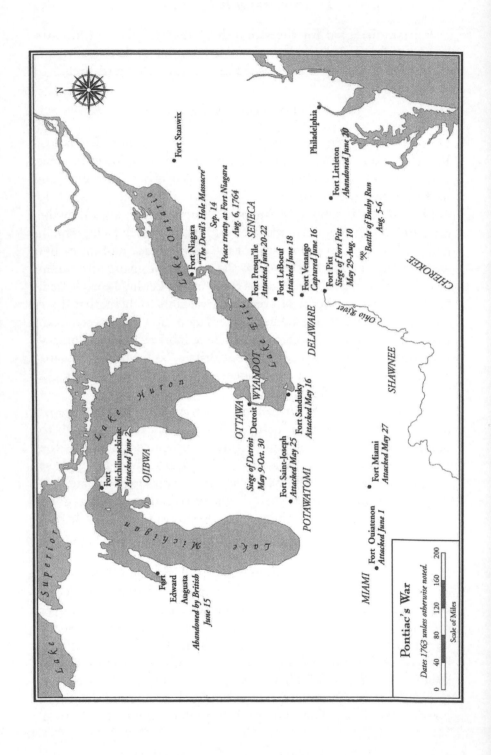

Pontiac's War

Dates 1763 unless otherwise noted.

0 40 80 120 160 200

Scale of Miles

frugality as preparation for war. "How it may End, the Lord Knows," wrote Croghan.[6]

Arrogant and ignorant of Indian ways, the British commander-in-chief Jeffery Amherst viewed an empire as something to be governed, not negotiated and cultivated by giving gifts to Indians. He demanded the return of prisoners, many of whom had been adopted and were now, in Indian eyes, Indians. His soldiers and his forts threatened Indian lands, and British traders entered Indian villages to turn a quick profit, not to conduct an exchange between allies. Now that the war was over, he wrote Sir William Johnson in April, "I Cannot See any Reason for Supplying the Indians with Provisions; for I am Convinced that they will never think of providing for their Families by hunting, if they can Support them by begging Provisions from Us." The letter was in part a lecture: Johnson was notorious for his liberality with Indian gifts. While Amherst maintained that Indians would not hunt as long as the British supplied them, Indians told Johnson they could not hunt *unless* the British supplied them: "having no Ammunition," they were in a "deplorable Situation." Johnson warned that stinginess would alienate the Indians and compromise the safety of British outposts, but found "it is not in my power to Convince the General thereof." By insisting on retrenchment, Amherst radically altered British-Indian relations and placed British soldiers, settlers, and traders in Indian country in a precarious position. For some of the little garrisons in the West, his policies constituted a death sentence.[7]

British victory in the French and Indian War "rendered our regard to this people still less, which had always been too little," *The Annual Register* observed; "decorums, which are as necessary at least in dealing with barbarous as with civilized nations, were neglected."[8] Amherst's insistence on implementing a policy of postwar retrenchment removed the only alternative to war.

Famine and disease stalked the trans-Appalachian West at the end of the war. Sick and hungry Indians blamed the parsimonious trespassers.[9] The voices of militant warriors drowned out sachems' words of caution. Runners carried war belts from village to village.[10] Indian fighters who had not been defeated refused to accept the conditions of peace that Britain imposed and France accepted. French wampum belts and speeches sent to the western Indians fueled their anger at the many posts the British occupied in their country and the "cool Treatment" they received from the redcoats.[11]

The Delaware prophet Neolin gave spiritual force to Indian discontent, preaching that they could redeem themselves as Indians only by casting off alien influences and returning to traditional ways. Neolin dreamed he had journeyed to see the Master of Life, who told him: "This land where ye dwell I have made for you and not for others. Whence comes it that ye permit the Whites upon your lands? Can ye not live without them?" Indians had become so dependent on the white man's things that the Master of Life had led the wild animals to the depths of the forests, leaving the Indians to depend on white men. But if they would "become good again," he would bring back the animals so that Indians could once again live by the bow and arrow. Neolin exhorted Indians "to live without any Trade or Connections with ye White people, Clothing & Supporting themselves as their forefathers did," to give up drink, to take only one wife, to not fight among themselves, and to pray. He had "a Vission [*sic*] of Heaven where there was no White people but all Indians."[12]

In 1763, the Ottawa war chief Pontiac took up the message and directed it against the British but not the French:

> It is important for us, my brothers, that we exterminate from our lands this nation which seeks only to destroy us. You see as well as I that we can no longer supply our needs, as we have done, from our brothers, the French. The English sell us goods twice as dear as the French do, and their goods do not last. Scarcely have we bought a blanket or something else to cover ourselves with before we must think of getting another; and when we wish to set out for our winter camps they do not want to give us any credit as our brothers, the French, do.[13]

Meeting with delegates from the Ottawas, Potawatomis, Ojibwas, and Wyandots at Detroit in April, Pontiac related Neolin's journey and vision. He urged the delegates to pick up Delaware war belts and expel the British.[14]

The next month, Pontiac's warriors tried to take Detroit by ruse. Warned in advance, possibly by a soldier's or even the commander's lover ("I was luckily informed the night before," was all Major Gladwin said), the British foiled the attempt. Reluctant to sustain the casualties necessary to take Detroit by storm, the Indians kept it under siege for six months. Ninivois at the head of the Potawatomis and Takay and Teata at the head of the Hurons laid siege on one side, while Pontiac invested Detroit on the other.[15] General Amherst approved Gladwin's handling of things, but regretted that when Pontiac, "the Principal Ringleader of the Mischief" and "the Other Villains Returned with the Pipe of Peace, they were not Instantly put to Death." Whenever hostile Indians fell into British hands, he instructed, "a Quick Retaliation may be made" without hesitation.[16]

The Indian alliance took the British posts at Sandusky, St. Joseph, and Miamis in May. As historian Matthew C. Ward points out, British garrisons fell victim to surprise in part at least because of familiar and even intimate relations between soldiers and Indians. Fort Miamis fell when Ensign Robert Holmes was killed leaving his post after his Indian mistress came to the fort and told him that another Indian woman "was very ill and wanted him to bleed her."[17] On June 2, Ottawas and Ojibwas captured Fort Michilimackinac at the juncture of Lakes Huron and Michigan, a key trading and fishing center as well as a strategic site. Staging a game of *baug-ah-ud-o-way* or lacrosse in front of the fort, the players lobbed the ball over the palisade and rushed after it through the open gates. Grabbing weapons from women who had concealed them under their blankets, they seized the commanding officer and turned on the garrison of thirty-five officers and men who had been watching the game. They killed fifteen soldiers, an officer, and a trader, and took the rest of the garrison and all the English traders prisoners. Half a dozen of the captive soldiers were later killed. The forts at Venango, LeBoeuf, and Presque Isle fell soon after. On June 19, General Amherst warned against abandoning posts like LeBoeuf and Venango since it would give the Indians "Room to Imagine themselves more Formidable than they really are." Better never to establish posts "in what they call their Country," said Amherst, than to abandon them every time there was an alarm. Amherst was too late: LeBoeuf and Venango had already fallen, one and three days before he wrote.[18]

At Venango, the Senecas wiped out the garrison of fifteen or sixteen men. Before they killed the commanding officer, Lieutenant Francis Gordon, they made him write down a list of their grievances: they cited lack of trade and high prices and the presence of the British fort on their lands, which "induced them to believe they intended to possess all their country." Amherst was amazed that the garrison had "been massacred by letting the Indians come into the Post as Friends; strange Infatuation that an officer can put a confidence in these treacherous Devils, that no Man but a Mad man would do to any civilised body of men that had Arms with them."[19] Delaware and Shawnee chiefs also made sure the commander at Fort Pitt understood the causes of the conflict: "You marched your armies into our country, and built forts here, though we told you, again and again, that we wished you to move," Turtle's Heart told Captain Simeon Ecuyer; "this land is ours, and not yours."[20]

At its height, the war encompassed a vast region between the Great Lakes, the Appalachians, and the Mississippi. Five hundred British soldiers and hundreds more settlers died. Britain's hard-won empire in the West was all but swept away: only Fort Pitt, Detroit, and Niagara remained "of all that had been purchased with so much blood and treasure."[21] There was little Amherst could do until reinforcements arrived from the decimated regiments in Havana; even then he had to scramble to cobble together an effective fighting force from regiments battered and broken by war and disease.[22]

Nor could the commander draw on united support from the colonies. The New England provinces had had plenty of experience with Indian wars and "for more than a Century having tasted of this bitter Cup," the Massachusetts legislature "heartily commiserate[d] the poor Inhabitants on the Frontiers of the Southern Provinces at present more immediately exposed." But they flatly refused General Gage's request that they levy 700 provincial troops and Massachusetts took no part in the fighting. The Connecticut General Assembly likewise took the position that they were "but very remotely interested" in an Indian war raging to the south and west and, still in debt after the last war, "it is not at this present time Expedient to raise Men in this Colony."[23]

Even at its height, the Indian revolt was never total either. While Indian forces invested Fort Pitt, for instance, British Indian agent Alexander McKee was in contact with Indians who divulged intelligence, made peace overtures, and offered assistance.[24] William Johnson worked through the Iroquois to prevent to war from spreading, to split the Indian confederacy, and to pit the Iroquois against the western tribes.[25] The Indian town of Stockbridge in western Massachusetts sent warriors but Amherst refused the services of Indian allies.[26]

Instead, Amherst ordered his officers to employ whatever measures were necessary to "extirpate" the Indians. "I wish to hear of no prisoners," he told Henry Bouquet as the colonel prepared to march to the relief of Fort Pitt. He ordered every commander "to Defend his Post to the Last Extremity; and to take Every Occasion he Can of putting them to Death." Dispatching Lieutenant Grimble of the 15th Regiment of Foot to Seneca country, he ordered him to "Destroy their Huts and Plantations, putting to Death everyone of that Nation that may fall into your Hands." Other western tribes were equally guilty and should be treated "as the Vilest Race of Beings that ever Infested the Earth & whose Riddance from it must be Esteemed a Meritorious Act for the Good of Mankind." Amherst offered £100 reward for Pontiac, "a Cowardly Villain."[27] His successor, General Thomas Gage, who had commanded the vanguard in Braddock's defeat, continued Amherst's policy of total war against the Indians.[28]

Historians have long debated whether Amherst ordered the use of germ warfare against the Indians. There is no doubt he would have liked to do so. In July, Amherst asked Colonel Bouquet: "Could it not be contrived to Send the Small Pox among those Disaffected Tribes of Indians? We must, on this occasion, Use Every Stratagem in our power to Reduce them." Bouquet promised to do his best. In fact, the deed appears to have been done before Amherst gave expression to it. Smallpox broke out among the garrison at Fort Pitt in June and Captain Ecuyer appears to have read his commander-in-chief's mind. On June 24, two Delawares, Turtle's Heart and Mamaltee, came to within hailing distance of the walls and tried to talk the British into giving up the fort. Alexander McKee went out to talk with them, and trader William Trent confided to his diary, "Out of our regard to them we gave them two Blankets and a Handkerchief out of the Small Pox Hospital. I hope it will have the desired effect." That same month Levy, Trent, and Company submitted an invoice for "Sundries got to Replace in kind those which were taken from people in the Hospital to Convey the Smallpox to the Indians." Ecuyer certified it and General Gage approved it. Turtle's Heart evidently did not succumb to the disease—he appeared in councils later in the year—but smallpox ravaged Indian villages that spring and summer.[29] Germ warfare was a dangerous game for the British to play, however, since the dreaded disease might easily strike them.

It was a bloody summer and fall. In July, Captain James Dalyell reached Detroit with a reinforcement of 260 men. "I . . . should not be surprized to hear he had lost the Skin of his head," John Watts wrote to General Monkton, a prediction that was rapidly realized.[30] Within days, Dalyell led an assault against the Indians. Pontiac's warriors ambushed them as they crossed a bridge over a creek. Dalyell and twenty men died and the creek earned the name Bloody Run. In August, at Bushy Run in southwestern Pennsylvania, the Indians mauled Colonel Henry Bouquet's army of 460 men, but sustained heavy casualties and were unable to prevent Bouquet's command from making it through to relieve Fort Pitt.[31] In September, Seneca warriors cut to pieces a British supply train and two companies of infantry at Devil's Hole near the whirlpool at Niagara Falls on the Niagara, killing five officers and sixty-seven men.[32] In November, a flotilla en route to relieve Detroit was hit by a storm on Lake Erie and seventy men drowned.[33]

Nevertheless, the Indian war effort began to falter. The Seven Nations of Canada had made their own peace with the British in 1760. In August 1763, they sent an ultimatum to the western tribes, warning them that if they persisted in "behaving badly" the king of England would cut off their trade; as he now controlled the entrance of the two great rivers that led from the sea into Indian country (the St. Lawrence and the Mississippi), he could prevent any other nation from trading with them. Although Amherst preferred not to enlist Indians as allies—"Their Assistance is rather a Dangerous Expedient," he said—William Johnson nevertheless used his influence to get Indians to take up arms against "the ill disposed Indians." Meeting with the Kahnawake Mohawks at Johnson Hall in September, Johnson reaffirmed the alliance with the Seven Nations. He had buried the axe the French gave them, he said. In its place he handed them "a good English Axe, made of the best stuff, which I desire you will give to the Warriors of all your Nations, with directions to use the same against these Covenant breakers." Assaragoa, a war chief, accepted the axe, and the next year Seven Nations warriors went on a campaign against Pontiac's warriors.[34]

Disease, shortage of supplies, and the separate agendas of individual tribes undermined the Indian war effort. Early in October, the Missisaugas, Potawatomis, and some of the Ojibwas abandoned the siege of Detroit. At the end of the month a messenger arrived from Major Neyon de Villiers, the French commandant in Illinois, to whom

Pontiac had sent an appeal for help. De Villiers had finally received news of the Peace of Paris. "[L]eave off spilling the blood of your brethren, the English; our hearts are now as one," his message read. The next day, October 30, Pontiac dictated a note to a Frenchman to be delivered to the fort, informing Major Gladwin that he was lifting the siege. Pontiac withdrew southward to begin the winter hunt.[35]

William Johnson made peace with the Senecas—in his view the key to securing peace—but many Ohio Indians kept fighting.[36] Two British armies invaded Ohio in 1764, carrying the war "into the heart" of the Indians' own country.[37] John Bradstreet marched south from Fort Niagara in the summer and offered the tribes preliminary, and unauthorized, peace terms. Bouquet marched west from Fort Pitt that fall with 1,500 men and dictated terms to the Delawares, Shawnees, and Mingoes. The French could no longer assist them, he said; the other tribes had made peace, and the Six Nations had joined the British; "It is therefore in our power totally to extirpate you from being

Pontiac's dictated note to Major Henry Gladwin, October 10, 1763, lifting the siege of Detroit. Translation: "My Brother, The word which my father has sent to make peace I have accepted; all my young men have buried their hatchets. I think you will forget the bad things that have taken place for some time past. Likewise I will forget what you have done to me, in order to think of nothing but good. I, the Ojibwas, the Hurons, we are ready to go speak with you when you ask us. Give us an answer. I am sending this resolution to you in order that you may see it. If you are as kind as I, you will make me a reply. I wish you a good day. Pontiac." William L. Clements Library, University of Michigan.

a people." Bouquet demanded that the Indians hand over all their captives.[38] They did so with "the utmost reluctance" and many of the captives shed tears at their liberation.[39]

In the Illinois country, Pontiac rejected the wampum belts the British sent him. "We want none of them," he said. "Tell your general to withdraw all of his people promptly from our lands. We do not intend to allow any of them to set foot there."[40] Charlot Kaské, a Catholic Shawnee war chief, son of a German father and married to an English woman who had been taken captive as a girl, was even more insistent on continuing resistance in the West and seems to have eclipsed Pontiac in the Illinois country.[41] During his peace embassy to the region in 1764, Captain Thomas Morris's life was threatened on several occasions.[42] But the Indian war of independence had lost its momentum. Sir William Johnson's deputy, George Croghan, who had recently returned from London, negotiated peace with Pontiac in 1765. Pontiac then made peace with Johnson. "[T]he War," he said, "is all over."[43] Charlot Kaské moved across the Mississippi along with many French refugees. Pontiac died several years later at the hands of a Peoria Indian.

The Indians did not win the war of 1763, but they asserted their power and wrung some concessions from the greatest empire in the world. The British demanded rights to the posts they had taken from the French, rights of free passage through Indian country, the return of prisoners, and hostages as a guarantee that the terms would be met. But there was none of the massive retribution Amherst had threatened. The British stepped back from Amherst's insistence on treating Indians as a conquered people. Instead, they stepped into the role of "fathers" formerly occupied by the French and learned to deal with the Indians as allies.[44]

THE SETTLERS' WAR

As they had during the Seven Years' War, frontier settlers bore the brunt of Indian attacks in 1763.[45] "Our Indian Affairs seem to grow worse & worse," wrote New York merchant John Watts in July, and news of Pontiac's War permeated his correspondence; "these wretched Savages still continuing to murder the poor defenceless frontier Settlers without Mercy, God knows what it will come to at last."[46] The explosion of hostilities in the West sent settlers reeling back across the mountains, leaving the frontiers of Pennsylvania, Virginia, and Maryland deserted. "Thousands of hopeful settlements, the labour of years," were suddenly abandoned. Carlisle, Pennsylvania, became the new frontier, "not a single inhabitant being beyond it." Newspapers reported refugees crowding "every stable and hovel in the town," reduced to living as beggars. The streets were "filled with people on whose countenances might be discovered a mixture of grief, madness and despair"; and "the sighs and groans of men; the disconsolate lamentation of the women and the screams of children, who had lost their nearest and dearest relations," could be heard.[47] Many did not make it to the safety of the settlements.

Settlers in western Pennsylvania struck out against Indians—any Indians—and against their elected assemblies, which they felt had done little or nothing to protect them. The war finally shattered some patterns of coexistence that had survived even the French and Indian War. At the beginning of 1763, wrote Moravian missionary John Heckewelder, Indians living on the north branch of the Susquehanna River "traveled as usual through the settlements of the white people without fear." The Christian Indians in the region enjoyed peace and prosperity. "But in the fall of this year the scene suddenly changed."[48]

Exasperated by raids on their frontiers, Pennsylvanians accused local Indians of complicity in the war; some denounced them as "Canaanites, who by God's commandment were to be destroyed." Christian Indians in the Moravian mission town sent an address to the governor of Pennsylvania, "testifying their abhorrence of the cruelties committed by their countrymen, and begging his excellency's protection." As had happened in King Philip's War in New England in 1675–76, Christian Indians wore "a mark to distinguish them from the enemy, lest some of them, while out on business, might be taken for enemies, and be molested." Like other Indians they lived in fear for their lives.[49]

At the end of the year, a group of Scots-Irish farmers calling themselves the "Paxton Boys" took matters into their own hands. In Governor John Penn's words, they "got it into their heads that one Indian should not be suffered to live amongst us."[50] On December 14, they murdered half a dozen Conestoga Indians. Two weeks later, they marched on the workhouse in Lancaster where the magistrates had given refuge to fourteen other Conestogas. While the Indians sat in a circle and prayed, the Paxton Boys "shot, scalped, hacked and cut

[them] to pieces." A month later, they marched on Philadelphia and demanded that the legislature raise more troops for defense of the frontiers. The authorities tried to remove about 140 other friendly Indians out of harm's way, and a detachment of Highland troops, then in Philadelphia, escorted the Indians toward New York, to place them under Sir William Johnson's protection. But Governor Colden and the New York Council refused passage to the Pennsylvania Indians and they were returned to Philadelphia, where they lived in barracks, guarded by British regulars.[51]

Francis Parkman, who rarely had much sympathy for Indians, observed, "The *Pennsylvania Gazette,* usually a faithful chronicler of the events of the day, preserves a discreet silence on the subject of the Paxton riots."[52] But Benjamin Franklin would not be silent. In "A Narrative of the Late Massacres" Franklin denounced the conduct of supposed Christians. In emotional terms, he identified some of the murdered Indians: Shehays, "an exceeding good Man"; his daughter Peggy, who looked after her aged father "with filial Duty and Tenderness"; Betty, "a harmless old Woman"; Sally, "a Woman much esteemed by all that knew her." Though the colonists appear to have suspected one of the Indians, Will Sock, of harboring anti-English sentiments, the only crime of which the victims were guilty, Franklin proposed, was that "they had a reddish brown Skin, and black Hair," as did the Indians who were raiding the frontiers. "If it be right to kill Men for such a Reason, then should any Man with a freckled Face and red Hair, kill a Wife or Child of mine, it would be right for me to revenge it, by killing all the freckled red-haired Men, Women, and Children, I could afterwards anywhere meet with." The Paxton killers retorted: "In what nation under the Sun was it ever the custom that when a neighbouring Nation took up Arms, not an individual should be touched but only the Person that offered Hostilities?" Despite Franklin's pleas, and despite Governor Penn's proclamations and orders that the ringleaders be seized, none of the perpetrators was brought to justice.[53]

The Conestoga Indians wore English clothes, went by English names, and lived under the protection of the governor and assembly. Sheehays had participated in a treaty with William Penn in 1701, and both Conestoga and Lancaster had served as council grounds. But the middle grounds that Indians and Europeans had constructed were shrinking fast in an atmosphere of escalating race hatred. If the Conestogas' Christianity could not save them from the wrath of

Christians, what basis could there be for coexistence? The Paxton men looked beyond the Conestogas' adoption of English forms and saw only Indians. In historian James Merrell's words, the bloodshed at Conestoga and Lancaster repudiated "the council culture and all that it stood for."[54] General Thomas Gage noted somberly that there was little point negotiating peace with any Indian nations so long as the frontier people were intent on "killing every defenceless Indian they met with."[55] Colonel Henry Bouquet regarded back-country settlers as Indian killers, not Indian fighters; "they have found it easier to kill Indians in a Goal [*sic*], than to fight them fairly in the woods," he said.[56]

But the Paxton insurgents were not just out to kill Indians. They also had "great Grievances to Complain of to this Government." Infuriated by the Quaker-dominated assembly, they raised about 500 armed men and in January 1764 marched on Philadelphia, which, according to one correspondent, "flustered Philadelphians very much."[57] Benjamin Franklin and other civic leaders managed to avert the crisis by going out to meet the mob's leaders and persuading them to disband on the promise of a meeting to discuss their grievances. For men like Franklin and Governor Penn the challenge to colonial authority and the breakdown of law and order was as worrying as the murder of innocent people. "In fine," Franklin wrote to a friend, "every thing seems in this Country, once the Land of Peace and Order, to be running fast into Anarchy and Confusion. Our only Hopes are, that the Crown will see the Necessity of taking the Government into its own Hands, without which we shall soon have no government at all."[58] Not as large or as dramatic as the Regulator Movement in which, a few years later, several thousand backcountry settlers took it upon themselves to try to "regulate" or reform the government of North Carolina, the Paxton "rebellion" nonetheless pitted backcountry settlers against eastern elites and institutions.[59]

Despite the increasing racial violence, and in the midst of the fighting, many settlers were taken captive and lived with the Indians their countrymen seemed determined to destroy. Eliza Carter, for instance, had migrated to America from the north of England with her family. In the fall of 1763 Delawares killed her mother and took Eliza and her sister captive. Her captors "often beat her & knocked her down," although after they sold her to the Senecas, the Senecas "used her well." Eliza was liberated the next year. She was ten years old.[60]

Others evidently experienced good treatment from the Senecas. A white man who had lived among them and "was formerly delivered up" went back to the Senecas and fought against the British during Pontiac's War. He was later captured and Sir William Johnson threw him in jail.[61]

One captive woman who was living with the Senecas in 1763 related her experiences in her old age. Twenty years old in 1763, Mary Jemison had been captured in western Pennsylvania in 1758 and had seen her parents murdered. The memory of her family connected her to her backcountry home, but her Seneca sisters, who had adopted her in place of a dead brother, eased her pain and helped her build a new life. She spent her days in 1763 much as Seneca women had done for generations. Living in a village on the banks of the Ohio River, she cared for children, planted, hoed, and harvested corn, pounded corn into hominy, cooked, baked, and occasionally joined the men on hunting trips. "Our labor was not severe," she recalled, "and that of one year was exactly similar, in almost every respect, to that of the others." When a party of Senecas had visited Fort Pitt, the inhabitants began to ask Mary questions: Who was she? When and where was she captured? Mary's adoptive sisters "became alarmed, believing that I should be taken from them, hurried me into their canoe and recrossed the river—took their bread out of the fire and fled with me, without stopping, till they arrived at the river Shenanjee. So great was their fear of losing me, or of my being given up in the treaty, that they never once stopped rowing till they got home." Mary never left the Senecas.[62]

As colonial authorities knew, and feared, it was not uncommon for young settlers who fell into Indian hands to "turn Indian." Many forgot their family names, some their native language. When Colonel Henry Bouquet invaded the Ohio country in 1764, he gave the tribes twelve days to deliver to Fort Pitt "all the prisoners in your possession, without any exception: Englishmen, Frenchmen, women and children; whether adopted in your tribes, married, or living amongst you under any denomination and pretence whatsoever; together with all negroes." The Delawares and Shawnees brought in 200 prisoners by mid-November, and Bouquet expected 100 more from the Shawnees. Some of the captives had been with the Indians so long, he said, "that they are become Savages & they are obliged to tie them to bring them to us."[63] Not all English captives wanted to return home after the war and many stayed in Indian country.

David Owens returned of his own accord, however. Owens had deserted during the Seven Years' War and taken up living among the Indians. His father had been a trader among the Shawnees and Delawares. Owens married a Delaware woman named Maria, sister-in-law to Teedyuscung and formerly a Moravian convert. In 1764 he came back carrying five scalps and accompanied by a white boy. Traveling with his Indian wife, another woman, five men, and two children, Owens had seized the opportunity to murder his companions as they slept. He shot two of the men, killed a third with his hatchet, and tomahawked to death the women and children. The other two men escaped. Owens scalped the adults "and bid the white Boy scalp the Children; but he declin'd it; so they were left." Scalping was common on the frontiers and Pennsylvania offered bounties on Indian scalps, but Owens's act made an impression on Indians and whites alike. "The Above Bloody Scheme of D: Owen to Atone for His Desertion is very Shocking," wrote Benjamin Franklin. "What must the Five Indian Nations Think of the White Men Who Vie with them in Cruelties[?]" As historian Jane Merritt suggests, Owens may have been wrestling with "inner demons of identity": attached to individual Indians in a world of increasing race hatred, he cleansed himself of those attachments and killed the "Indian lover" inside by his grisly act.[64] Henry Bouquet promptly employed Owens as an interpreter in dealing with the Delawares and Shawnees.

By 1763 William Penn's "peaceable kingdom" had become a zone of vicious racial violence. Pontiac's War, the Paxton massacres, Owens's cold-blooded killing of his relatives, atrocities and rumors of atrocities on both sides killed any hopes of peaceful coexistence between the new settlers and the original settlers and revealed "the final incompatibility of colonial and native dreams about the continent they shared."[65] In many frontier regions, trade and mutual dependence had brought Indians and colonists together; now Indians and colonists alike argued for boundaries to keep them apart.[66] But where would the boundaries be?

THE REDCOATS' WAR

The reverses suffered by British forces in the early stages of the Seven Years' War damaged the reputation of British regular soldiers among American colonists. Before the war was over, the British army had more than recovered lost ground, but then Pontiac's War erupted. Again, it seemed, the redcoats failed to protect American settlers. To make things worse, by the end of the year, redcoats seemed to be protecting the Indians. In 1763, British garrisons represented a threat to Indian liberties; before long, British redcoats symbolized a growing threat to American liberties.[67]

The things that earned the British soldier a reputation as an effective instrument of war and empire often cloud our ability to see him as an individual. Rank and file redcoats left few records: "I have no news of your Son," John Watts wrote to an anxious parent in July; "Soldiers don't often write."[68] The redcoat's role as "ally in 1756" and "enemy in 1776" provides little place for his experiences in 1763, a year of supposed peace for others but not for him, and a year that would cast him in the role of villain. Hollywood's stereotyping of British officers as cruel and arrogant but not very bright, and foot soldiers as brutalized and brutal, leaves no room for individual human experience in a redcoat's uniform. The historical image of ranks of redcoats bound by training, discipline, steady courage, and devotion to king and country leaves little place in our imagination for the sergeant who died when Indians caught him outside the walls of Fort Sandusky "planting something in his garden,"[69] for officers who kept their private fears and despondency in their journals, and for men who, by 1763, just wanted to go home.

Fighting in America was like combat nowhere else. "Those who have only experienced the severities and dangers of a campaign in Europe, can scarcely form an idea of what is to be done and endured in an American war," *The Annual Register* for 1763 advised its readers; "in an American campaign every thing is terrible; the face of the country, the climate, the enemy." Indian terror tactics and psychological warfare frequently unnerved British regulars. Soldiers who served in Indian country may have been "decentered" by the severing of traditional ties and the new ways of living and killing they experienced.[70]

Many soldiers fought in the North American campaigns, the West Indies, where they participated in the capture of Martinique from France and Havana from Spain, and in Pontiac's War. Redcoats suffered appalling casualties in these years. Yellow fever and malaria killed 40 percent of the 1,400 British soldiers involved in the siege of Havana; according to Thomas Mante, who was there, the army was "quite melted down by the West-Indian service." As usual, Highland regiments bore more than their share of the casualties. John Watts saw troops from Havana arrive in New York: "never did I see such a Spectacle," he said. One ship left Havana with "One hundred & ten Royal Highlanders" on board "& in Sixteen days landed here hardly alive thirty odd." Another correspondent in New York said that less than one-third of the Royal Highland Regiment (the 42nd or Black Watch, which had been decimated at Fort Ticonderoga in 1758) returned from Havana and the survivors seemed "dejected and enfeebled, with little hopes of recovery." Encamped on Staten Island, the survivors of the 42nd and the 77th Regiment (Montgomery's Highlanders) suffered from diphtheria, scarlet fever, dysentery, broken bones, rheumatism, venereal disease, wounds, coughs, chest pains, and smallpox. The surgeon of the 77th Regiment was himself so ill that local physicians had to tend the sick; they then presented the surgeon with their bills and he had to obtain reimbursement from the army. When Pontiac's War broke out, British commanders had to piece together a fighting force from among the sick and wounded. Many men were fit to march only if assisted by wagons. Of more than 2,000 Highlanders who had sailed for the Caribbean in 1761, only 245 remained fit for active duty in late August 1763, after the Battle of Bushy Run. The Black Watch was "reduced to a mere skeleton": Out of 1,200 men in the regiment, "only seventy-six survived to see their country again." Some of those who failed to return home stayed in America to take advantage of government land grants for veteran soldiers. Nevertheless, the casualty rate was appalling. Dr. Samuel Johnson, touring the Western Highlands some years later, said: "Those that went to the American war, went to their destruction."[71]

Like many of his fellow officers, Lieutenant Thomas Stirling of the Black Watch thought North America was no place for a British soldier: "long may Peace reign here," he wrote his brother from Montreal in 1760, "for sure god never intended any war should be carried on by any other besides the natives." Stirling hoped his regiment would be sent home, then to Germany, "for I am heartily tired of this Country as is every officer in it." Instead, the Black Watch remained in America another seven years: they were sent to the Caribbean, then back to the mainland to confront Pontiac's warriors. In 1765, Stirling himself led a detachment of the Black Watch on a 3,000-mile round trip from Fort Pitt to receive the surrender of Fort Chartres in the Illinois country.[72] (Stirling commanded the Black

Watch during much of the American Revolution and was severely wounded. But he did get to go home: when his elder brother died, he inherited the baronetcy of Ardoch in Pethshire.)

Many British officers treated rank-and-file soldiers as the scum of the earth. The British army was notorious for the brutality of its discipline even in a brutal age. But many British soldiers were skilled artisans—weavers, tailors, cobblers—who had been forced into service by wrenching economic changes. They had expectations at the end of the war, and protested forcefully and effectively when those expectations were not met. When news came in June 1763 that Cuba was to be returned to Spain, the troops disembarked and headed for home. Eight days into their voyage the fleet was overtaken by orders to return the regiments to North America. Invalids from Havana stepped back into the ranks to fight in Pontiac's War. Soldiers in North America experienced pay stoppages, shortages of clothing, and, they felt, betrayal of their rights. Mutinies broke out in regiments in Nova Scotia, Newfoundland, and Quebec, and spread. The garrison at Quebec mutinied when they received orders to pay 4 pence for provisions: "the men of the 45th represented they could not live if they were to pay 4 pence for their provisions, by which they had but 13 pence per week remaining. Washing cost them 6 pence, spruce beer 4½, barber 1; a little tobacco took the rest, and they wanted to know who would pay for their Leggins, Shirts, Stockings and Shoes which they were obliged to buy yearly or starve with cold." By staging what was essentially a labor strike, and laying their lives on the line to do so, the mutineers managed to extract some concessions from the government and assurances that they would soon be going home.[73]

Even among soldiers who did not mutiny, morale and discipline were at low ebb by 1763, especially among garrisons on the frontier. The barracks of the officers and men who occupied Pensacola in November were "nothing more than miserable bark hutts, without any sort of Fire places, or windows, void of every necessary utencil."[74] Complaints about food were universal. Soldiers frequently described their bread as mainly dust, or in some cases dust and bugs. The commanding officer at Fort Tombigbee felt the bread there was "excessive bad," even by British army standards: "no Bread in the world deserves Condemnation more Justly, which makes my men murmer [*sic*]."[75] Officers longed for home, drank heavily, and submitted requests for transfers; rank-and-file soldiers, resentful at being kept beyond the terms of their enlistments, longed for home, drank heavily when they could, and deserted, some to the Indians.[76] John Harries, a captain in the 9th Regiment, served in the siege of Havana and was placed in command at Apalache (St. Marks) in Florida in 1763. He wrote letters to his commanders-in-chief, first Jeffery Amherst and then Thomas Gage, requesting leave to return home. He missed his wife and daughter, and now that he was "the worst side of fifty" he was "anxious to see Great Britain once more before I dye." His anxiety was exacerbated by a rupture he had suffered during the siege of Havana: "possibly I might find a proper remedy in London, or at least be supplied there with a truss to prevent the parts descending into the scrotum, the reduction wherof [sic] to their natural situation is attended with some pain & difficulty." A soldier in the regiment had improvised a truss for him but it "doth not effectually answer." Gage granted Harries leave, although it is not known whether he found the relief he sought.[77]

The conditions that British soldiers endured were surely responsible in part for the presence of deserters among the Senecas and other western tribes at the end of the Seven Years' War.[78] Indian country and Indian communities offered some men a welcome escape from the hardships, discipline, boredom, isolation, and punishments that were the lot of British soldiers in frontier garrisons in 1763.

British actions in 1763 reflect the attitudes of Jeffery Amherst and his kind: arrogant, ramrod straight officers who despised Indians, Frenchmen, and common soldiers. But many who wore the king's red coat did not fit the stereotype. Captain Donald Campbell, stationed at Detroit, was a plump, gray-haired, shortsighted, and amiable fellow. He appears to have liked the Indians and enjoyed Pontiac's respect, got on well with the French, and looked out for the interests of those lower in the ranks. Writing to Colonel Bouquet in April 1763, Campbell told his superior that from "the moment the Soldiers heard of the Peace," all those entitled to discharges had been pestering him. "I hope they will not be forgot," he added. He then argued the case of "Poor Lieut Mac Donald," his second-in-command, who had "been troubled with a melancholy disorder for some time past." The lieutenant's condition "proceeded from a Love Affair with one of our young Lady's" (Campbell did not say whether she was French, Indian, or métis) and the doctor thought "he woud get the better of it if he left this place, and if he continued here it would still be worse with him."[79] James MacDonald remained at Detroit, and it fell to him to report Campbell's fate to Bouquet.

Campbell had come to Detroit with Major Robert Rogers in 1760 and held command until Major Henry Gladwin arrived. He received no directions on how to deal with Indian affairs. He feared the consequences of Amherst's policies of retrenchment among the Indians at the outposts "as our small Garrisons are at their Mercy." He tried to keep the news secret but could not.[80] His fears were well-founded. When the garrison foiled the Indian attempt to take Detroit by surprise, the Indians attempted to parley. Campbell, as second-in-command to Gladwin, and Lieutenant John McDougall went out to talk with them. The Indians took them hostage and detained them in a Frenchman's house two miles from the fort. McDougall managed to escape and made it to the fort, but Campbell, overweight and short-sighted, "could neither run nor see, and being sensible of that failing I am sure prevented him from attempting to escape."[81] A few days later, on July 4, the Indians tomahawked Campbell, cut out his heart and ate it. Campbell's killer was probably a Saginaw Chippewa chief named Wasson, exacting revenge for a son or nephew who was killed in a skirmish with the British. According to different accounts, the Indians threw the body into the river or chopped it up and made a pouch from the skin of his arms.[82]

"Thus lamentably one of the best hearted Men in the world ended his days to the concern of every body," wrote merchant John Watts to a business associate. "God grant you and I tho' we must be worm eaten at last, a more civilized exit."[83] Campbell's death caused Lieutenant James MacDonald "pain beyond expression." "I must own I never had nor never shall have, a Friend or Acquaintance that I valued more than him," he told Bouquet, which was something for a MacDonald to say about a Campbell.[84]

Exposed to Indian anger in Indian country, British soldiers endured harrowing experiences. The garrison at Detroit dug in for a long siege. An anonymous letter from the fort written on July 6 described their position: "We have been upon the watch Night and Day, from the Commanding Officer to the lowest soldier, from the 8th of May, and have not had our Cloaths off, nor slept all Night since it began." "[S]carce a night in bed," Scottish soldier John Bremner wrote in his journal. Even after the siege was lifted the garrison was in a miserable situation the following spring, short of clothing and "in want of every necessity to make them appear like soldiers."[85]

Major Henry Gladwin had survived the slaughter of Braddock's army in 1755, but now he suffered under the strain of the siege. By

October he was despondent. "I am brought into a scrape, and left in it," he confided in a letter to William Johnson; "things are expected of me that cant be performed; I could wish I had quitted the service seven years ago, and that somebody else commanded here."[86] He told Henry Bouquet he was "heartily wearied" of his command; "I hope I shall be relieved soon, if not, I intend to quit the service for I would not chuse to be any longer exposed to the villainy and treachery of the settlement and Indians."[87] Ten years later, Gladwin was in another world, "very happy" back in England with his "wife and two little children, upon a small paternal estate, and fond of farming and rural amusements."[88]

A Swiss officer provided the British with what victories they could claim in Pontiac's War. Colonel Henry Bouquet was a hard-bitten soldier's soldier, who had learned his trade through twenty years of service in the armies of Holland and Piedmont-Sardinia. He had tasted combat in the War of the Austrian Succession and experienced guerrilla warfare in the rugged mountain terrain of northern Italy and Piedmont. He seems to have despised all Indians, had no qualms about infecting them with smallpox, and recommended bringing bloodhounds from England to track down Indian raiding parties: "As it is a pity to expose good men against them I wish we would make use of the Spanish Method to hunt them with English Dogs, supported by Rangers and Some Light Horse, who would I think effectually extirpate or remove that Vermin," he wrote to Amherst in 1763.[89] At the same time, he seems to have kept his word to them: as commander at Fort Pitt in 1762 he refused an offer of 25,000 acres from the Ohio Company to allow settlers into the Ohio valley, denouncing the bribe as a "scandalous breach" of treaty.[90] He had no time for backwoods settlers who shrank from joining redcoats on campaign and he relied on regulars to get the job done. He cobbled together a force of 460 English, Highland, and German soldiers to go to the relief of Fort Pitt. It included two light companies of the Black Watch, recalled to the mainland after horrendous campaigning in the West Indies.

Sir William Johnson, who had fought with redcoats and Indians, said that "altho' British soldiers have infinitely more bravery than any Indians, the loss may be very considerable in a woody country should they come up with them."[91] Bouquet and his redcoats proved their courage at Bushy Run but the battle also bore out Johnson's warnings about engaging Indians in forest warfare. About one o'clock in the afternoon of August 5, after they had already marched seventeen miles that day, Bouquet's army was ambushed by Shawnee, Delaware, and Mingo warriors at Edge Hill, or Bushy Run as it came to be known, twenty-six miles from Fort Pitt. A bitter "running kind of fight" ensued: the exhausted soldiers tried to dislodge the Indians, but, wrote Bouquet, "as soon as they were driven from One Post, they appeared on Another, 'till, by continual Reinforcements, they were at last able to Surround Us, and attacked the Convoy Left in our Rear." The soldiers drove off their attackers with fixed bayonets but suffered more than sixty casualties. The fighting lasted until nightfall, by which time, according to one sergeant in the 77th Regiment, the hollow square, the traditional defensive formation of the British army, was shattered. "And We Expect to Begin again at Day Break," Bouquet wrote to Amherst, hunkered down with his men behind hastily constructed ramparts of flour sacks on the crest of a hill. "Whatever Our Fate may be, I thought it necessary to give your Excellency this early Information." He commended his men for their "Cool and Steady Behaviour."[92]

The Indians attacked early next morning, 500 of them by Bouquet's estimate. Faced with the prospect of being overrun, Bouquet executed a desperate feint. Pulling troops back in the center, he gave the impression of an impending collapse. When the Indians rushed forward to seize the opportunity, the redcoats flanked them, poured a devastating fire into them, and then charged with their bayonets. The Indians, reported Bouquet, "could not Stand the Irresistible Shock of our Men." The battle exacted a heavy toll on the troops: fifty killed and another sixty wounded. "I Hope We shall be no more Disturbed," wrote Bouquet, "for, if We have another Action, We shall hardly be able to Carry our Wounded."[93] Later, Bouquet and others would call his pyrrhic victory a "thrashing" that shattered the Indians' "Boasted Claim of being Invincible in the Woods." In reality, it was a close thing.[94]

Bouquet's men staggered on to Fort Pitt. "You may be sure the Sight of the Troops was very agreeable to our poor Garrison," said a letter written at the fort on August 12, "being penned up in the fort from the 27th of May to the 9th Instant, and the Barrack Rooms crammed with Men, women, and Children, tho' providentially no other Disorder ensued than the Small-pox."[95]

People in the colonies would not be so happy to see redcoats for long. The British military felt they had fought the Seven Years' War to defend the colonies against French and Indian assault. But army officers and common soldiers had done little to endear themselves to the colonial populace. Old attitudes and antagonisms resurfaced and new

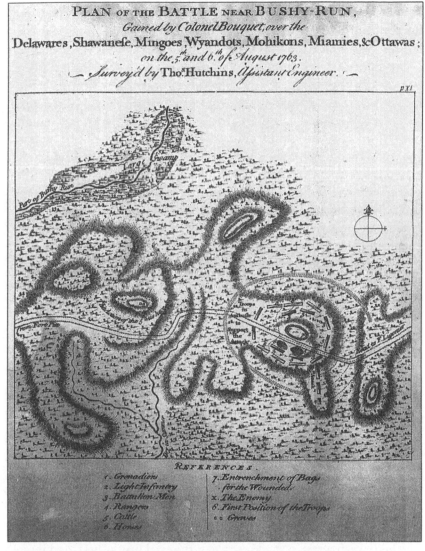

Map of the Battle of Bushy Run by Thomas Hutchins, 1765. Pennsylvania Historical and Museum Commission.

tensions emerged over issues of supply, quartering, and recruitment. British officers regarded colonial assemblies as tight-fisted and uncooperative, colonial militia as unreliable and ineffective. "I am so much disgusted at the Backwardness of the Frontier People in assisting us in taking Revenge of the savages who murder them daily with Impunity, that I hope this will be the last time I shall venture my

Reputation and Life for their Sake," wrote Bouquet in 1764.[96] He got his wish: appointed commander of Pensacola, Bouquet died of yellow fever in September 1765, shortly after his arrival.[97]

For their part, colonists resented the arrogance of redcoat officers, pointed out the failure of regular troops to defend the frontier settlements during Braddock's campaign and Pontiac's War, and regarded the common soldiers as a threat to their liberty, property, and daughters.[98] The army was an institution that stimulated settlement: veterans received land grants and soldiers wrote letters home telling of the fertile lands they had seen.[99] But now, the redcoats seemed to be siding with the Indians. With provincial governments unwilling and unable to enforce the British government's restrictions on settlement, it fell to the army to try and protect Indian lands.[100] The army lacked the manpower to systematically eject settlers who trespassed beyond the Appalachians, but at least in theory redcoats stood between colonists and the rich lands to the west. Policing the empire they had helped to win earned them the hostility of British subjects they had helped to defend. In 1763, the government decided that the forces for America needed to be increased to 10,000 men. The measure was intended to defend the new empire but colonial Americans feared its purpose was to create a police force. Britain had not maintained a standing army in America when the French threatened the colonies; why do so now when there was no French threat? Enterprising colonial merchants stood to benefit from the presence of the army as a major market, but most colonials saw a need for fewer, not more, troops. Meanwhile the cost of maintaining the army in North America—almost 4 percent of the entire national budget according to one estimate—helped drive Britain and its colonists apart: "There was good reason for British resentment at what was believed to be the tax-free state of the colonies."[101]

The British army in the West was a thin red line at best, and by the end of 1763 the redcoats were "wore to the Stumps" after campaigns against the French in Canada, the Spanish in the West Indies, and the Indians in the West. Most British soldiers in 1763 were more interested in going home than in policing Indian lands. Jeffery Amherst, the conqueror of New France, was one of them, and he got his wish. He returned to England in November, but he hardly enjoyed a hero's homecoming. "It is a matter of Concern to His Majesty," Lord Halifax wrote Amherst the month before, "to find that the measures you had taken for putting an end to the Indian war, have not yet produced the desired effects."[102] William Johnson wished him bon voyage and relief from "the cares & anxieties in which your station must necessarily involve You during the present unhappy ruptures in this Country."[103] George Croghan, Johnson's deputy who was in London early the next year, said Amherst's reputation was ruined. "Gineral Amhirsts Conduct is Condemd. by Everybody and has been pelted away in the papers the army Curse him in publick as well as the Merchants," Croghan wrote to Johnson. Knowing there was no love lost between Johnson and Amherst, Croghan embellished on the general's fall from grace for the superintendent's satisfaction: "in Short," he added, "he is No body heer Nor has he been askt aquistion with Respect to the affairs of America Sence he Came over which a gentleman might nott ask his footman."[104] In fact, Amherst was appointed commander of all Crown forces in 1778. Footsoldier John Bremner also got his wish. Bremner had joined the army in Scotland in 1756, was shipped to North America, served through both the Seven Years' War and Pontiac's War, and was discharged after participating in Bradstreet's campaign. "I hop[e] it will be forever for thought I had Enough of soldiering," he wrote in his journal.[105]

In 1763, a year of escalating racial violence, British soldiers were sometimes the last defense of colonists' lives against Indian attack and of Indian lands against colonial aggressions.[106] But colonists would come to regard redcoats as the oppressed military arm of a regime that was becoming increasingly oppressive toward its own subjects. In 1772 the British abandoned the western posts, thinking that eastern cities needed more policing than western frontiers. Citizens in Boston and Philadelphia who had complained about the presence of a standing army on the western frontier now confronted redcoats on the streets. Indian peoples who had opposed the presence of redcoats on the western frontier now confronted settlers in their homelands. In eastern cities and on western frontiers, conflicts were not long in coming.[107] Pontiac's Revolt was not the last American war for independence—American colonists launched a rather more successful effort a dozen years later, prompted in part by the measures the British government took to try to prevent another war like Pontiac's.

CHAPTER 4

Setting Boundaries

*A*S SETTLERS AND SPECULATORS LAID CLAIM to territory they regarded as the fruits of victory, the British government endeavored to restrain them. As Indians and whites fell on each other with escalating fury, the British government endeavored to separate them. Westward expansion would occur, the government said, but it would follow a measured British pace, not a frantic American one, and it would be checked by clear boundaries dividing colonial settlers and Indian nations. Boundary lines were essential to keep Indians and colonists from each other's lands and throats.

In the fall of 1763, Britain attempted to impose a new imperial order in North America and to prevent the outbreak of bloody frontier conflicts like Pontiac's War. It did so with minimal resources and massive consequences. The British army was charged with defending the empire it had won but lacked the resources to stem encroachments on Indian land. The concept of an Indian boundary line was established, but the line was porous and impermanent.

A LINE IN THE MOUNTAINS

In October 1763 King George issued a proclamation establishing the Appalachian Mountains as the boundary between British settlement and Indian lands. The Royal Proclamation reflected the notion that segregation not interaction should characterize Indian-white relations.[1] Pontiac's War confirmed the opinion of British ministers that boundaries and imperial regulation of the frontier were essential. Plans to implement a boundary line between Indian lands and colonial settlements were hurried forward so that Indian alliances could be restored and peace could be preserved once the Indians had been "reduced to due Submission." As evidenced by the Royal Proclamation, Britain continued to regard Indians as under imperial dominion but modified its policies to the demands of Indian country.[2]

The British recognized that peace in the West required extending royal protection to Indian country, fulfilling promises to protect Indian land, and regulating the activities of traders.[3] The British had assured Ohio Indians at the Treaty of Easton in 1758 that their lands would be protected when the war was won. The Articles of Capitulation agreed upon by General Amherst and French Lieutenant-Governor Marquis de Vaudreuil at Montreal in 1760 stated that France's Indian allies were to "be maintained in the Lands they inhabit, if they chose to remain there; they shall not be molested on any pretence whatsoever, for having carried arms, and served his most Christian Majesty."[4]

Royal officials tried to stem trespass on Indian land even before the war ended. Early in 1763, ministers in London read several documents and memoranda articulating the need for reforms in the old colonial system. The author appears to have been Henry Ellis who, on the basis of having served four years as governor of Georgia and spent two of those years dealing with the Creeks, was considered an "expert" on America and Indian affairs. Secretary of State Lord Egremont, who "like most of the noble lords ... was almost entirely ignorant about America," relied on Ellis for advice. Ellis argued that if population were allowed to spread unchecked into the vast American heartland Britain eventually would be unable to maintain dominion over them. The colonists considered themselves "intitled to a greater measure of Liberty than is enjoyed by the people of England, because of their quitting their Native Country, to make Settlements for the Advantage of Great Britain in the Wilds of America." But Britain's wealth from America lay in trade with the coasts, not in settlement in the West. A boundary line restricting settlement east of the Appalachians would limit the costs of administering new territories, prevent the colonies from growing to the point that they became ungovernable, encourage settlers to move north to Nova Scotia or south to the Floridas, and remove Indian apprehensions about British intentions. "Such an Instance of our goodwill to the Indians, would fix them more firmly in our Interest, than all the Talks we can give them, or all the Presents we can bestow on them."[5] Egremont told Amherst that the king had it "much at heart to conciliate the Affection of the Indian Nations, by every Act of strict Justice, and by affording them His Royal Protection from any Incroachment on the Lands they have reserved to themselves, for their hunting Grounds, & for their own Support & Habitation."[6]

The president of the Board of Trade as it deliberated policy for the West in 1763 was Lord Shelburne. Only twenty-six years old, Shelburne developed "a reputation for insincerity exceeding that of any man of his insincere age." He had no intention of permanently halting the westward expansion of the colonies; he hoped to be able to advance the interests of the expanding colonies and at the same time protect the rights of the Indians. He envisaged a boundary line as a device for regulating, not eliminating, frontier expansion, something that would eventually be abolished as old colonies grew and new ones were created. He also hoped to relieve some of the population pressure in colonies abutting the Appalachians by diverting settlers to Nova Scotia and the new colonies of East and West Florida. Shelburne and his colleagues presented their ideas in a report to the king on June 8, by which time Pontiac's warriors were already wreaking havoc in the West. The proclamation was hurried through to its final form and drafted in just six days, a remarkable achievement given the snail's pace at which eighteenth-century government usually operated. The king signed it on October 7 and the packet sailing for New York was detained until October 11 so that printed copies of the document could be sent to America without delay.[7]

The Royal Proclamation established the Appalachian Mountains as the boundary line between Indian and colonial lands. It also stipulated "that no private Person do presume to make any Purchase from the said Indians of any Lands reserved to the said Indians within those parts of our Colonies where, We have thought proper to allow Settlement." Only the Crown's representatives acting in formal council with Indian nations could negotiate land transfers, and only licensed traders would be permitted to operate in Indian country. By such measures, the government sought to prevent "all just Cause of Discontent, and Uneasiness" among the Indians in the future. The governors of Quebec and the Floridas were authorized to grant land to help populate their new colonies. Veterans of the war were entitled to free land on a graduated scale according to rank: 50 acres for privates, up to 5,000 acres for those holding the rank of major and above.[8]

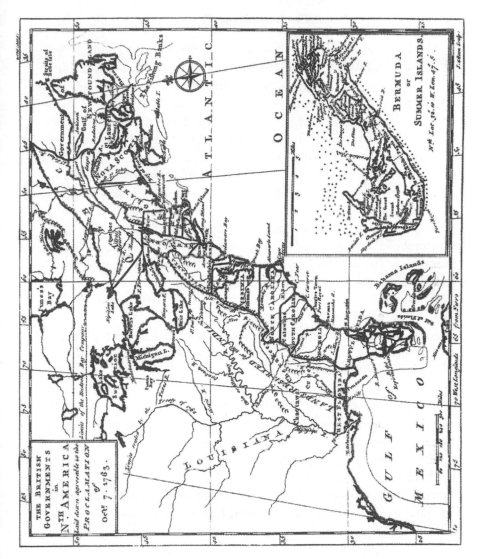

The British Governments in North America Laid Down Agreeable to the Proclamation
of Oct. 7, 1763.

The Proclamation of 1763 has been described as the Indians' "Bill of Rights." Courts in both the United States and Canada have sought to interpret its meaning and its terms have been seen as a model for the 1840 Treaty of Waitangi with the Maori in New Zealand. But scholars disagree on whether the proclamation recognized or undermined tribal sovereignty. L. C. Green and Olive Dickinson point out that it regulated Indian relations with settlers rather than with the Crown. Native legal scholar Robert Williams sees the Crown's claim to centralize land policy by the Proclamation as derived from the "Doctrine of Discovery," which vested in the Crown "inchoate rights of conquest and ultimate title to infidel-held territories." Anthony Pagdon acknowledges that the Proclamation granted Indian nations "a measure of legal autonomy," but repeated references to the Crown's sovereignty and dominion make it clear that "this was to be severely limited." Historian Gregory Dowd argues that it "effectively denied native sovereignty."[9]

Anishinaabe political theorist John Borrows argues that the Proclamation should be understood as a charter of Indian rights rather than as a unilateral declaration by the Crown that undermines Native rights of self-determination. Scholars and lawyers usually concentrate on the text of the document, but, Borrows points out, the Proclamation must be read and understood in tandem with the exchange of wampum that took place at Niagara the following summer.[10]

The Proclamation reaffirmed for Indian peoples the commitment the British had made in the Articles of Capitulation in 1760 to protect France's Indian allies in the lands they inhabited. It delineated boundaries and defined jurisdictions between Indian nations and the Crown. It reiterated assurances made many times in recent years that British colonists would not encroach on Indian lands, but it simultaneously opened the way for the Crown to acquire lands. It outlined the foundations for a relationship between Britain and the Indian nations now that France was removed from the scene. The British were learning what the French had known, that in Indian country imperial policies often depended on negotiation and agreement.

In the winter after the Proclamation was promulgated, Indian delegates carrying copies of the document and strings of wampum traveled Indian country from the Northeast to the Midwest, summoning the tribes to a council at Niagara in the summer. There, said Sir William Johnson, the British and the Indians would make "a treaty of Offensive and defensive Alliance" that would include protection of Indian lands and guarantees of free trade. "The invitation to treaty, with the accompanying promises that were to govern the parties' relationship," says Borrows, "demonstrates the intent of the British to enter into momentous negotiations with the First Nations of North America."[11]

Two thousand Indians, representing twenty-four nations, from Nova Scotia to the Mississippi and as far north as Hudson Bay, assembled at Niagara in July and August 1764.[12] William Johnson read the provisions of the Proclamation as "the terms of what he hoped would prove a Pax Britannica for North America"; the Indians pledged themselves to peace. Gifts and wampum belts were exchanged to seal the agreement, with the *Gus Wen Tah*, the two-row wampum belt reflecting the Indians' understanding of the Niagara treaty and the Proclamation. The belt consisted of two parallel rows of purple beads, representing the separate paths and independence of the Indians and the British, embedded in three rows of white beads, representing mutual respect, sharing, and interdependence. Britain and the Indian nations of the Great Lakes entered into a new era of alliance. Indian communities preserved copies of the Proclamation and wampum belts as records of the agreement, and they honored the terms of the alliance by siding with Britain in subsequent conflicts with the United States. The Proclamation, and the treaty-making principles derived from it, established a foundation of First Nations legal relations in Canada. Whereas Canadian courts have often regarded the Proclamation as a unilateral declaration of the Crown's will in dealing with Indian peoples and their lands, First Nations regard it, in tandem with the Niagara council, as a treaty agreement and cite the Proclamation as a reaffirmation of their preexisting rights of self-government.

The Proclamation's most important feature was its recognition that Indian peoples held rights to unceded lands in British North America, and that those rights could be surrendered only to the Crown or its duly appointed agents in public council. Although usually considered as applying to the lands west of the Appalachian Mountains and east of the Mississippi, the Proclamation's provisions also applied to territories that today comprise almost the whole of modern Canada. The Proclamation was incorporated into the Constitution Act of 1867 and still forms the basis for dealings between Canada's government and Canada's First Nations. Lord Denning declared in 1982 that the Proclamation was as binding "as if there had been included in the statute a sentence: 'The aboriginal peoples of Canada shall continue to have all their rights and freedoms as recognized by the royal proclamation of 1763.'"[13]

However, the Proclamation failed to stop the advance of non-Indian settlers onto Indian lands. A "simple watershed boundary did not fit the actual human geography of 1763."[14] Many settlers already lived west of the mountains, and many Indians still lived east of them. The British government knew that adjustments to the boundary line would have to be made (and they were, under the authority of William Johnson and John Stuart, superintendents of Indian affairs north and south of the Ohio River, respectively). The British also fully intended to keep moving the line of separation westward. But Americans were impatient and brooked no restraints. A plan formulated to prevent Indian wars by offering protection of Indian lands and rights signaled the opening chapter in another war, in which Indian lands and freedom were threatened more than ever before. A plan formulated in England produced an unprecedented "American" reaction.[15]

Settlers could, and did, ignore the Proclamation Line. Four years after the Proclamation, Indians complained that settlers were making "more incroachments on their Country, than ever they had before."[16] But speculators could not ignore the Proclamation: their ability to make profits in the West depended on being able to convey clear title to the lands in which they invested and they could not, now, buy and sell western lands legally. The new measures adopted in 1763 "infuriated Virginia land speculators" who saw their opportunities being undermined. George Washington, Thomas Jefferson, Arthur Lee, Patrick Henry, and others saw tyranny in Britain's interference with their freedom to make a killing in the West. In their eyes, it seemed a new British and Indian barrier had replaced the old French and Indian barrier. Colonists who had fought and bled in the war were not about to be deprived of the fruits of victory by a distant government. Land speculators would not watch their investments in Indian country slip away. The clash of French and British ambitions gave way to a clash of British and American ambitions.[17]

Writing to Captain William Crawford in 1767, George Washington said:

I can never look upon that Proclamation in any other light (but this I may say between ourselves) than as a temporary expedient to quiet the Minds of the Indians & [one that] must fall of course in a few years especially when those Indians are consenting to our Occupying the Lands. [A]ny Person therefore who neglects the present opportunity of hunting out good Lands & in some Measure Marking & distinguishing them for their own (in order to keep others from settling them) will never regain it.[18]

Washington and other future fathers of American independence were still loyal subjects of George III in 1763 and, as Washington's letter to Crawford indicates, they did not see the Proclamation as an insurmountable obstacle. Nevertheless, the ties that bound were being stretched. For Washington and other debtor-planters, revolution would provide both unrestricted access to western land and an escape from London creditors.[19]

Even as the Royal Proclamation announced that the lands beyond the Appalachians were to be set aside as an Indian reserve, speculators petitioned the government for land grants in the reserved territory. In late 1763, a group of merchants who had suffered losses to Indians in the war met at the Indian Queen Tavern in Philadelphia. The traders were mainly from Lancaster and Philadelphia and included Sir William Johnson's deputy, George Croghan, and his brother-in-law, William Trent (who had handed out smallpox blankets at Fort Pitt in the spring), as well as the Quaker firm of Baynton, Wharton, and Morgan. They selected Croghan, who was going to London on business, to present their claims for compensation to the Lords of Trade or the king in Council. The trip was financed by a group of capitalists known as the Burlington Company, headed by William Franklin, governor of New Jersey and illegitimate son of Benjamin Franklin. Despite General Amherst's disapproval of the trip "at a time when surely his presence is necessary in his Department, if it ever was so," Croghan set sail in December; despite a shipwreck he made it to London. But then he was kept waiting for three months: "there has been Nothing Don Sence I Came to London by the Grate ones butt Squebeling & fighting See who will keep in power," he wrote to Johnson. Dismissing them as a pack of rogues, Croghan looked forward to going home: "I am Sick of London," he said. Even so, he was not sorry he came; "it will Larn Me to be Contented on a Litle farm in America if I Can gett one when I go back." Back in America, the memory of that lesson faded. The "suffering traders" and their supporters felt that if they could not get compensation from the government, they should secure it in the form of Indian lands. Sir William Johnson determined to do the group "an essential Piece of Service" when he next met with the Indians to renegotiate the boundary line.[20]

At the Treaty of Fort Stanwix in New York in 1768, Johnson delivered on his promise. Meeting with the Iroquois he obtained their agreement to bulge the Proclamation line westward and negotiated a huge session of land.[21] The treaty made the Ohio River the dividing line between Indian and white land, but the hunters, traders, and settlers who crowded onto Indian lands were, in General Gage's words, "too Numerous, too Lawless and Licentious ever to be restrained." Britain could not keep its subjects off Indian lands on the western rim of the empire, and Indian chiefs could not control young warriors angered by the invasion of their lands.[22] The Shawnees and other Indians in the Ohio Valley rejected the Treaty of Fort Stanwix as a deal concocted between the British and the Iroquois to deprive them of their lands. Confronted by the influx of settlers and then by a growing nation on the move, however, they fought to preserve the Ohio River boundary for the next twenty-seven years.

THE TREATY OF AUGUSTA AND THE SOUTHERN INDIANS

The dramatic events in Indian country in 1763 occurred in the Northeast, where the Indian war of independence attributed to Pontiac set frontiers ablaze, sent settlers reeling back across the mountains, and gave the British a bloody lesson in the importance of forest diplomacy. But as in the Northeast, so too in the Southeast the power shifts of 1763 generated new circumstances and increased tensions in Indian country. Two key Indian leaders met violent deaths in 1763: in the Northeast, Teedyuscung was murdered; in the Southeast, Hagler was killed by Indian raiders from the north. For a dozen years, the Catawba chief had pulled off an individual balancing act, building diplomatic relations with Crown and colonial officials, maintaining peace with Virginia and North and South Carolina, and yet consistently pursuing Catawba interests and remaining loyal to Catawba traditions. His death was symbolic: there was less room after 1763 for the kind of middle-ground maneuvering Hagler had practiced with such skill.[23]

At the beginning of the year, Governor James Wright of Georgia reminded the Upper Creeks of their treaty obligations and their dependency on the English: "You know you cannot do well without us, but we can do without you." No one could supply the Indians' needs like the English could, he said. If the Creeks behaved well toward the King's subjects "we can pour in Goods upon you like the Floods of a great river when it overflows." Conscious of their dependency, the Gun Merchant, "a Man of by far the greatest interest & influence of any Indian in the Nation" and other Upper Creek headmen promised to keep their young men in line. In private conversations and public talks with the Creeks, Wright saw "no Appearance of any Uneasiness amongst them." Things were quiet and the province was flourishing, Wright wrote the Board of Trade in February.[24]

But this quiet threatened to be the calm before the storm. Over the previous two generations the Creeks had skillfully preserved their political autonomy in a context of competition between rival European powers. The British victory in 1763 removed the competition and necessitated a shift in Creek foreign policies. Creeks hated to see the French and Spanish go, and "bristled at the idea of a new imperial order featuring only one rather than three European powers." Creek warriors made threatening gestures toward British garrisons and Creek headmen demanded to know the boundaries of British claims. The *South Carolina Gazette* reported that the Creeks insisted the British "have noe right to possess the lands that were never given to us, and they will oppose all our attempts that way."[25] In April, Upper Creek headmen protested to Wright that Virginian "People Cattle and Horses" were crossing the river and driving away game, contrary to previous agreements "that white People were to drink upon one Side of Savannah River and red People on the other." Creeks called all the people who encroached on their lands "Virginians"; it was not a term of respect. Unable to supply their families by hunting, Creek hunters killed cattle they found on their lands. Wright warned the Board of Trade that the French and Spanish were "still infusing bad notions amongst the Indians," saying the British intended to destroy them. The governor assured visiting Creek delegates that this was not true but the Creeks were angry and feared that the English were intent on taking their lands.[26]

The contest for land south of the Altamaha River, which had constituted the northern border of Spanish Florida, was between colonies as
well as between colonists and Indians. Prior to 1763, South
Carolinians, Georgians, and Spaniards had all used the area to a
limited extent. Now that Spain was out of the picture, South Carolina
and Georgia each claimed the lands. South Carolina claimed them
under colonial charter and Governor Thomas Boone proceeded to
issue land grants; Georgia felt its geographic proximity provided a
stronger claim, and Governor Wright tried to halt the land grants,
hoping that the region would be granted to Georgia. He feared, or
claimed to fear, that South Carolinians intruding on lands south of the
Altamaha might bring on Creek hostilities: "a great Number of armed
Men riding all over the Southern Part of the Country has alarmed
them very much," he wrote the Board of Trade in June. The Royal
Proclamation in October granted the disputed lands to Georgia.[27]

Although the Proclamation established a line on paper separating
the British colonies from the southern Indian nations, the physical
boundary was established in a series of treaty conferences negotiated
in the months and years that followed.[28] Anxious to dispel any notions
put about by the French and Spaniards that the British were intent on
"extirpating the whole Indian Race, with a View to possess & enjoy
their Lands," Henry Ellis advised, and the king ordered, that the governors of Virginia, North and South Carolina, and Georgia hold a
multi-tribal congress at Augusta in Georgia to discuss the issues that
threatened to disrupt peace.[29] John Stuart, who assumed office as
superintendent of Indian affairs for the Southern District early in
1763, joined the governors at Augusta in early November. They met
more than 700 Indians. Attakullakula, Ostenaco, and the Prince of
Chota came with about 300 Cherokees; Colonel Ayres brought a small
delegation of Catawbas; and Red Shoes led the Choctaws. Paya Matta
came with a delegation of Chickasaws, although James Colbert, a
Scottish trader who had lived among the Chickasaws for thirty years
and served as their interpreter, said they received "insolent" treatment
on their way through Creek country and were anxious to return home.
Captain Alleck led a delegation from the Lower Creek towns but few
Upper Creek headmen attended. Prominent headmen like the Mortar
and the Gun Merchant stayed away, saying they did not trust the
English, and even those Creeks who did attend the treaty were suspicious of British intentions. Emistisiguo, a headman from the town of

Little Tallassee, led the Upper Creeks but he was still a lesser chief and acknowledged that he could not speak as "the mouth of the nation." For Emistisiguo, as for Stuart, this was his "debut on a major stage." Stuart feared a Creek war was imminent and felt hampered in his efforts to prevent it: Amherst's policy of cutting back on Indian gifts "would give a very unfavourable impression of me at my first Entrance on the Execution of My Office," he wrote; the Indians would likely walk out in disgust.[30]

They did not. By the time the conference began, traders like Lachlan McGillivray and George Galphin had had more than ten days to confer with the assembled Indians and the main business—getting the Creeks to agree to a land cession—seems to have been carried in these meetings, with Emistisiguo playing a key role.[31] Stuart opened the conference on November 5 by assuring the Indians that His Majesty's goodness was "as extensive as the Dominions" he now possessed. "At a time when he has nothing to apprehend from any enemies he opens his arms to receive his red children." Stuart explained the new political situation. Knowing that "the perfidious and cruel French" had been spreading lies among the Indians, the King had insisted in the Peace of Paris that the French and the Spaniards remove beyond the Mississippi so that the Southeastern Indians and the English could live in peace and friendship. It would be the Indians' fault if this did not happen.[32] Paya Matta, Attakullakulla, Ostenaco, and Red Shoes gave belts of wampum and pledged their allegiance. Attakullakulla gave strings of wampum to keep the path open and clear. Paya Matta declared his heart was as white as any white man's. But the Indian speakers also voiced complaints against British traders and expressed concerns about encroachments on their lands.[33]

After the ritual exchanges of good words and white beads, the parties agreed to "a perfect and perpetual Peace and sincere Friendship." The governors and superintendent promised to continue trade so long as the traders were guaranteed safe passage. Adhering to an agreement evidently worked out before the formal conference proceedings began, the Creeks ceded a huge tract of territory between the Savannah and Ogechee rivers; in return the British guaranteed the Creeks' rights to their remaining lands in Georgia. Governor Wright hoped to settle the ceded lands with "the Middling Sort of People, such as have Families, & a few negroes."[34] Wright negotiated more than 2 million acres out of Indian hands in 1763 and made additional purchases in the years that followed. Between 1763 and 1775, Georgia acquired more than 5,500,000 acres of land in three cessions. As historian Edward Cashin notes, "the year 1763 was a watershed in Georgia history." Georgians formerly had looked to the backcountry for trade; now they poured into the Ogechee strip clamoring for land. The Augusta conference unleashed a land hunger that would culminate in a revolution to open more Indian lands to settlement.[35]

Stuart and the colonial governors probably knew that something was up when the Creeks agreed to cede land, and they certainly had notice that Emistisiguo, Captain Aleck, and the other headmen lacked authority to make such a cession. "Nothing done here will be confirmed by the absent leaders, in comparison of whom the present chiefs are inconsiderable," a Chickasaw headman warned them. Stuart had to convene five more congresses in the next decade to confirm the business at Augusta. As Steve Hahn argues, 1763 constituted a turning point in Creek history. The Creeks had to abandon their strategy of maintaining neutrality among competing powers and deal instead with a single and expanding power. Disputes over land replaced imperial intrigues at the core of Creek political life and foreign policy.[36]

The Catawbas did well to hold on to what little land they had left. Colonel Ayres, their spokesman, needed no interpreter but he had little to say—"he lives among the White People and came to hear the Talks of Others." All he asked was confirmation of a fifteen-mile-square reservation protected from encroachments by colonists. Although Creeks and Choctaws were still able to operate from positions of power, Catawbas in 1763 negotiated survival from a position of weakness. Once a force in the piedmont region, Catawbas had fought with the Iroquois to the north and they had proved useful to the infant colony of South Carolina. They assisted South Carolina in the Seven Years' War, but returning warriors brought smallpox in 1759 and the Catawbas "suffered grievously" from the ensuing epidemic, losing as much as two thirds of their population. Catawbas volunteered to fight in the Cherokee War but they were a spent force and had no more than seventy men capable of bearing arms. With both the French and the Cherokees defeated, South Carolina no longer needed Catawbas as allies; with the tribe reduced to a shadow of its former strength, South Carolina no longer feared them as enemies. The Catawbas, on the other hand, were "absolutely dependent" on South Carolina. Colonists pushed onto Catawba lands and, said chief Hagler, "they say they will continue to do so unless we show them a paper to restrain them." It was the end of an era in which Catawbas survived by diplomacy and the beginning of an era in which they survived because of their weakness. They agreed to live on a small reservation, with boundaries clearly surveyed and marked, as a refuge from impending destruction. Hagler, their most experienced and effective diplomat, died in August 1763. Three months later, the Catawba delegates were "last to be introduced, last to be addressed, and last to speak" at Augusta. They confirmed "an agreement heretofore entered into with the White people" and declared, "We will remain satisfied with the Tract of Land Fifteen Miles Square a survey of which by our Consent and at our request has been already begun." The Catawbas obtained the paper they needed to protect their land against trespassers. South Carolinians no longer courted them. By and large they ignored them. Like many other Indian peoples in the East, Catawbas now survived by keeping their heads down.[37]

Stuart remained at Augusta after the governors had departed. He distributed presents "and had the pleasure to send the Indians of every Nation away, with all the Marks of Satisfaction and good Humour." The new superintendent was figuring out the lay of the land in southern Indian country, learning the "who's who" of Indian politics and cultivating key players. Handing out presents afforded him the opportunity to confer separately with each tribe and ascertain their relations with other tribes. The Creeks were the main problem, Stuart wrote. Before the war, they had been courted by Britain, France, and Spain, "from whence they conceived high Ideas of their own Importance, and became Insolent and haughty to their Indian Neighbors, who I believe would gladly Join to humble them." The Cherokees hated them; the Choctaws had suffered often at their hands and only lack of guns and ammunition prevented them from taking revenge; the Chickasaws were firmly allied to Britain "and consider our Enemies as theirs." In Stuart's estimation, the Creeks' claims to lands bordering on the Floridas "must render these Provinces extremely limited, if the Indians cannot be prevailed upon to recede from them. They prevent any settlement being made to the Westward of Saint Johns River or above Fort Picoletta."[38] Governor Wright of Georgia agreed that the Creeks posed a threat. His province was "nearest, weakest & most exposed" to the Creeks and if they went to war would need help: "if an Handfull of Indians" in the North were able to inflict such distress on Pennsylvania and other colonies where there were plenty of His Majesty's troops, he wondered, "What may or may not, be the fate of Georgia, if attack't by the Creeks only, who alone consist of at least 3000 Gun Men."[39]

The most problematic individual in this problematic nation in 1763 was Yahatatastonake, a headman from the upper town of Oakchoy known to the French as the Loup and to the English as the Mortar. Governor Wright described him as "a Creek Indian of Considerable Family Connections Amongst them, a Man of Great Influence and who for Several years past has been our greatest & most active Enemy."[40] In the spring meetings with Wright, the Mortar was the most vocal opponent of further land cessions. He said he had heard the white people were "going to take all the Lands which they lent the French and Spaniards" and the Indians were "surprized how People can give away Land that does not belong to them." He declared that "he and his Family were Masters of all the Land, and they own no Masters but the Master of their Breath; but he thinks the White People intend to stop all their Breaths by their settling all round them." Prior to 1763, the Creeks had controlled the flow of British goods to their western rivals. The Mortar swore that he would kill every British trader who tried to pass through Creek country to reach the Choctaws and Chickasaws.[41]

The Mortar boycotted the Augusta conference. Stuart described him as the head of "the French party" in the nation. He had served as a French emissary during the war, had been "instrumental in the Murder of so many English," and was "bold and enterprising." Now that the Mortar's French backers were gone, Stuart cautiously courted him. He did not send him presents but did send the King's offer of pardon, granted "upon a Supposition of His having been Actuated by a mistaken Principle of serving his Country, founded on the Abusive Misrepresentations of the French." Stuart invited him to meet at Fort Augusta the next April and explained his actions to his superiors: "I took this Step upon considering that this Man may possibly continue to be troublesome, from a Dispair of being forgiven and received into favor. I think if he could be fixed in our Interest, there would be no Danger of any Rupture with the Creeks."[42] In addition, Montault de Monberaut, whom Stuart employed as his deputy, exerted his influence, sending his son into Creek country, to persuade the Mortar to make his peace with the British.[43]

Stuart's diplomacy paid off. By the next summer, the Mortar came around and accepted an alliance with the British and the government's program of frontier regulation as the best option for the Creeks. Two of his brothers had been killed by the Chickasaws, and this may have contributed to his change of heart. The Handsome Fellow and other Upper Creek headmen brought "a Peaceable Talk" to Stuart and the governors of Georgia and South Carolina in the name of the Mortar, who begged forgiveness for "the Many Outrages and hostilities that I have Committed Against the English, during my Attachment to the French interest." He sent a white wing as a pledge of his future friendship and a string of white beads on behalf of the chiefs of the nation. They asked "that the Great Old Path between Augusta and the Nation, may be kept White and Clean, and that they may be Supplied with goods etc. by that Path, as they want to know no other."[44] The Mortar told Stuart in the summer of 1764 that he would have nothing to do with West Florida, but the next spring he attended the treaty the British held at Pensacola. Montault de Monberaut claimed credit for the Mortar's change of tune,[45] but, as Governor Wright had predicted in April 1763, the Creeks could not do without English trade.[46]

A closer look at the Creek confederacy shows how imperial adjustments in 1763 generated shifts in power within Indian nations and produced adjustments to international changes at the community level. When the British took over Mobile and Pensacola from France and Spain, the Creeks were left with fewer diplomatic options and their towns looked to be encircled by British power. But the British takeover also brought some new opportunities. Prior to 1763, towns in the southern part of Upper Creek country lacked direct connection to the British because the paths linking them to Charles Town and Augusta ran through Lower Creek or northern Upper Creek country. Now, British traders moved into Mobile and diverted much of the traffic that had formerly made the long trek to Charles Town and Augusta. Southern Upper Creek towns had a direct path to new sources of British power and trade at Mobile and Pensacola, and the chance to control the flow of goods from the Gulf Coast to their northern neighbors.[47]

The Treaty of Augusta included an agreement that any Indian who murdered a colonist would be "immediately put to Death, in a public manner, in the presence of at least Two of the English who may be in the Neighbourhood where the Offence is committed." On Christmas Eve, seven Lower Creek warriors, "a Parcell of young Fellows," killed fourteen whites in the Long Canes region of South Carolina. Stuart demanded the Creeks comply with the terms of the treaty and the British considered imposing a trade embargo to force compliance although they recognized that such a step might push the Creeks into full-scale war. At first the Lower Creeks at Coweta blamed the Cherokees, among whom the perpetrators lived. A week later, however, meeting at the town of Chehaw, the Lower Creek chiefs agreed to execute the murderers after their men returned from hunting. The White King, a chief from Cussita, signed the agreement, even though two of the murderers were his sons. The incident reflects how political influence within the nation was shifting southward from Coweta and Cussita to Hitchiti-speaking towns like Chehaw.[48]

The Wolf's King, "a noted Warriour" and "a great chief amongst the Creek Indians" received immediate attention when the British took over West Florida: among other gifts to the chief, Major Robert Farmar's expense account at Mobile that fall listed "3 Gallons of Claret for the Wolfe King." But gifts could not compensate for trespass. Farmar believed Wolf's King was a friend to the English, but the chief made clear the English might have only the land lying under the guns of Pensacola; "that all the land round was their hunting ground, and hinted that as soon as the English should begin to settle the land they would declare War & begin to Scalp the Settlers."[49]

In Florida, too, the British had to deal with Indians as a first step in taking over in the province. "I think that the Indians will give them some work," observed Governor Kerlérec of New Orleans in October 1763.[50] He was right. Although Spain had claimed East Florida, Indians had confined Spanish population to the immediate vicinity of St. Augustine and two posts at Picolata and Apalachicola. In 1763, while Creeks in Georgia and South Carolina protested against trespass and trade abuse, other Creeks, primarily from the lower towns, continued to migrate into northern Florida. They maintained only tenuous connections with their relatives along the Chattahoochee and Tallapoosa rivers and were in the process of becoming a separate nation, the Seminoles. John Stuart and another Scotsman, James Grant, who had invaded Cherokee country in 1761 and was now the first British governor of East Florida, held conferences to decide the extent of Indian lands in Florida. They met with the Creeks at Picolata in 1764–65, and later with Cowkeeper, leader of the Seminole community at Cuscowilla on the Alachua prairie. The Indians accepted British medals, gave up the ones the Spaniards had given them, and gravitated toward British traders and agents in the St. Augustine region.[51]

Yet Spanish fishermen from Cuba continued to fish off the coast and off the Florida Keys (which Britain and Spain continued to dispute as they were not mentioned in the Peace of Paris). Spanish fishing boats continued to carry Indian chiefs and Spanish goods between Florida and Cuba. Seminoles paddled large seagoing canoes made from cypress trunks to Cuba, the Keys, and the Bahamas, trading deerskins, honey, and dried fish for coffee, rum, sugar, and tobacco. When traveler William Bartram traveled through Florida a full ten years after the Spanish withdrawal, he met Seminoles whose manners and customs were "tinctured with Spanish civilization." Most spoke Spanish and some wore silver crucifixes.[52] In Seminole country as in much of Indian country, some things remained unchanged by the Peace of Paris.

The Peace of Paris opened up new opportunities in the southern Indian trade; the Royal Proclamation gave greater numbers of men access to the opportunities. The Proclamation ostensibly closed Indian country to settlers but at the same time opened it to traders, declaring the Indian trade "free and open to all our Subjects whatever," provided they obtained a license from the colonial governors. By removing limitations on the number of licenses issued, the Proclamation compelled colonial governors to license virtually anyone who applied. It also neglected to impose regulations on the licensed traders. A host of newcomers flooded the Indian trade. Trader James Adair called giving general licenses a "most impolitic step," and reckoned there were "at least five times the number of trading houses in all the western Indian nations, since general licenses, through the wisdom of our civil rulers, were first introduced." Formerly a limited number of "orderly reputable traders" operated in Indian country; now it was overrun with riffraff. A young Scot in Charles Town in 1763 complained that the Indian trade was "overstockt" with traders.[53]

Prior to 1763, traders transacted business in the principal towns as ritual exchanges of gifts with chiefs who controlled the distribution of guns and other trade goods to the warriors. Now, aggressive and profit-driven traders traded directly with anyone who had deerskins to

sell. Amid stiff competition, many of the newcomers were unscrupulous in their methods. "The Times are much Altered and not now as
they used to be," Emistisiguo told Governor James Wright. "Many
Unruly Bad White People," carrying "great Quantities of Rum" peddled
goods in the woods and anywhere else they could make a deal. They
got their customers drunk, cheated them, and abused their women.
Wright described them, with some understatement, as "not the
honestest or Soberest People." In the scramble for profits, they
undercut one another and told the Indians that other traders were
cheating them (which was probably true). "Clear I am beyond a doubt,"
Wright wrote to the Board of Trade, "that almost every disturbance &
injury that has happened from the Indians has in great measure, if
not totally Proceeded from the great Misconduct & abuses Committed
Amongst them by the Traders & Packhorsemen Employed there."
Some ran up Indian debts as a means of getting Indian lands, whose
value they knew would increase as settlers pushed west. (Forty years
later, President Jefferson confidentially applied the same practice as
national policy.) "[P]eople is mad to be Settelling upon the Indians
Land," George Galphin warned John Stuart, "it is bringing the hole
Contrey in to troblle."54

Many traders shifted their operations to West Florida. West Florida
merchants shipped huge quantities of deerskins to London from
Pensacola and Mobile. As the deerskin trade expanded in volume,
Indians became increasingly dependent on European manufactured
goods. Hunters slaughtered white-tailed deer as never before,
exchanging deerskins for guns and rum and neglecting rituals and
restraints that formerly maintained reciprocal relationships between
hunters and hunted. Deer herds became depleted. Unprecedented
amounts of alcohol caused social disruption. Chiefs lost authority: in
less than a decade, Choctaw chiefs were pleading poverty, asking their
British father to take pity on them.55 The hunters and traders were
destroying the basis of a way of life that had sustained Choctaws for
generations. Once a bond of peace, the southern Indian trade became
marked by disruption and violence.

In its "Plan for the Future Management
of Indian Affairs," drawn up in 1764, the Board of Trade recommended
establishing two superintendencies, restoring the practice of gift-
giving, and regulating trade. "The most superficial View of the nature

and disposition of the Indians and of the manner in which they regulate their civil concerns, will suffice to show that a steady and uniform
attachment to, and Love of Justice and Equity, is one of their first
principles of Government," the Commissioners of Trade reminded
John Stuart.[56] A close friend of Attakullakulla and the father of several
Cherokee children (Cherokee society was matrilineal, so his children
inherited clan membership through their mothers), Stuart needed
little convincing. In his view, frontier whites, not Indians, posed the
major threat to peace, and he attempted to extend imperial control
over the frontier as the best means to preserve it. Stuart regarded
Indians as potential subjects of the crown; many colonists saw them
as obstacles to valuable resources. Stuart's insistence on curbing the
activities of aggressive traders and on restricting colonial access to
Indian lands alienated many southerners. Britain's efforts to regulate
the frontier and to establish Indian boundaries fueled anti-imperial
sentiments that would lead to revolution and fueled the revolution-
aries' hunger for Indian lands.[57]

CHAPTER 5

Endings and Endurance in French America

"CANADA IS NOW SURROUNDED ON EVERY SIDE," Montcalm had written in 1758; "without the peace we need Canada is lost."[1] France got peace in 1763, but the price was the loss of Canada and more. "The disaster did not end with the substitution of one flag for another," wrote historian Guy Frégault. New France was dismembered, Canada transferred to the British empire, and the Province of Quebec established by the Royal Proclamation of October 1763. The defeat was economic, social, and cultural as well as military and political and it set in motion "a deep and complex transformation." The British world acquired an immense field of action in America, but "the French world, shorn of its American wing and confined within its European boundaries, had no longer scope for those broad movements which were to be, henceforth, the requisite of real power."[2] For the next two decades French foreign policy focused on securing revenge for the losses sustained in the Seven Years' War and the Peace of Paris.[3]

The collapse of the French empire in North America, however, did not mean the end of French presence and influence. Long after the Peace of Paris removed the French nation from North America, French, French Creole, and French-Indian populations, social systems, and cultures survived across large swaths of Canada, the Great Lakes, and the Mississippi Valley. French-Canadian fur trade society, French-Canadian folkways, language, foods, architecture, clothing, and relations with Indian people persisted from the mouth of the St. Lawrence to the mouth of the Mississippi.

In 1762, the governors of Quebec, Trois Rivières, and Montreal each surveyed his district and submitted reports and censuses to help the British government ascertain what they had conquered. They recorded a total of just over 79,000 Canadians, of whom more than half lived in the Quebec region.[4] Yet the people the British called French were a diverse lot. They included soldiers; habitants; traders who traveled between Montreal and the *pays d'en haut* (the lands to the north and west of the St. Lawrence) or between New Orleans and the Mississippi Valley; settlers at Detroit, Michilimackinac, and other frontier communities; the "interior French" living in and around Indian villages in the Great Lakes and beyond; and inhabitants of the Illinois country and Louisiana.[5] In 1763, France and Britain agreed to transfer an empire and create a new order in North America. French peoples from the St. Lawrence to the Mississippi now lived under a new regime. But imperial authority diminished the farther it reached from the center. Neither the government in Paris nor the government in London was able to dictate what French people on the peripheries of a North American empire would make of their changed circumstances.

QUEBEC

Like their Indian allies, many French-Canadians were shocked by news of the Peace of Paris. It was not unusual for colonial conquests to be returned at peace talks, and many colonists expected that France would insist upon, and Britain would accede to, the return of Canada as part of the peace settlement. "Many of the Canadians consider their Colony to be of the utmost consequence to France," Jeffery Amherst reported on his return to London, "& cannot be convinced either by the Definitive Treaty of Peace or by the information of Canadian Officers who have returned from Europe, that their Country has been ceded to Great Britain, they look upon it as a report spread on purpose to keep them quiet & to discourage the Indians from molesting Our frontiers."[6] The people of Canada had fought and suffered in the cause of the French king. They could not believe they were being abandoned, and that France would agree to a peace that did not include the return of Canada.

The Duc de Choiseul "had other plans for Canada," however. According to Canadian historian William Eccles, Choiseul's foreign policy was simple: obtain peace as soon as possible, rebuild French military power, strengthen the alliance with Spain, and renew war with Britain at the earliest opportunity. "Canada and Louisiana were intended to play vital roles in this scheme, but they were not roles the colonists would have chosen." France gave Louisiana to Spain to cement the Family Compact. Canada was allowed to remain in English hands in expectation that, without French power in the north to hold them in check, the American colonies would attempt to break away from the British Empire and disrupt British commerce.[7]

The Peace of Paris guaranteed the French inhabitants of Quebec security of property and the right to practice their Catholic religion. Those who refused to change their allegiance to the king of England were free to return to France. About 1,600 people left New France as result of the British conquest, many of them civil administrators, wholesale merchants, and military officers who accompanied French troops when they sailed for home. "Their fortunes were tied to the French empire, and the British empire's administration offered no employment to Roman Catholics."[8] But while many of the Canadian elite returned to France, ordinary Canadians found that a transatlantic crossing on British ships charging exorbitant fares was out of their reach. Only 270 French-Canadians left the colony.[9] This was as the British wanted. "Nothing is more essential to His Majesty's service," wrote Lord Egremont, "than to retain as many French subjects as possible and to prevent them from leaving their homes to go off to the colonies that may remain in France's possession."[10]

Canada had been under martial law since 1760. Amherst divided the conquered colony into three districts: Quebec under Brigadier James Murray; Trois Rivières under Lieutenant-Colonel Ralph Burton, and Montreal under General Thomas Gage. Each reported to Amherst as commander-in-chief. Amherst issued a "placard," posted on public buildings and church doors, that announced the ways in which the districts would be governed, assured the inhabitants of fair treatment, and urged his occupying forces to live "in harmony and good fellowship" with them.[11] The military governments at Quebec, Montreal, and Trois Rivières were hardly tyrannical, at least to hear the governors tell it. When General Gage succeeded Amherst as commander of the British forces in North America in October 1763, he believed he left the government of Montreal "in as good a Situation as can be wished; the People happy & contented, & the Savages in good Temper." In Quebec, James Murray claimed that no military government had ever been "conducted with more disinterestedness

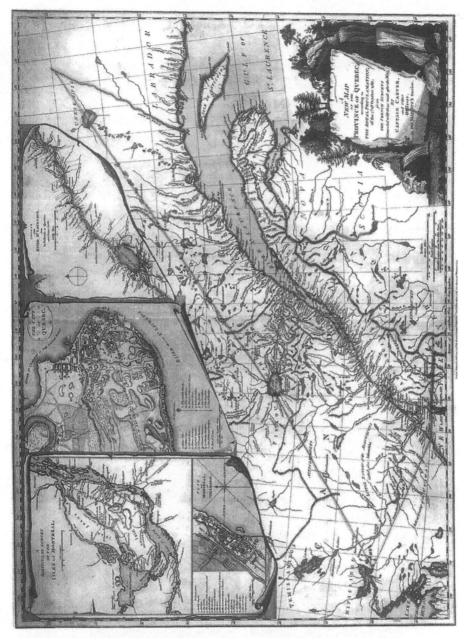

A New Map of the Province of Quebec according to the Royal Proclamation of the 7th October 1763.

and more moderation" than his, although, he added pointedly, he was not responsible for what went on at Montreal or Trois Rivières.[12]

The Royal Proclamation in October 1763 united the three districts into the province of Quebec, which encompassed both banks of the St. Lawrence River from about the Ottawa River to Anticosti Island. The Proclamation line defined the borders of the province, coming to their western point at Lake Nipissing. This was the limit to settlement but few settlers ventured that far west—most lived in the lower St. Lawrence Valley. Civil government for Canada was proclaimed in Britain in November 1763 but was not restored until the following August (the Peace of Paris stipulated that French-Canadians be allowed eighteen months in which to leave).

James Murray was appointed governor of Quebec. A career officer from an aristocratic family, Murray had served in Europe and with Wolfe. He had been made governor of the garrison of Quebec after

James Murray (1712–1794), ca. 1770. Artist unknown. Library and Archives Canada. C-002834.

Wolfe's death and had come perilously close to losing the city back to the French. As governor of the province, he was supposed to have been assisted by two lieutenant governors, but the positions were discontinued after Burton and Gage declined to serve. Issues of performance and promotion grated on old friendships. Burton was placed in command of the troops in the province and growing friction between Murray and his former friend contributed to both of them being recalled to England in 1766.[13] Murray hoped that his wife of fifteen years would join him in Canada now that he was governor. She made preparations to sail by the first ships in the spring but was "under great fears and apprehension of falling by the way."[14]

Murray's charge was to bring Quebec into the British imperial system. It was a formidable task. Disbanded Scottish soldiers settled along the St. Lawrence River but the British government's hope that English-speaking Protestant settlers would immigrate from the south proved to be a pipe dream (at least until the American Revolution produced an influx of displaced loyalists). Canada's economy lay in ruins after years of war and blockade. Now that it was part of the British Empire, its overseas trade flowed to England and England's colonies, not to France. British traders moved in to take advantage of the new opportunities and a new British elite dominated the towns. In Quebec, British officers and colonial officials lived in the upper town, while the lower town and suburbs remained heavily Canadian, although most of the merchants, wholesalers, and small traders who did business there were now English. Many French seigneuries, lands originally granted by the king to French nobles who emigrated to New France, passed into British hands. Some were confiscated; some were bought for a pittance from seigneurs who returned to France; some were obtained by marriage to the daughter of a seigneurial family.[15]

British debates about Quebec prior to the peace settlement had focused primarily on the value of the colony and the cost of governing it. How the French-speaking Roman Catholic inhabitants would be brought under British imperial rule received far less consideration. Anglicizing Quebec proved to be more difficult than most of the politicians anticipated—like some twenty-first-century Americans, many eighteenth-century Britons were convinced of the superiority of their way of life and assumed that other peoples would happily embrace it, given the chance. In reality, incorporating an alien population into the imperial system controlled from London constituted a major challenge.[16]

The British government hoped that establishing British-style laws and institutions in Quebec would help attract British immigrants. The Royal Proclamation declared that the newly acquired colonies were to be organized "as near as may be agreeable to the laws of England." Surprisingly, given the situation in modern-day Quebec, language was not much of an issue in 1763. French was regarded as the language of culture and the British educated classes, including army officers, spoke it regularly. Not until 1790 did the British government plan to impose the English language on the conquered population.[17]

Murray's commission as governor was accompanied by eighty-two detailed instructions regarding military defense, the composition of his council, trade, religion, Indian relations, land grants, timber harvests, suppression of piracy, information gathering about soil and climate, and a host of other issues.[18] Murray could be arrogant and authoritarian, but he soon began championing the people he was supposed to incorporate into the empire and stuck his neck out trying to temper the effects of the Anglicization policies formulated in London. He developed a genuine liking for French-Canadians, identifying with them ("The Canadians are to a man Soldiers," he wrote), rather than with the newly arrived British merchant class ("the Licentious Fanaticks Trading here") whom he saw exploiting them.[19] Writing to the Lords of Trade in April 1764, Murray described the difficulties he faced in trying to govern the inhabitants of Quebec:

> The People ... are composed of a Conquering Army who claim a sort of right to Lord it over the Vanquished, of a distress'd people Stript of almost all their Substance real and Imaginary, dreading the fate of their Religion and accustomed to an Arbitrary Government, and of a Sett of free British Merchts. as they are pleased to Stile themselves, who with the prospect of great gain have come to a Country where there is no money & who think themselves Superior in Rank and Fortune, to the Soldier and Canadian, deeming the first voluntary and the second born slaves.[20]

In particular, Murray tried to protect the inhabitants of Canada in their religious practices. In Britain, Roman Catholicism was associated with attempts to place a Stuart back on the throne—the last Jacobite Rebellion had occurred less than twenty years before. In the fourth article of the Peace of Paris, King George granted "the liberty of the

Catholick religion to the inhabitants of Canada ... as far as the laws
of Great Britain permit."[21] English laws prohibited Catholics from
voting or from holding political office. The oaths of office Murray
administered required candidates to disavow Catholicism and swear
loyalty to the Protestant Hanoverian monarchy, thereby effectively
excluding Canadians from any role in the new government. Canadians petitioned the crown, requesting that they be readmitted to
government. Writing to Lord Eglinton, Murray declared that he
would gladly do anything to defeat the King's enemies:

> but I cannot be the Instrument of destroying, perhaps, the best and
> bravest Race on this Globe, a Race that have already got the better of
> every National Antipathy to their Conquerors, and could they be
> indulged with a very few Privileges, which the laws of England do
> not allow to Catholics at home, must in a very short time become the
> most faithful & useful Set of Men in this American Empire.

He continued:

> If the Popular Clamour in England will not allow the humane Heart
> of the King to follow its own dictates, and the Popish Laws must be
> exerted w. Rigour in Canada, for God's Sake procure my Retreat, and
> reconcile it to Lord Bute, as I cannot be Witness to the Misery of a
> people I love and admire.[22]

The original intent of the Royal Proclamation and of Murray's
commission had been to replace the old counciliar form of administration with an elected assembly, as in the thirteen southern colonies.
British merchants were accustomed to representative government and
wanted an elected assembly that excluded Catholic Canadians. But
Murray kept his council and refused to summon an assembly.

The Royal Proclamation stipulated that English criminal and civil
laws should apply in Quebec, but the vast majority of Quebec's population were Canadians, and whereas English criminal law could be
adjusted to local needs, English civil law was not appropriate for
Quebec, as attorney general Charles Yorke and solicitor general
William de Grey recognized. If the inhabitants of Canada were to be
left undisturbed in their possessions, the old seigneurial system, the
social system that depended on it, and the Custom of Paris that governed the inheritance of property had to be preserved. (When New

France became a royal province in 1663, Louis XIV had decreed that it should follow the Custom of Paris, the body of laws governing the region around Paris.) Under the Custom of Paris, when a seigneur died, half his estate went to his eldest son and the other half was divided equally among the other children, a system of inheritance that protected the landed aristocracy against excessive subdivision of estates. On commoners' land, the Custom of Paris provided for equal division of property among all children of a deceased parent. In the superior court established in 1764, cases were decided according to the laws of England, but in cases between French-Canadians heard in inferior courts, French laws and customs governing the ownership, transfer, and sale of property were recognized and maintained. Catholics were allowed to serve as jurors, although English judges might have tended to view inheritance cases from an English point of view and favored the rights of fathers to dispose of their property by will.[23]

Murray also had to deal with an economic crisis. During the last years of the French regime, in an effort to remedy the chronic shortage of cash the authorities had issued more than 1 million livres in paper money. In 1760 the French government suspended payment on this paper, causing a currency crisis and threatening to wipe out the savings and business capital of the Canadians. Murray was unable to enforce the use of cash. He argued that "the People of this Country will hardly ever be reconciled to British Government while such sums of French paper money remain with them," but he was unable to get the home government to substitute a British equivalent. Instead, he registered the money in circulation, instructed the inhabitants to make a full declaration of the paper money they possessed, and implemented measures to limit speculation. Even that process took longer than expected: an early thaw in 1764 caused flooding that temporarily cut off some parishes from communication.[24] Murray also established a system of price controls to counter the inflationary effects of speculators who hoarded goods to drive up prices. But Murray would be home in England before Canada was on the road to economic recovery.

English merchants who were already suffering from the effects of Pontiac's war and the frustrations of obtaining licenses as required by the Royal Proclamation, resented Murray's apparent favoritism toward French-Canadians. They adopted a truculent attitude in dealing with the governor and used their connections in London to convey their discontent. Things came to a head in Montreal, where relations between merchants and the military were always tense. On the night of December 6, 1764, a group of soldiers wearing disguises and blackened faces broke into the house of Thomas Walker, roughed him up, and sliced off one of his ears. Immediately the question of who should try the perpetrators and where became contentious, and merchants accused Murray of obstructing justice. Quebec merchants sent a petition to the king, characterizing Murray's administration as "Vexatious, Oppressive, unconstitutional, injurious to civil Liberty and the Protestant Cause," and urging that the governor be removed.[25] Murray was told he would have to account in London for the disturbances in Montreal and for his administration in general and he was recalled in 1766. The charges against him were dismissed but he did not return to Quebec; instead he resumed his military service and then took a posting as lieutenant governor of Minorca. When Murray was appointed governor of Quebec, it looked as if the colony would be turned into an anglicized society. His "ultimate achievement, or failure," concludes one biographer, "was that he helped to impede this movement."[26]

Murray's successor, Sir Guy Carleton, continued in much the same direction. He continued the council form of government, and the Quebec Act of 1774 ratified it. Like Murray, he believed that the French-Canadians must be "inspired with a cordial attachment and zeal for the king's government."[27] The mixture of French and English legal practices caused such confusion and "chicanery" that in 1767 Carleton recommended revoking the Royal Proclamation and leaving the "Canadian laws" intact for the time being, or at least a modified version of them. English criminal justice would remain but French civil law would continue with respect to issues such as property, inheritance, matrimonial rights, and paternal authority. The Quebec Act of 1774 entitled Roman Catholics to practice their religion, provided a new oath of office that was inoffensive to Catholics, and stipulated "in all Matters of Controversy, relative to Property and Civil Rights, Resort shall be had to the Laws of Canada." Carleton interpreted this to restore the entire body of French civil laws, even in commerce. "In this way," writes historian Peter Moogk, "the British government's humane pragmatism combined with one governor's naïve enthusiasm for the French regime to bring about a continuation of French civil law in the Old Province of Quebec and in its successor, the modern Province of Quebec."[28]

In 1763 in Canada, there were new economic as well as new political leaders. A new merchant class operating under a more open economic system and pursuing new opportunities brought a shift in the balance of power from the old political, ecclesiastical, and military capital at Quebec to the new center of economic activity at Montreal. Yet, a dozen years later, Quebec did not become the fourteenth colony to rebel. Instead French-Canadians continued to live under the power of a nation whose religion, customs, language, and laws were very different from their own.[29] Thomas Douglas, Fifth Earl of Selkirk, offered a Scotsman's comments on the state of affairs he saw in 1803:

> The English at Quebec & Montreal cry out in the true John Bull style against their obstinate aversion to institutions which they have never taken any pains to make them understand—& are surprised at the natural & universally experienced dislike of a conquered people to their conquerors & to everything which puts them in mind of their subjection.[30]

In Guy Frégault's words, "an English society had closed around the Canadians without absorbing them.... Generations of Canadians succeeded one another in a British empire, a British continent, a British state."[31] The bulk of Canada's inhabitants remained *French*-Canadians.

In conceding "that the French-Canadians could be British without becoming English," the Quebec Act laid down a new principle of empire and established a precedent for "the creation of multi national empires." But the act also extended Quebec's boundaries through Lake Ontario and the Niagara River to Lake Erie, down to the Ohio River, and down the Ohio to the Mississippi. American colonists viewed the act as restoring the old boundaries of New France and blocking their growth with a Roman Catholic, French-speaking province under the British thumb. As a result, the act "did much to ensure that one portion of North America should remain British, while it contributed largely to the loss of the rest."[32]

THE INTERIOR FRENCH

The tolerance and even in some cases paternalistic affection that British officials displayed for former enemies in Quebec was not matched by their attitudes toward the people they called "the interior French," French-Canadians who lived in and beyond the Great

Lakes country. The Royal Proclamation was supposed to keep Europeans out of the West but Frenchmen had been living in Indian communities there for a century. They now found the lands they inhabited assigned to the trans-Appalachian Indian reserve.[33] Many were descendants of French fathers who had married Indian women. Many had lived "in these upper Countrys for these twelve, twenty, or thirty years," said one British officer at Michilimackinac; they had "adopted the very principles and ideas of Indians," and differed from them "only a little in colour."[34]

In the St. Lawrence Valley, the British found "a land of white-washed cottages clustered around high-spired churches in quaint rural villages with their long, thin, cultivated strips of land reaching back from the river banks toward the forest"; an orderly, rural, and ranked society composed of former soldiers and industrious farmers. In the West, they saw idle Frenchmen leading semi-nomadic lives, spreading disorder and inciting unrest, living like and with Indians. In Quebec, the British found much to admire and preserve in French society; in the West, they found much to detest and destroy. Frenchmen living in the Great Lakes and Illinois country had aroused the suspicion of French colonial authorities who could not control them; British colonial authorities who were suspicious of their own backcountry settlers were doubly suspicious of French interior settlers they "inherited" by the Peace of Paris. Several British officials advocated rounding up the interior French and expelling them from the country.[35]

The French had built their North American empire on a network of carefully cultivated Indian alliances and they earned a reputation for good dealings with Indian peoples. Frenchmen usually had little choice but to pursue good relations with the people whose world they entered and whose power could permit or prevent France's great goal of linking the settlements in Canada, Illinois, and Louisiana. By the middle of the eighteenth century, the French had asserted their hold on the Mississippi, French trade was seeping through to New Mexico, French traders were active on the Missouri, and French eyes had looked on the distant peaks of the Rocky Mountains.

But the French were spread thin in the West. Only at Detroit, at Kaskaskia, Cahokia, and Vincennes in the Illinois country, and on the lower Mississippi, were they able to establish agricultural settlements, and these were small. Kaskaskia contained about eighty houses;

Cahokia between forty and fifty. Small Indian villages, inhabited by members of the once-powerful Kaskaskias, Cahokias, Peorias, Michigamias, and Tamaronas, existed close by and Indians and French inhabitants mingled freely.[36] Elsewhere, French presence consisted of small fur-trade posts, usually a few log buildings surrounded by a palisade. In such circumstances, French commanders usually tried to avoid rather than wage war with Indians, and to prevent or negotiate an end to intertribal wars that jeopardized French presence and purposes.[37] For the most part, Frenchmen lived in the West on Indian sufferance or as individuals married into Indian communities.[38] The French defeat not only deprived Indian nations of allies, but it also meant difficult readjustments for communities and families in the Great Lakes and beyond where French and Indians lived side by side.

In July 1763, Governor D'Abbadie of Louisiana sent dispatches from New Orleans to Peter Joseph Neyon De Villiers, French commandant in the Illinois country at Fort Chartres, informing him that the country had been ceded to Britain. In September, Neyon sent a message to all the Indian nations in the region. "The great Day is come at last," he announced, putting a good face on the situation, "whereon it has pleased the Master of life to inspire the great King of the French, and him of the English to make Peace between them, Sorry to See the Blood of Men Spilt so long." The two monarchs had each ordered all their warriors to lay down their weapons.

> What Joy will you have in seeing the French & English smoking with the same Pipe, and Eating out of the same spoon, and finally living like Brethren. You will see the Roads free, the Lakes, and Rivers unstopped; Ammunition, and Merchandize will abound in your Villages, your Women, and Children will be Clothed as well as you; they will go to Dances, and Festivals, not with Cumbersome, and heavy Cloaths, but with Shirts, Blanketts & Ribbons. Forget then, My Dear Children, all the *evil Talks*. May the Wind carry off like Dust all those which have proceeded out of evil Mouths.

The King had not given up the Indians' lands, he added disingenuously, only those the French possessed, "in Order to avoid War for the future, and that you may always enjoy Tranquility, and Abundance of Merchandize in your Villages." It was time to stop shedding English blood. "Our Hearts are now but one."[39]

No doubt writing with gritted teeth, Neyon painted an idyllic future under British rule. Few Indians bought it. When the British took over the stone fortress of Fort Chartres and introduced new trade regulations, French and Indian inhabitants alike abandoned their homes and property and moved west. Communities like Kaskaskia, Cahokia, and Chartres became depopulated as some 2,000 people crossed the Mississippi and took up residence in the new towns at St. Louis and Ste. Genevieve. French merchants refocused their attention from the North to the West, and channeled pelts to New Orleans instead of Montreal. *Coureurs de bois* who had formerly operated in the Illinois country now traded with Indian peoples up the Missouri River, although on occasion they still traded east of the Mississippi in defiance of British authority.[40]

General Amherst had dispatched Major Robert Rogers, accompanied by Irish trader and Indian agent George Croghan, to take over the French posts around the Great Lakes.[41] Detroit was transferred to Britain on November 29, 1760. By the terms of the surrender of Canada, French settlers at Detroit were allowed to remain on condition they swore allegiance to King George. Detroit's residents became nominally British subjects but Detroit remained a predominantly French community. Captain Donald Campbell thought they seemed happy with the change of government, despite "being in great want of everything." Campbell got on well with them. He held parties at his home on Sunday evenings when he and his French guests played cards until midnight. He noted: "The Women surpasses our expectations, like the rest of America the men very Independent."[42]

But French influence among the Indians remained strong and the British knew it. "I am convinced that while they are permitted to trade here," wrote Lieutenant Edward Jenkins from Fort Ouiatanon on the Wabash River in March 1763, "the Indians here will never be in our Intrest [*sic*], for although our Merchants sell them a Stroud for 3 Beaver, they will rather give six to a Frenchman."[43] Pontiac's War increased the Francophobia of British officers. The French had for so long been *the* enemy that British officers and officials attributed any and all problems to the influence and intrigues of French settlers and traders. "The French are at the bottom of this affair," pronounced Major Henry Gladwin.[44] Some historians also have seen the Indian war of independence as a French-inspired conspiracy. British conduct certainly generated nostalgia for the French, and rumors of an imminent return of the French king's forces to North America filtered through Indian country and into the history books. Some French residents lent a hand to undermining British control. British prisoners after the war testified to seeing French inhabitants provide Indians with food, and even, in the case of a few young Frenchmen, "dressing the heads and painting ... in the Indian manner." But it was the Indians who tried to persuade the French to join them, not vice-versa, and they fought the war for Indian, not French, reasons. Indians went to war hoping to wake up the French king, who must surely have fallen asleep.[45] But their French fathers refused to stir. Secondhand information related by a party of Potawatomis indicated that Governor Neyon returned Pontiac's war belt requesting French assistance. When Pontiac presented it again and pressed the matter several times, Neyon "grew angry and kicked it from him."[46]

According to a French source from Detroit, many of the settlers "were torn by conflicting feelings." Some "groaned over the foolish enterprise of the Indians" and wanted to see it stopped; others "would gladly have cast their lot with the Indians had it not been for the fear of public contempt." Others vacillated. During the siege of Detroit, Indians went to the French-Canadian houses along the river, demanding food and occasionally threatening the settlers if they refused. A delegation of settlers complained to Pontiac about their treatment and asked that the Indians desist from killing their livestock. Describing himself as "French Pontiac," the Ottawa chief assured them the Indians meant them no harm. His fight was with the English, who were as much enemies to the French as to Indians. All he wanted from the French, he said, was provisions. The French agreed to let Indian women grow corn in their fields and fallow lands.[47]

George Croghan visited Detroit during his peace embassy to Pontiac in 1765. Accustomed to viewing French as enemies, as well as competitors in trade, Croghan blamed them for inciting the Indian revolt in 1763 in breach of their oath of allegiance to the British crown, and he was free with his prejudices. Nevertheless, his description revealed a persistent French community whose interethnic fabric remained intact:

> the country is thick settled with French, their plantations are generally laid out about three or four acres in breadth on the river, and eighty acres in depth; the soil is good, producing plenty of grain. All the people here are generally poor wretches, and consist of three or four

hundred French families, a lazy, idle people, depending chiefly on the savages for their subsistence; though the land, with little labor, produces plenty of grain, they scarcely raise as much as will supply their wants, in imitation of the Indians, whose manners and customs they have entirely adopted, and cannot subsist without them. The men, women, and children speak the Indian tongue perfectly well.[48]

When the inhabitants of Detroit spoke French rather than Algonquian, they incorporated "Gallicized" Indian words in their speech.[49]

Croghan found another French community on the St. Joseph River, where nine or ten French houses clustered around a Miami village of forty to fifty cabins had formed "a runaway colony from Detroit, during the late Indian war."[50] Many Indians were happy to pin blame for the recent revolt on the French, and Croghan was predisposed to believe the French were at the bottom of it. Yet, he wrote to his boss, Sir William Johnson, after his mission, "it has not changed the Indians affections to them, they have been bred up together like Children in that Country, & the French have always adopted the Indians customs & manners, treated them civilly & supplied their wants generously, by which means they gained the hearts of the Indians."[51]

Most French adjusted slowly to the new regime; some no doubt resolved to wait and see how things played out; but many kept their connections in Indian country and Indian communities. According to trader Alexander Henry, who narrowly escaped death when the Ojibwas captured Michilimackinac, the French traders and inhabitants stood back from the slaughter. "I observed many of the Canadian inhabitants of the fort, calmly looking on, neither opposing the Indians, nor suffering injury." When Henry begged Charles Langlade, his next-door neighbor, to shelter him, Langlade shrugged his shoulders and asked "Que voudriez-vous que j'en ferias?" ("What do you want me to do about it?") Langlade's Indian slave hid Henry in the garret but when the Indians questioned Langlade directly, the Frenchman gave him up. An Indian named Wenniway took Henry and named him after a brother he had lost, but another Indian, Wawatum, who had befriended Henry before the attack, "bought" him and adopted him as his brother.[52]

The British commander at Michilimackinac, Captain George Etherington, was taken prisoner early in the assault. In contrast to Henry, he was grateful to Langlade for "many good offices."[53] In fact, Langlade had warned Etherington of the danger the fort was in and rescued him from the stake, at considerable personal risk. Langlade's allegiance was in transition. The son of a French trader and an Indian mother, he had led a French and Indian attack on the Miami village at Pickawillany in 1752. He had led Indians at the defeat of General Edward Braddock in 1755 and he was at the siege of Quebec in 1759. But he adjusted to the shift in political realities that occurred with the British defeat of France. During the attack on Michilimackinac, he ignored pleas for help from Henry, "who was only a competitor to Langlade and inconsequential to the British," but "strode out of the fort in the midst of the attack and seized the officers" as the Indians were preparing to burn them. The event, as Langlade's most recent biographer suggests, may have been stage-managed, to convince the British of his loyalty and value. With the assistance of his Ottawa allies and family, Langlade was able to get the survivors, including eventually Alexander Henry, to safety in Montreal. Invaluable to the French before 1760, Langlade now made himself invaluable to the British—and to the Indians— as a trader, cultural broker, and leader of warriors. Like many individuals on the borderlands of empires and cultures, Langlade was a man of flexible and concentric identities. He worked for the British Indian department and served Britain until his death in 1802.[54] The British Indian department recognized French experience and expertise in Indian country and routinely employed French and métis as agents.[55]

According to Anishinaabe historian William Warren, another French trader, Jean Baptiste Cadotte, was instrumental in keeping the Ojibwas of Lake Superior out of Pontiac's coalition. He warned them "the war would only tend to thin the ranks of their warriors, causing their women to cover their faces with the black paint of mourning, and keep them miserably poor, for the want of traders to supply their wants."[56]

By 1763, English, Scots, Irish, Scots-Irish, and Yankees settled in the Great Lakes and brought British capital into the fur trade. British goods replaced French goods as the products of Britain's industrializing society and expanding commercial empire flowed into Indian country: rum made from West Indian sugar, tobacco grown in Virginia, steel knives manufactured in Sheffield, guns made in Birmingham, textiles from Yorkshire, linen from Ireland, and a host of other items from the mills and factories of England.[57] But many of the personnel conveying those goods were French. The kinship networks Indian women had created with French men resisted British penetration and continued to dominate the western Great Lakes fur trade. Hundreds of French traders arrived at Michilimackinac each summer to exchange pelts. Four years after the Peace of Paris, 85 percent of men identified as Michilimackinac traders were French. Indian women and their French husbands still controlled the exchange process.[58] Prairie du Chien fell under British sovereignty in 1763 but French-Canadians, many of them métis, developed it as a trading post "and stamped the community with their character."[59]

St. Louis was not founded until the end of the French regime and grew up under Spanish dominion, but it was a French town. In an effort to revive Louisiana's flagging economy, Governor D'Abbadie granted a number of business monopolies in 1763. He gave New Orleans merchant Gilbert Antoine Maxent a six-year trading monopoly with the Indian tribes on the Missouri River and the west bank of the upper Mississippi. Pierre de Laclède Liguest joined the new company as a partner with a quarter share in the venture. Maxent, Laclède and Company were to establish a post in the Illinois country to stimulate and tap this trade. Laclède and his future son-in-law, Auguste Chouteau, a thirteen-year-old clerk, left New Orleans in August 1763, made the 700-mile voyage upriver with a heavily laden boat, reached Ste. Genevieve in early November, and selected the site for their operations in December. They chose an elevated location that offered protection from flooding and easy access to the Mississippi, Missouri, and Illinois rivers. "So many advantages were embraced in this site, by its locality and its central position" that Laclède predicted the settlement he built there "might become, hereafter, one of the finest cities of America." In February, Chouteau and thirty workmen started building the post. By spring they had erected cabins, had plans for building a town, and announced the new settlement would be named St. Louis in honor of King Louis XV's patron saint, Louis IX.

Many French-speaking inhabitants from the east bank of the Mississippi immediately crossed over to escape British rule and took up residence in the new settlement. St. Louis was a town of forty or fifty French families by December 1764 when news arrived that it had been built on land that was now Spanish territory and its citizens were about to become subjects of the Spanish crown. Despite the transfer, more French people fled to St. Louis in the fall of 1765 when the

British took possession of Fort Chartres. Some people dismantled their homes and transported them across the river. The first Spanish officials did not arrive until 1767. By then, notes Jay Gitlin, "St. Louis had passed through its infancy. It grew up speaking French, and its new imperial guardian made no attempt to change it."[60]

St. Louis was laid out on a grid-iron plan similar to New Orleans: "the plan of Upper Louisiana's capital was in fact a smaller version of Lower Louisiana's capital." But the town soon acquired the pattern of settlement and land usage common in the Illinois country.[61] St. Louis was "Spanish" for almost the next forty years but its distinctive French character changed little: French-style buildings with their steep architecture, French Catholicism, French customs, and the French language remained predominant.[62] It still had a distinctly French character after the United States acquired it. Washington Irving described its population as "motley": traders, backwoodsmen, and river boatmen mingled with Indians, métis, and the descendants of the original French colonists. The strains of old French songs and "the happy Gallic turn for gayety and amusement still lingered about the place" amid the hustle and bustle of a growing American frontier market.[63]

The key to St. Louis's birth and growth was trade with the Indians. In November 1765, Sir William Johnson warned the Lords of Trade that a Frenchman near the mouth of the Missouri was carrying on "a vast Extensive Trade, and is acquiring a great Influence over all the Indian Nations."[64] Johnson was probably referring to Laclède, but it was Auguste Chouteau who spent the rest of his life at St. Louis, prospering with his younger brother Pierre in the Indian trade that built the city. The Chouteaus catered to the powerful Osages and other tribes on the Missouri and upper Mississippi rivers. Two dozen tribes from both sides of the Mississippi—Kansas, Otos, Pawnees, Sauks, Foxes, Missouris, Sioux and others—came to St. Louis to receive gifts and trade.[65] Like William Johnson in the Mohawk Valley, the Chouteau brothers exploited their niche as traders and culture brokers. Operating between their Osage customers and the Spanish authorities, the two Frenchmen built personal fortunes and put St. Louis on the map as a pivotal location in the shaping of the American Midwest.[66]

More than two years after the Peace of Paris, the British were still a long way from cracking the French hold on the Indian trade in the Illinois country and the Mississippi Valley. Sir William Johnson told the Lords of Trade that Indians would rather pay more to French traders than deal with British traders. By "their superior address, and knowledge of the different languages," Frenchmen "maintain their Influence, enjoy the major part of the Trade, whilst our Traders are considered as Interlopers, and have it not in their power to acquire the good opinion, or even a proper acquaintance with the Indians." Johnson had "little reason to expect that our People in general will ever treat the Indians with the like kindness and civility," yet he hoped that with the proper men at the posts, regular inspections, annual presents, and time, the Indians might be weaned from their attachment to the French.[67] Captain Henry Gordon was not so optimistic. "The French carry on the Trade all round us by Land and by Water," he complained in 1766. "Coop'd up at Fort Chartres only, We make a foolish figure, hardly have the Dominion of the country, or as much Credit with the Inhabitants as induce them to give us any thing for Money, while our Neighbors have plenty on trust."[68]

In the northwestern fur trade, the presence of Frenchmen seemed to increase rather than diminish after 1763. The West had always attracted young Frenchmen searching for adventure and freedom from the social constraints and sedentary lifestyle they could expect in the colonial settlements. The end of New France did not end French mobility in North America.[69] The fur trade now depended entirely on British organization, British capital, and British goods. British personnel monopolized the higher ranks of the trade. But French-Canadian voyageurs continued to provide the muscle of the fur trade. Other French-Canadians, freed from the financial and bureaucratic restraints of the French colonial regime, joined Scots merchants and Yankee traders in challenging the position of the English Hudson Bay Company. "By 1764, the western trading routes were once again crowded with Montreal canoes."[70]

Imperial politics did not always or immediately alter existing social realities. On the peripheries of empire, many of the same people continued business as usual. In their newly acquired territories, both Britain and Spain relied on locally influential individuals and families with established connections in Indian communities. That often meant Frenchmen with Indian wives.[71] In their postwar dealings with the Choctaws and other tribes in the lower Mississippi Valley, the British appointed as their liaison Montault de Montberaut, a Frenchman who had masterminded Indian attacks on South Carolina during the Seven Years' War. The cession of Louisiana east of the Mississippi to Britain placed Montberaut in a dilemma: he had either to give up his home and considerable property or his allegiance to France.

"Being thus reduced to the alternative of losing my possessions or changing allegiance," he wrote, "It is not astonishing that I accepted a position which could procure me considerations equivalent to those which I had in my native country, which I loved and only quitted under duress and with regret." He took an oath to King George and negotiated the terms of his appointment as Britain's Deputy Superintendent of Indian Affairs in West Florida. During his brief tenure in office he played an important role in British-Indian diplomacy (though probably not as important a role as he claimed) and developed a stormy and antagonistic relationship with Governor George Johnstone and Indian Superintendent John Stuart.[72]

The British barely affected the traditional French Creole way of life in the Illinois country. French and French Creoles predominated until after the American Revolution, as did the settlement patterns they had developed in the first three decades of the eighteenth century from traditional rural practices in northern France. They lived in nuclear villages, with open-field arable agriculture and common areas for pasturing livestock. This system of communal agriculture was unique in French colonial America. The elongated strips of farmland in the Illinois country resembled the ribbon farms in the St. Lawrence Valley, but whereas the St. Lawrence longlots were independent plots, each containing a residence and serving multiple uses, the strips in the Illinois country were plowlands, clustered together in a system of open-field agriculture. The system survived the British period intact and began to break down only when Anglo-American settlers flooded into the region toward the end of the century.[73]

The fleur-de-lys no longer flew in North America after 1763. But the French left a string of trading posts that grew into cities as Quebec and Montreal had done, and across large stretches of North America French people remained, French-Canadian lifestyles survived intact, and Indian families traced descent from French fathers and grandfathers. In some areas, the imprint of the British takeover was minimal. When the United States took over the Illinois country in 1783, they found communities shaped by almost 200 years of French presence in North America, not by two decades of British colonial administration. When the United States acquired Louisiana in 1803, they found French communities that showed little evidence of having been in Spanish territory for forty years. They also found new French communities, remade out of the upheavals of 1763.

CHAPTER 6

Louisiana Transfer and Mississippi Frontier

T
HE NATIONS THAT SIGNED THE PEACE OF PARIS made one of the largest land transfers in history but "showed little desire for a million square miles of territory west of the Mississippi." Small West Indian sugar islands that produced profits were far more desirable than huge swaths of territory that cost money. Louisiana was considered valuable insofar as it afforded or barred access to other, richer regions. It was "the prize proffered for favors." Choiseul offered it to help get Spain into the war and, when Spanish participation failed to stem the British tide, to help get Spain out of the war. He was willing to hand over Louisiana to get Spain to agree to the peace terms before, he feared, Pitt and the war hawks returned to power in Britain. France offered it to Spain, partly to ease Spain's losses in the war but mainly to keep it out of British hands. "The cession was given all the appearance of an impulsive, generous, and even quixotic gesture, but it was a calculated move of selfish national policy, carefully staged by a statesman intent on deriving every ounce of advantage for his own country." Carlos III hesitated: Spain hardly needed another unprofitable chunk of territory in an already burdensome empire. He accepted the expensive proposition primarily because Spain was just as committed as France to keeping Britain out of the heart of North America, and Louisiana would help keep the British away from the rich silver mines in Mexico.[1]

France's transfer of Louisiana did not have as immediate or as dramatic an impact as its cession of territories in Canada and the Midwest. The Spanish takeover produced nothing equivalent to Pontiac's Revolt. European presence west of the Mississippi was still relatively slight and the effects of changes negotiated in European capitals dissipated in regions where real power on the ground lay with the Indian nations. The great river continued to roll unchecked to the sea and French traders still plied its waters. Nevertheless, the Louisiana transfer did produce a revolt in New Orleans, it necessitated reforms in Spain's frontier defenses, and it made the Mississippi an imperial border as well as a trade highway. After 1763, British traders operated west of the Mississippi in increasing numbers; French traders continued to work there; and Spain claimed the region. Britain replaced France as the major threat to New Spain. Powerful Indian nations held back, and at times pushed back, its northern frontiers. In some cases, Indian nations continued to live, trade, and fight as and where they had before, and compelled the Europeans to adjust to their reality and dance to their tune. In others, they shifted their locations, their allegiances, or their expectations as they took stock of challenges and opportunities produced by decisions made in Paris and London. Although it featured secondarily in the negotiations, Louisiana felt the impact of the peace in years to come. As historian Daniel Usner notes, in the Lower Mississippi Valley, the treaties that ended the Seven Years' War "affected the inhabitants . . . far more than did the war itself."[2]

A New Order in Lower Mississippi Indian Country

The removal of one European power from the heart of the continent, and the efforts of the two remaining powers—Britain in the East and Spain in the West—to regulate their empires in new ways produced repercussions throughout Indian country. In the Lower Mississippi Valley and the Gulf South, news of the Peace and the impending transfer of power generated considerable anxiety, a flurry of delegations, and a series of movements among many of the "petites nations." When news of the preliminary peace terms reached New Orleans in April, Governor Kerlérec feared trouble from the Indians as the French left Mobile, Tombigbee, and other posts. But when the French evacuated Mobile in November, Kerlérec's successor, Governor D'Abbadie, complained that the English gave him "more trouble than the Indians," as they wrangled over the terms of the evacuation. "What a commission to have to deal with people intoxicated with their success who regard themselves as the masters of the world!" he lamented.[3]

Nevertheless, D'Abbadie cooperated with the British in communicating the new world order to the Indians. He had been on the job less than a month when, in July 1763, chiefs of the Biloxis, Chitimachas, Houmas, Quapaws, and Natchez, as well as Choctaws, visited him in New Orleans "to sound out rumors circulating among them" about the cession of Louisiana and, they said, to express their undying devotion to the French. D'Abbadie confirmed eastern Louisiana's cession to Britain, urged the Indians to live in peace with the newcomers, and assured them the British would supply their needs. The Indians remained skeptical and the delegations kept coming. Biloxi Indians declared their intentions "to die among the French" and told the governor they wanted to abandon their settlements on the east bank of the Mississippi and migrate to the western bank. Pascagoulas Indians joined them. "Mastabé," a Choctaw chief from the village of Yellow Canes, told D'Abbadie "that he could not become accustomed to the absence of the French in his village and that everything was melancholy for them." Two hundred thirty Mobilians, Taensas, and members of other small bands from the Mobile region traveled to New Orleans early in the spring to request refuge in French territory. They expressed their love for the French, but D'Abbadie knew it was fear of the English that drove them to him. When D'Abbadie reproached a Tunica chief for not following his advice and receiving the English in peace, the chief replied that "the English had sinister hearts" and treated the Indians with contempt. The Tunicas had retaliated and struck against them, "but they had not done it on French soil." D'Abbadie settled the Tunicas and Panacas (probably Alabama Koasatis) among the Acolapissas until the fall, when he planned to relocate them in the vicinity of Red River. Meanwhile, intertribal killings and tensions complicated the situation. In September 1763, for example, eighty Apalachee Indians (who had originally inhabited the Florida panhandle but resettled on the northwest shore of Mobile Bay early in the century) fled to Mobile "with their wives, children and baggage," seeking "a refuge from the fury of their pursuers," Atalapouche Creeks from the Tallapoosa River.[4] The next year, said D'Abbadie, Indians on the Mississippi remained "restless from everything which they see and from everything which is told to them."[5]

Within a few days of Colonel Augustine Prevost's arrival at Pensacola in August 1763, some 200 Indians from five different nations visited him. Prevost spoke fair words and dispensed a little rum but had few presents to give them.[6] Major Robert Farmar took possession of Mobile in October and promptly disembarked his troops—who had been on board ship for almost six weeks, with only a brief break at Pensacola. Unfortunately, the British arrived just as a contingent of Choctaws, who had been summoned by the French, arrived. The next day D'Abbadie and Farmar met jointly with the Alabamas and Choctaws to announce that their two kings had ended their quarrels and to explain the terms of peace. "You Tchataws, who are Born freemen equally with the white People," they harangued the Choctaws, "Open well your Ears to hear the great words of Truth which we are about to speak to you from the Great Emperor of the English, and the Great Emperor of the French; take good care not to let the winds blow these words away; open your hearts to receive them; and believe us, that we are only labouring in good affairs, for the Tranquility of You, of your Old Men, and of your women and children." The Indians would now be under British, not French, jurisdiction, and would receive all their trade from the English. The Indians surrendered their French medals and were given British ones in their place.[7]

Before 1763 the powerful Choctaws had played the rival colonial powers against one another and shaped the terms of their relationships with Frenchmen and Englishmen. Now, the Choctaw homeland had become part of the British colony of West Florida. They were amazed to see the French settlements east of the Mississippi given to the British without a fight, and even more amazed to hear the British claim Indian lands as a result. Choctaws who had become accustomed to being courted by French, British, and Spanish emissaries during the war now had to adjust their tactics to deal with a single European power.[8]

But the British had to make adjustments too. The Choctaws were not a people to be slighted. Major Farmar said they "inhabit this Country for four Hundred Miles North of this place, and all to the Westward as far as the River Mississip[p]i," and the French told him they numbered 14,000 people, "whereof six Thousand are fighting Men." In Patricia Galloway's words, the Choctaws were "a multiethnic confederacy of autonomous towns" that constituted "the largest population unit in the Old Southwest, the single native group with whom all whites were compelled to deal." And the Choctaws expected the British to deal with them as the French had done, adhering to Choctaw protocols and lubricating their diplomacy with ample supplies of gifts.[9] At the joint meeting with Governor d'Abbadie in Mobile in November 1763, Farmar promised the Choctaws "that the English would in all respects use them as the French had done." Farmar promised more than he knew and exceeded his authority. The

Choctaws now expected regular and generous supplies of presents at a time when British policy was to cut back on Indian gifts. Worse, notes historian John Juricek, since the Choctaws knew better than the British how they had been treated by the French, Farmar had "put the British into the position of needing direction from the Choctaws on what their policy toward these Indians ought to be." The Choctaws left happy, but the British had to deal with other nations who were disgruntled by the commitments made to the Choctaws. "Major Farmar's naïve and open-ended promise to the Choctaws, which could be neither repudiated nor fully honored, complicated all aspects of British relations with the southeastern Indians for the rest of the colonial era."[10]

In March 1765, Choctaw delegates came to Mobile again, this time to negotiate land cessions in the vicinity. It was a learning experience for the British. The Choctaw chiefs had spent their lives mastering the intricacies of intercultural diplomacy; the British were still learning the ropes. The British claimed to be meeting with representatives of the Choctaw nation; in reality, the meeting was "a political drama played out by certain Choctaws who sought to gain advantage for their own faction beyond the constraints of their traditional authority." The Choctaws who attended were mainly from the western division of the confederacy, which tended to favor the British; few chiefs attended from the eastern division, which had formerly favored the French. The British employed the fictive kinship of Indian diplomacy and were pleased to hear Choctaw speakers refer to them as "fathers," but for the matrilineal Choctaws the term conveyed expectations of indulgence rather than acknowledgment of authority. "If I am to become their Son, they must Act the Father by Supplying my Wants by proper presents," pointed out a Choctaw chief named Tomalty Mingo. The British thought the purpose of the meeting was to confirm the King's domination and transfer land; the Choctaws thought they were sharing the land and saw the meeting as an opportunity to negotiate the shift in allegiance and secure better rates of trade.[11]

As their Creek enemies realized, Choctaws enjoyed improved access to superior British trade goods and guns now that Mobile had changed hands. The smoldering rivalry of Creeks and Choctaws shifted to open conflict in 1763. The war is usually attributed to British meddling, of which there was plenty. John Stuart had his hands in things and it suited British interests to have the two most powerful

Native nations in the South at odds with each other. But Choctaw chiefs also saw in the war an opportunity to bolster their prestige with the warriors by protecting a precarious trade relationship with Britain. The British would give the chiefs the guns they needed to distribute to their warriors if they were to be turned against the Creeks. Hostilities continued, on and off, until the outbreak of the Revolution, at which time the British Indian Department scrambled to try to end the conflict and unite the tribes against a new enemy.[12]

Lingering French and Reluctant Spanish

Europeans were slow to implement in Louisiana the changes in sovereignty dictated by the Peace of Paris. On paper, the Peace of Paris ended the French regime; in practice, Spain was in no hurry to occupy its new territory. In 1763, Louisiana was placed under the first minister of the Spanish government rather than the minister of the Indies, who supervised Spain's New World possessions. French laws, institutions, and practices were to remain in effect until the king deemed it necessary to change them. British observers looking across the Mississippi saw "a Strange Mixture of French and Spanish Government . . . so that there is no knowing to whom the Country belongs." Sir William Johnson advised the Lords of Trade that "although the Spaniards should possess N. Orleans &c. and are a less active people yet the French will still remain and act the same part under the Spanish Government which they practise under their own."[13]

The first Spanish officials did not arrive until 1766, and Spain did not take effective control of the province until 1769. For six years after 1763, nominal power and effective local government remained in the hands of the French governors, Jean-Jacques Blaise d'Abbadie (1763–65) and Charles-Philippe Aubry (1765–69), the Superior Council, and Attorney General Nicolas Chauvin de Lafrénière, an elite Creole who opposed the transfer to Spanish rule. Louisiana suffered a severe postwar economic crisis, while Spanish resources were committed to rebuilding Havana and strengthening Mexico rather than to administering the new province.

When Jean-Jacques Blaise D'Abbadie arrived in Louisiana in June 1763 he had a lot on his plate. He was to restore order to the government of Louisiana, which had been reduced to a shambles by feuding between the previous governor, Louis Belouart de Kerlérec, and his commissaire-ordonnateur, Vincent de Rochemore, both of whom had been recalled to France. D'Abbadie was instructed to settle the royal accounts, which had been in arrears since 1755. He was to oversee the orderly transfer of Louisiana west of the Mississippi to Spain, the portion that lay east of the Mississippi to Britain. He transferred all but 200 regular troops to St. Domingue (present day Haiti). French colonists in Louisiana who chose to live under British or Spanish rule were permitted to do so, but those who wanted to relocate would be transported at government expense to the French colony of their choice. D'Abbadie's instructions also urged him to maintain good relations with the Indians and "to avoid the problems which a change of domination could occasion."[14]

Carlos III appointed fifty-year-old Antonio de Ulloa, captain of the royal navy, as first governor and captain general of Spain's new province. Ulloa sailed from Havana and arrived in New Orleans the first week of March 1766. Ulloa was a scientist rather than an administrator. At nineteen, he had accompanied a French astronomical expedition to Peru in an effort to determine the shape of the earth. In 1748 he had published a book of natural history and travel, in which he described, among other things, the pre-contact irrigation systems of the Incas and the impact of the 1687 earthquake. He was also a proponent of the first natural history museum in Spain.[15]

Ulloa had to defend the province, but he came with only ninety soldiers, not enough even for effective police duty. Plans to induce French soldiers to reenlist in Spanish service proved fruitless. Ulloa felt he could not take formal possession of the province until he received reinforcements. He worked out "a peculiar arrangement" with Governor Aubry, who remained in command of the soldiers. The Spanish flag was raised at Balize at the mouth of the Mississippi and at other posts in the colony, but not at New Orleans. The French governor remained in nominal control of Louisiana and issued orders in the name of the Spanish King. "My position is most extraordinary," Aubry wrote in January 1768. "I command for the King of France and at the same time I govern the Colony as if it belonged to the King of Spain."[16]

Ulloa did his best with limited resources. He built new posts and settlements along the Mississippi as defenses against British threats. He cultivated good relations with Indians in the Illinois country, inviting them to meet him in council and offering them gifts and inducements to relocate to Spanish territory. He continued the French

Governor Antonio de Ulloa (1716–1795) by Andres Molinary, 1910. Courtesy of
the Louisiana State Museum.

system of dealing with Indians by largesse and license. At the same
time, Ulloa tried to keep the tribes hostile to the English who were
intruding on the west bank of the Mississippi and up the Missouri.
"The Missouri River belongs to the domain of his Majesty in its
entirety, as is stipulated in the last treaties of peace between France and
England," Ulloa wrote in secret instructions in 1767 regarding the
building of two forts at the mouth of the Missouri.[17] That summer,
two barges of Spanish soldiers arrived and Captain Don Francisco
Ríu began the work of strengthening fortifications at the mouth of the
Missouri to thwart anticipated British threats.[18]

Louis St. Ange de Bellerive, the former French commandant at Fort
Chartres, reestablished his headquarters at St. Louis and made it the
seat of his temporary government in Upper Louisiana until Spain

assumed control. The French-Canadian captain had seen more than forty years of service on the frontier. Ulloa thought it "necessary to keep him in the same command which he has held not only on account of his conduct but also because of the credit and reputation which he has among the Indians." St. Ange was an elderly man, "and when he comes to the end of his days, the officers of our troops naturally will have more knowledge of the management of the Indians."[19] Ulloa called St. Louis "Pencur," from the French nickname for the place, Paincourt (short of bread), but the town prospered in the Indian trade and had more than 300 residents by the time Spain took over in 1767.[20] The Laclède-Chouteau family and most of the residents of St. Louis took an oath of loyalty to Carlos III of Spain ("under the supervision, paradoxically, of the Frenchman, St. Ange,") and went about their business.[21] Spain was happy to let them. "The advantages of trading with the Indians with equity and justice are well proven in this city," wrote Ulloa's successor, Alejandro O'Reilly. "Daily Indian canoes, laden with food, skins, and other trifles, which they sell publicly at their just price, arrive, and the Indians buy afterwards, by means of them, what they need in the shops and stores and go away well satisfied."[22]

But Ulloa was unable to remove root causes of unrest among the resident French population. New Orleans merchants were reluctant to relinquish the freedom from commercial regulation they had enjoyed in the years between French cession and Spanish possession. Ulloa imposed price controls on goods from the West Indies in an effort to protect Louisiana consumers but instead alienated Louisiana merchants who made profits importing West Indian goods. And Ulloa was pinched for funds. "Everybody is without pay, troops, officials, offices, and purveyors," he wrote from New Orleans on Christmas Day, 1767. They had suffered patiently in the hope things would improve, "but now that they have seen the contrary come to pass, it is inevitable that this will result in some very serious disaster."[23]

The disaster came in 1768. Led by prominent Louisiana Creoles, including Attorney General Lafrénière, discontented citizens rose in revolt. Ulloa fled to Havana for refuge. Spain replaced him with General Alejandro O'Reilly, an Irish soldier of fortune turned Spanish subject, who promptly sailed to New Orleans with 2,000 troops and quelled the rebellion. A dozen ringleaders were put on trial, six of them condemned to death. One died in prison "and as there is no hangman here, five of them were shot." Lafrénière was among those executed. The others were imprisoned at Havana, one for life, two for ten years, and three for six years.[24]

Some inhabitants of Louisiana found the transition to Spanish rule unsettling, and some fought against the imposition of the new regime. For many, life went on much as it had before. The majority of Louisiana's inhabitants were slaves: according to a census taken shortly after Ulloa's arrival, 5,940 out of a total population of 11,476. When Spain and Britain took over the Gulf coast, they inherited a well-established system of slavery. Slaves regularly ran away to Indian country and, as they did in other colonies and as the French had before them, the new colonial authorities regularly required Indians to return them, and paid them to do so.[25] Since African slavery was an accepted part of life in Spain's other American colonies, Spanish officials saw no reason to interfere with it in this one. Ulloa did not attempt to introduce Spanish slave laws; O'Reilly did. Some Spanish governors attempted to reduce the cruelty of the system but generally Spanish officials did not want to antagonize the planters who constituted the most important class in the province.[26] As did the British in West Florida, the Spanish in Louisiana encouraged the immigration of new settlers and slaves, with the result that plantation agriculture spread and the population of the Lower Mississippi Valley trebled in twenty years.[27] Indian slavery too was common in Louisiana when Spain took possession but African slaves obviated the need for Indian labor. In 1769, O'Reilly outlawed Indian slaving-taking, "under any pretext whatever, even though there be an open war against that Indian nation," and ordered a census of Indian slaves in the province the following year.[28]

Frontier Defenses and Indian Power in the West

The transfer of Louisiana greatly increased the range of Spanish contacts with Indian peoples, from the Gulf of Mexico to Canada. In the words of Borderlands historian Herbert Bolton, "Spain now had on her hands an enormous Indian problem."[29] For Spain, Louisiana was a vast defensive borderland in which Indians dominated, even after epidemics had torn through their populations.

For much of the eighteenth century, Spain lacked the manpower and resources to keep their frontiers closed to French intruders and to contain Indian raids. Comanches and Apaches tormented the northeastern frontier of New Spain while Frenchmen exchanged guns, metal weapons, and cloth for Comanche hides, horses, mules, and war captives. Spaniards had feared that France intended to take over the area, cut off Spanish expansion by way of New Mexico, threaten the silver mines in Mexico, and ultimately acquire domination of the continent. For most of the war, France and Spain had kept a watchful eye on one another over vast stretches of the southern plains while Indians moved at will across the intervening zones of competition.

Now the French were gone and Spain held Louisiana. Texas was no longer the frontier against France; it was, in effect, an interior province. Texas was part of New Spain, but Louisiana was administered from Havana, a situation that made it difficult to apply a consistent policy toward the Indian peoples whose lands and movements transcended administrative borders. Britain, not France, was now the major supplier of guns to Indians and the major threat to Spain's possessions. Spain needed to implement wide-ranging reforms to defend the enlarged empire, and the impact of the reforms reverberated through the Spanish Southwest and northern Mexico. The end of the Seven Years' War "brought true commotion to the Mexican viceroyalty."[30]

The new situation demanded new Indian policies. Spanish-Indian relations had changed much since the armies of Francisco Vasquez de Coronado and Hernando de Soto rampaged through Indian country in the 1540s. Eighteenth-century Spaniards understood that diplomacy, not force, was the key to their success, even to their continued presence, in Indian country. They had learned how to deal with capable Native politicians who in turn understood that the key to their success and survival lay in playing off rival European powers. Governor Ulloa did not make the same mistake General Amherst had made: he knew that to conduct relations with the Indians Spain had to meet their expectations and budget for annual gifts as well as for gifts to be presented at councils and other special occasions.[31]

With British power looming across the Mississippi, Spain needed Indian allies on its northeastern borders more than it needed Indian converts. Instead of relying on a system of missions and presidios as Spain had done elsewhere, governors Ulloa and O'Reilly followed the French system of cultivating Indian alliances through fur trade and gift-giving. They attempted to ensure that only licensed traders operated in Indian country, placed restrictions on trading guns to Indians, and barred British traders from Spanish territory. O'Reilly also

outlawed trading for Indian slaves and trading for livestock, most of
which was probably stolen from Spanish herds in Texas and New
Mexico. Nevertheless, Spaniards found that Indian, not European,
expectations often dictated the terms of allegiance, and Indians
expected Spaniards to be the kinds of allies the French had been. Individual officers, agents, and chiefs had to build new relationships on the
edges of empires.[32]

When news of the Peace of Paris reached the Indian West, the
French and Spanish both had some explaining to do. Now that
French Louisiana and Spanish Texas were colonies of the same
crown, French and Spanish officials began telling Indians that they
were one people. Indeed, there was relatively little change at the
grassroots level. Ulloa and O'Reilly left operation of Indian affairs
largely in the hands of French agents, and they licensed French
traders to go freely among the tribes of Louisiana and Texas. The
Spanish continued to operate out of the French trading centers at
St. Louis, Arkansas Post, and Natchitoches. Arkansas Post dealt
with the Quapaws and other tribes in the region; Natchitoches was
the center for the Caddos, Hasinais, Wichitas, Tonkawas, and other
nations.[33] St. Louis dealt with the Osages.

Governor Alejandro O'Reilly, an Irishman, enlisted Athanese de
Mézières, a Frenchman, to serve as Spanish lieutenant governor of
Upper Louisiana. Born in Paris, Mézières had come to Louisiana
thirty years before and had worked his way up through the ranks to
become a captain of infantry, but he was discharged from the French
service in September 1763. He was also an Indian trader and man of
property in Natchitoches, and he held both African and Indian slaves.
Like many French traders and officials he transferred his allegiance to
another flag. The former soldier and Indian trader was an effective
broker—between French and Spanish, Spanish and Indians. His job
now was to get the Indians to accept the Spanish takeover, keep out the
English, arrest renegade French hunters, and make allies of the
Norteños, the tribes on the northern edges of Spanish settlement in
Texas. A major component of Mézières's peace plan involved inducing
Norteños to settle closer to Spanish settlements in order to consolidate
the frontier from Louisiana to New Mexico and provide a buffer
against the British and their Indian allies. He called on other well-
placed Natchitoches French traders to exert their influence among the
tribes. "[T]here are now no Frenchmen in these lands," the Frenchman

told the Indians; "we are all Spaniards." He embarked on a series of peace embassies deep into Indian country, to the upper Brazos River and Red River, and persuaded some groups to relocate nearer to the Spanish settlements.[34]

In many areas the fact that one distant king rather than another claimed their homelands made little difference to the Indian nations who actually occupied and controlled the territory. Osages, Caddos, and Comanches cared about access to European guns, not allegiance to European monarchs. The Osages had moved west as part of a migration that also carried Quapaws, Poncas, Omahas, Otos, and Kansas from the Ohio Valley to new homes beyond the Mississippi.[35] They took up residence on the prairies between the Missouri and Arkansas rivers. They inhabited large villages in the spring and fall, dispersed to hunt buffalo on the plains in the summer, and wintered near the forests. They could raise more than a thousand warriors,[36] had ample supplies of horses and guns, and earned a fierce reputation among Europeans and other Indians alike. They had met French traders at the end of the seventeenth century and were accustomed to dealing with Europeans on their own terms and from a position of strength. They exploited their geographic, economic, and numerical advantages at the expense of other Indian peoples, operated as middlemen funneling guns to some peoples, tried to keep guns out of the hands of their enemies, and preserved their independence and their dominance in a world of shifting international contests and territorial boundaries.[37]

The Peace of Paris had little immediate impact in Osage country. As tribal historian John Joseph Mathews wrote, the Osages did not know that their French allies, "the Heavy Eyebrows[,] had given up dominion over them, such as it was," to the King of Spain. Osages "saw the same Heavy Eyebrows traders, singing and sweating their way up the Smoky Waters [the Missouri] with their pirogues filled with trade goods." French officials and explorers continued to come upriver "with presents and effervescent friendliness when their numbers were few." The Osages saw no *I-Spa-Tho* (Spaniards) for six or seven years after the Peace of Paris.[38] When Spain did take over Louisiana, the Osages had no intention of observing new trade bans that threatened to undermine the hegemony they had constructed. They traded at St. Louis but they also did business with French-Canadian and British traders.[39] As the Osages themselves came under increasing pressure from Indian migrants to their northeast, they intensified raids on the Caddos and Wichitas to their southwest, stealing livestock, slaves, and pelts to trade for weapons to defend themselves. Spaniards blamed the Osages for keeping the region in turmoil.[40]

Osage pressure pushed Wichitas and Kichais south into Texas. Taovayas, Tawakonis, and other groups who had moved south from the Arkansas River to escape Osage pressure found themselves even more vulnerable after 1763. Cut off from access to French guns and ammunition, they kept moving into Texas. Wichitas appealed in vain to the Spaniards, who were having their own problems dealing with the Osages. Frustrated and angered by Spanish alliance with the Lipan Apaches in Texas, some Taovayas turned to committing hostilities against the Spanish.[41]

The Caddos, a group of confederacies located along the Red River region of Texas, had been a client nation of France and had bolstered their power with French weapons in an era when European and Indian contests rendered their homelands increasingly volatile. Now, the Caddos found themselves in a precarious situation. They were compelled to make alliances with the Spanish, but the Spanish proved ineffective in providing protection against powerful Indian enemies like the Osages, while diseases continued to ravage Caddo villages.[42]

The transfer of Louisiana to Spain and the movement of Indian groups disrupted the supplies of firearms that Comanches had obtained from French traders via their Wichita allies. Faced with growing competition from Osages and Pawnees, Comanches turned to Anglo-American traders for guns.[43] Governor of New Mexico Thomas Vélez Cachupin was working hard in 1763 to maintain the peace he had established with the Comanches, which was "also a means for the reduction of these heathen to our holy faith."[44] It was a precarious peace, and Spanish relations with Comanches were complicated by Spanish and Comanche relations with Apaches. Comanches attacked Apaches wherever they found them, pushing them off the plains and pursuing them into southern Texas. Some Apaches sought refuge at Spanish missions, and in 1763 Indians allied to the Comanches attacked San Antonio because Spaniards there provided protection to refugee Apaches.[45] The next governor did not share Cachupin's opinions or his diplomatic skills and there was more conflict to come with the Comanches, although it lessened later in the decade once Spain began to implement the Marquis de Rubí's

recommendation: make peace with the Comanches and wage geno-
cidal war against the Apaches.

The temporary but traumatic loss of Havana to Britain in 1762
emphasized the need for reform in Spain's American colonial system,
even if it was only "defensive modernization" to protect the colonies
from foreign commercial intrusion.[46] Carlos III appointed José de
Gálvez *visitador-general* (inspector-general) of New Spain in 1765
with instructions to reorganize the entire administrative system and
institute fiscal reforms. Gálvez went further and attempted to expand
military authority and centralize control over the northern provinces.
The Marquis de Rubí was assigned to inspect the presidios on the
northern frontier, from Texas to Sonora, and to report on the imperial adjustments and financial reductions necessary as a result of the
shift of international boundaries. In two years, Rubí visited almost
two dozen posts and traveled more than 7,600 miles through Indian
country where "we are admitted only as friends, but without any
authority." Spanish troops were vastly outnumbered and ineffective in
dealing with the hit-and-run warfare of Indians who obtained guns
through intertribal trade. To counter the Indian threat Rubí recommended reorganizing defenses and establishing a line of fifteen
presidios, located at 100-mile intervals, from the Gulf of Mexico to
the Gulf of California.[47] He "essentially posed European solutions
for American frontier problems"—mobile Indian raiders easily
penetrated the porous cordon of military posts—but the "New Regulations for Presidios" issued by royal order in 1772 largely followed his
recommendations.[48]

In the north, the Upper Missouri and Saskatchewan Rivers marked
the boundaries of Spanish Louisiana and British-claimed territory in
the West. These regions lay beyond Spanish influence, but developments stemming from 1763 drew increasing Spanish interest. Before
1763, the Hudson's Bay Company, which King Charles II had chartered in 1670, confined its operations to the shores of the bay, relying
on Indian trappers and traders from the hinterland who brought their
pelts to its posts. When New France fell, the Hudson's Bay Company
believed "their golden age of monopoly had finally arrived"; there
would be no French competitors in the interior to divert Indian traders
from the bay posts. In fact, the Company faced growing competition.
In 1763, control of the St. Lawrence River system passed formally
from France to Britain, and with it water access to the Great Lakes,

Lake of the Woods, Lake Winnipeg, and beyond. Scots and French-Canadians operating out of Montreal adopted the old French position that the Hudson's Bay Company's rights applied only to the shores of the bay. They pushed into the interior, intercepting Indian trappers as they canoed their pelts down to the Hudson's Bay posts. The government in London gave up trying to enforce a monopoly of the fur trade. The Hudson's Bay Company had no choice but to follow its competitors and extend operations inland. The western territories suddenly "were open to all comers," and a new era began. Before 1763, Crees, Assiniboines, and Ojibwas had virtually monopolized trade with the posts on Hudson Bay; after 1763, Montreal traders began dealing directly with most of the tribes of the Canadian West. Eventually, the Montreal interests formed the Northwest Company and their traders and explorers mapped the Canadian West as they pushed into new regions. What fur trade historian Arthur J. Ray describes as a "tumultuous period" of population shifting began, as Western Crees and Assiniboines migrated west in response to new developments in the fur trade, and Ojibwas moved in behind them.[49] The presence of traders on the ground, not the fact that the territory now appeared on English rather than French maps, was what mattered in Indian country.

As Crees and Assiniboines moved to keep ahead of the shifting fur trade, they linked up with a trade network centered on the Great Bend of the Upper Missouri River. There, Mandan, Hidatsa, and Arikara women planted huge fields of corn around their villages and produced surpluses of corn, beans, squash, and tobacco that they traded to hunters from the Great Plains. In the eighteenth century the Missouri River villagers began to exchange horses and guns as well as corn and meat and the Mandan-Hidatsa-Arikara rendezvous increased its business and its significance. From the northeast they obtained manufactured goods, either direct from French and British traders or via Cree and Assiniboine middlemen; from the west they received horses and the products of the plains; from the southwest came more horses, plus goods of Spanish and Pueblo origin. Indian traders returning from the villages passed on what they obtained to more distant neighbors, often at greatly inflated prices. Spanish Indian policy continued to prohibit trading guns to Indians but guns-for-horses trade networks ensured that southern plains tribes obtained firearms from the north and east. The Mandan-Hidatsa-Arikara trade center connected with other Native exchange centers on the southern plains, the Rio Grande, and the Columbia River, with Montreal and St. Louis, and, ultimately, with the mills and markets of Europe. French and Spanish traders from the new trade center at St. Louis pushed upriver to do business at the villages, and when they got there, they met British and Canadian traders. The villages were not only a hive of activity but also a key site for European governments planning explorations and seeking information about the world beyond. But even as Spaniards penetrated the upper Missouri, more mobile and better-armed Sioux enemies challenged the village traders and smallpox cut down their numbers. The horses, guns, and trade networks that enhanced the power and prosperity of the Mandans and their neighbors, in time destroyed their busy trade villages.[50]

Spain needed not only to protect its frontier against Indian attacks but also to prevent the invasions "which are to be expected from the nations protected by the English and in time of war from the English themselves."[51] It failed to contain the British or to control the Indians. British smugglers operated on the coast of Texas, British guns reached Comanches and the Taovayas on the upper Red River via Indian middlemen, and British traders in Texas boasted they could trade wherever they pleased.[52]

Like Britain, Spain after 1763 tried to tighten its imperial control over its American colonies and to improve relations with the Indian nations on its North American borders. As historian Henry Kamen observes, the North American empire after 1763 remained "a frail possession in Spanish hands."[53] Prior to 1763, Spaniards feared the French as a threat to their northern frontiers and Mexican silver mines; after 1763, they feared the British; after 1783, they feared the Americans, and with good reason. Spain gave Louisiana back to France in 1801. Two years later France sold it to the United States, and New Spain had a more aggressive neighbor than ever before on its northern frontiers.

CHAPTER 7

Exiles and Expulsions

 T HE END OF THE SEVEN YEARS' WAR, the news of the Peace of
Paris, and the shifts in imperial presence generated frequent and
sometimes far-reaching population movements in North America.
European emigrants crossed the Atlantic, settlers pushed toward the
West, and many slaves moved farther across the South. Some Indian
peoples migrated beyond the Mississippi. Indian customers and relatives went west with French traders or maintained ties with them by
crossing the river to trade. After the British occupied Illinois country
in 1765, most Illinois Indians moved west of the Mississippi, although
they seem to have shifted residence easily from one bank to the other.[1]
Migrant Indians generated chain reactions in the West, where indigenous peoples had to adjust to the presence of new Indian neighbors as
well as to a new imperial situation. The victory of Protestant England
over Catholic France and Spain was not followed by religious purges
in the territories Britain acquired; nevertheless, several groups of
Catholic people felt or found themselves compelled to move: Spanish
colonists evacuated Florida, many refugees from Acadia regrouped in
Louisiana, and even Jesuit priests were uprooted and expelled. Stripped
of its mainland empire, France offered French-Canadians no nearby
haven and little incentive to leave their homes in the St. Lawrence
Valley, which had been the heart of New France, whereas Spain, whose
North American empire was altered but not destroyed, provided transportation to relocate its own citizens from territory it had lost and to
attract others to territory it had acquired. Spaniards who sailed from
Florida to Cuba exchanged life in an outpost of the empire for life in
one of its jewels.

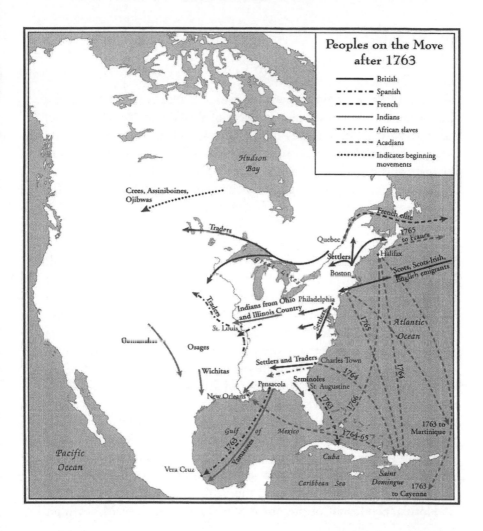

LEAVING FLORIDA

Without Havana, Spain's other possessions in North America and the Caribbean lay open to assault. Recovery of the Cuban capital was vital, but Spain would have to pay to get it back. Puerto Rico and Florida were both candidates for sacrifice but Puerto Rico was worth far more to Spain and Florida was handed over to Britain at the Peace of Paris. Spain was more than willing to exchange an unprofitable province for a prosperous Caribbean port. Charles Townshend, who resigned his brief tenure as Secretary at War in protest against the Bute administration's peace policies, complained that when the Peace was signed, instead of Puerto Rico, Britain got "an uninhabited country."[2] British troops sailed from Havana and took possession of Florida. For the first time in 200 years the Spanish flag was lowered in St. Augustine and the Union Jack raised in its place. Sick soldiers from the killing grounds of Havana found St. Augustine a welcome change. "It is remarkably healthy, perhaps the most so of any Town in America," noted one officer; "the Climate in Winter is pleasant, beyond the Idea of any man who has never been out of Europe."[3] But, climate aside, few Britons felt that giving up Havana for Florida was a good deal.[4]

The Royal Proclamation of October 1763 divided Florida into two provinces: the peninsula of East Florida, from the Atlantic to the Apalachicola River, which was governed from St. Augustine; and West Florida, from the Apalachicola to the Mississippi, governed from Pensacola. West Florida included the panhandle of the modern state of Florida, about half of present-day Alabama, much of Mississippi, and part of Louisiana.

The Peace of Paris stipulated that the 3,000 or so Spanish subjects living in Florida would be free to practice their Catholic religion and would not be molested if they chose to remain. But English antipathy toward Roman Catholicism was notorious. The Spanish crown encouraged its citizens to evacuate and offered to compensate them with other property elsewhere. Unlike the citizens of Quebec, the residents of Spanish Florida had the means to leave and saw little reason to stay. The province was not "much more than an outpost of Havana and a frontier refuge area; there was no body of deeply rooted colonists as in Canada." When Spanish officials offered assistance and land "on the real mainland, Cuba," Florida's Spanish population opted en masse to relocate. They were allowed eighteen months to settle their affairs and sell their property, much of it land acquired from Indians, to subjects of Great Britain. Royal officials in Cuba dispatched assistants to the governors of St. Augustine and Pensacola to help expedite the evacuations.[5] British officials complained that the Spanish government offered so many incentives to remove that, despite counterincentives and assurances, "no inhabitant will remain." But Major Francis Ogilvie, commander of the 9th Regiment, griped to the Board of Trade that their departure constituted "no loss to his Majesty's Government of East Florida ... as they were the least industrious of any people I ever saw, having depended entirely upon our colonies in Jamaica for supplies of provisions."[6]

Juan Elixio de la Puente was sent from Havana to oversee the removal of royal property and to assist Colonel Melchor Feliú, governor and captain general of St. Augustine, in evacuating the population. Juan de Cotilla, a Cuban engineer, was sent to calculate real estate values and facilitate sales of property within the stipulated eighteen-month period. He prepared detailed inventories of the houses in St. Augustine and produced estimates of property values as people scrambled to sell up and move out. The British complained that he inflated the estimates. Few houses were sold before the evacuation and property prices tumbled when British troops arrived and were quartered in private houses, "as there were no publick houses to receive them." Many property owners ended up entrusting their assets to Elixio de la Puente. He in turn transferred most of St. Augustine's houses and lots to Jesse Fish, resident land agent for the Walton Exporting Company in New York, and other lands to John Gordon of Charles Town, South Carolina, against future payment when the properties might be sold at a better price. But when the British took over, the government issued regulations authorizing the governor to grant lands, and required that all Spanish land claims other than those for property in St. Augustine be confirmed in London. The extensive claims of speculators like Fish and Gordon would have left little land for government grants. Governor James Grant argued that in reality, all lands beyond the immediate vicinity of St. Augustine belonged to the Creek Indians. Gordon traveled to London and spent many years defending his "pretended purchases," but the lands were granted to other British subjects. Secret transactions and shady dealings accompanied many property transfers, as both Spain and

England ignored the property provisions of the Peace of Paris: Spain tried to evade the limitations of the treaty; the British government denied land sales permitted by international agreement.[7]

In addition to shipping people to Cuba, Spanish officials in St. Augustine evacuated crown and personal goods, administrative records, military supplies and records, cannons, ammunition, tools, and equipment from the Castillo. "Not content with carrying away all the living," reported Governor George Johnstone, "they remove the dead; the bones of the late governor and of a number of Saints are carried to the Havanah." In addition, "Spanish Catholicism abandoned Florida." The evacuation involved shipping the personnel of the Parochial Church of St. Augustine, the Convent of St. Francis, altars, bibles, church records, and religious paraphernalia. Launches transported goods and people over the notorious St. Augustine sand bar to ships anchored beyond the bay.[8]

The exodus began in April 1763; the last transport departed in January 1764. Over the course of ten months, 44 transports loaded to overflowing with troops and stores carried more than 3,000 people— 952 men, 794 women, and 1,323 children—to Cuba, and 33 people to Campeche. St. Augustine's population went into exile mainly in family units: 364 Spanish families; 96 families of colonists from the Canary Islands, who had come to Florida between 1757 and 1761; 36 Catalan families from northeastern Spain who had come in 1762 with the Catalan Mountain Fusileers to reinforce the St. Augustine presidio; 6 German families, who probably had moved south from Georgia; 19 families of Christianized Indians; 16 free *pardo* (mulatto) families; 5 free African families, as well as 300 royal and private slaves, and 38 convict laborers.[9]

Troops and artillery received priority in scheduling transportation; St. Augustine's Spanish Creole population was given priority over the Catalans, Germans, and Canary Islanders, who received second-class accommodation as foreigners. Indians, mulattos and blacks were often segregated from the Spaniards.[10] Poor rations and yellow fever cut down the Indian evacuees: eighty-nine left for Havana in 1763; only fifty-one survived three years later.[11] The Spanish garrison at San Marcos de Apalache waited almost seven months for the British to arrive and take over the fort. Finally, in February 1764, the fifty soldiers, along with fifteen women and children, evacuated.[12]

The soldiers evacuated from Florida, 550 in total, were reassigned to other posts, but the civilian refugees posed a bigger problem. Initially, they were found temporary lodgings around Havana and each individual received a daily allowance of one *real*. Officials in Havana confronted an enormous task in feeding and housing the entire population of East Florida at the same time their overstretched treasury was also financing the reconstruction and fortification of the city after its siege and occupation by British troops. "Jesús, Maria y Joséf!" an exasperated official scrawled over the front page of a bundle of pension documents for the wives, widows, and daughters of displaced Floridians. Eventually the refugees assimilated and made new homes in Cuba. The St. Augustine census in 1786 showed that only fourteen of the hundreds of families who had left in 1763 and 1764 returned to Florida when it was handed back to Spain after the American Revolution.[13]

There was no immediate influx of British immigrants to repopulate East Florida. Governor James Grant did his best to promote the province and conducted Indian affairs with a view to creating an environment conducive to settlement. Nevertheless, when he returned to Britain in 1771, the colony had only 288 white inhabitants and 900 African slaves.[14]

Britain's new province of West Florida was created partly from what had been Spanish Florida and partly from territory that had belonged to French Louisiana. Lieutenant Colonel Augustine Prevost and 350 soldiers of the 60th or Royal American Regiment, veterans of the siege of Havana, entered Pensacola in the first week of August. Prevost described it as "a small Village surrounded with a Stockade." The residents lived close to the fort and in fear of the surrounding Indians, who were "numerous and near." Another soldier described Pensacola as "a few irregular houses and thinly inhabited."[15]

Following royal instructions, the governor of Pensacola, Diego Ortiz Parilla, organized a hasty evacuation. On September 3, 622 people boarded eight ships and accompanied Parilla to Vera Cruz. In addition to the governor and his officials, they included 160 soldiers, 118 civilians, 108 Christian Yamassee Indians, 105 convicts, and the families of the garrison. The Yamassees asked for permission to evacuate, apparently out of fear that other Indians would exterminate them once the Spaniards had left. It was a tough choice. In the winter of 1765, the Yamassees were resettled at a planned village called San Carlos, about twenty miles from Vera Cruz. There, they were required to live under a code of laws and were provided with land and farm implements in the hope they would become a self-sufficient community. A dozen Spanish soldiers accompanied their Indian wives, but only 47 of the 108 Yamassee refugees from Pensacola made it to San Carlos. Emigration and resettlement proved disastrous for Florida's Yamassee people.[16]

That part of French Louisiana east of the Mississippi and south of 32° 28' now became part of British West Florida. Major Robert Farmar and the 22nd and 34th regiments occupied Mobile in October. Unlike the Spanish residents of Pensacola and St. Augustine, the 350 French inhabitants of Mobile and the 90 French families in the surrounding areas stayed put and took oaths of loyalty to Britain.[17]

British military government in West Florida lasted slightly more than a year. George Johnstone, a Scottish naval officer, was appointed governor. He arrived at Pensacola in the fall via Jamaica, where he had served during the war. All four of the new governorships established in the British Atlantic world in 1763—Quebec, the Ceded Islands (Dominica, Grenada, St. Vincent, and Tobago), East Florida, and West Florida—went to Scots. At one level, 1763 marked the arrival of Scots—themselves no strangers to exile and diaspora—as key participants in the British empire; the appointments were made in London, after all. But like the others, Johnstone's appointment attracted criticism in the imperial capital, where anti-Scottish feeling ran high. [18] *The North Briton* denounced it as inappropriate and due only to the influence of a fellow Scot, Lord Bute. Johnstone responded by getting into a fistfight with the author, a relatively mild action from a man with a propensity for dueling. Johnstone's prickly character and naval ideas of authority and discipline hardly fitted him to establish civil government in the colony during a delicate period of transition.[19]

Few British people knew anything about West Florida, and images of the place were often negative: an exotic wilderness inhabited by Indians and wild animals. Writers in the British press complained that the region's barren and sandy lands were "good for nothing but destroying Englishmen." Some early migration efforts failed: in October 1763 the *Robert and Betty,* bound for West Florida from Liverpool, with 213 passengers on board, was driven on to the rocks at Madeira during a nocturnal storm. All but eight of the passengers perished. Nevertheless, despite setbacks and bad publicity, settlers and speculators flocked to take advantage of land grants the British government offered to render the colony an effective defense against Spanish Louisiana. The European population of West Florida expanded rapidly: it reached 1,473 by February 1765 and more than tripled in the next ten years.[20]

The black population in West Florida also increased dramatically. When the British government had encouraged settlement in Georgia in the 1730s, it had attempted to exclude slavery. It took a different approach in Florida in the 1760s. The governors of both Floridas issued proclamations offering 100 acres to any head of a household; they offered an additional 50 acres for every dependent accompanying him, whether male or female, adult or child, "white or negro." East Florida had no slave code until 1782, but West Florida adopted one almost immediately, mandating severe punishments for those who transgressed and imposing rigid restrictions on slaves' activities. The British did not introduce slavery into West Florida—when they arrived they found French residents who owned dozens of slaves—but African slavery expanded enormously under the British regime. African slaves were deemed essential to the economic transformation of the colony and the British required manpower to do the heavy and laborious work of the plantations. Slaves worked as field hands and as domestic servants; they worked in towns as well as on plantations, as coopers, carpenters, sawyers, brick makers, and boatbuilders. The British army used them as laborers and some slaves served as sailors. A few obtained their freedom; the vast majority did not.[21]

The transfer of Florida from Spanish to British hands occurred with relatively little conflict and tension between the two imperial powers. But for the people who gave up their homes and went into exile it was a traumatic, and sometimes, as in the case of the Yamassees, a catastrophic experience. British occupation proved short-lived. Twenty years after the Spanish inhabitants of St. Augustine and Pensacola crowded onto their overloaded transport ships and sailed to an uncertain future, the scene was repeated. In 1783, the Union Jack was lowered, Florida returned to Spain, and British inhabitants of St. Augustine crowded aboard ships headed for the West Indies, the British Isles, or Nova Scotia.

JESUIT EXPULSION AND ACADIAN REUNION

The Jesuit Order had been at the forefront of French penetration of North America for a century and a half. Jesuit missionaries, often traveling alone, had pushed deep into Indian country carrying their word of God; they established themselves in Indian villages from the mouth of the St. Lawrence to the mouth of the Mississippi and baptized thousands of Indian people. But events in Europe terminated the

Jesuits' work in America. The Order was suppressed in France and in 1763 expelled from Louisiana.

Once the militant arm of the Catholic Church, the Society of Jesus was on the defensive by the mid-eighteenth century. Their wealth and political power attracted enemies and the growing contest between the Church and the Enlightenment called into question the Order's values and position. The Jesuits were "struggling amid the rising waters of skepticism, deism, and atheism." Portugal suppressed the Order in 1759. In France, the Jansenists, political adversaries of the Jesuits since the 1640s, secured the support of the Parlement of Paris in the 1760s. The Parlement championed the independence of the French Church against control by the Vatican, which the Jesuits advocated. Louis XV tried to mollify the situation but his mistress, Madame de Pompadour, hated the Jesuits. When creditors sued the Jesuit superior of Martinique, Fr. Antoine Lavalette, for massive debts accumulated in unsuccessful speculation, the Society's affairs were exposed amid growing public outcry. The Parlement of Paris held the Society liable for payment and, citing the Order's record in amassing power and property when it should have been caring for souls, banned the Society from France. Several provincial parlements followed suit. In 1762, the Jesuits' colleges were closed and their religious houses put in charge of receivers. The King delayed the government's suppression of the Order but its fate was sealed.[22]

The Jesuits' overseas missions suffered a sharp decline during the assault. At the time of the suppression, the French had twenty-seven priests and brothers at work in the territory from Quebec to Louisiana. In Canada, ironically, the British who since the seventeenth century had viewed black-robed Jesuit priests as agents of Satan and instigators of Indian raids, honored the terms of the Peace of Paris and left them free to do their work. According to Father P. Watrin, the Jesuit superior in the district of Fort Chartres, who wrote a detailed account of their expulsion, Jesuits in New Orleans in June 1763 "were still between hope and fear as to their future fate." But the ship that brought the news of the peace also brought "orders for their destruction." On board were the new governor, D'Abbadie, and Nicolas Chauvin de Lafrénière, newly appointed attorney general/procurator of the superior council of Louisiana, who was charged with implementing the expulsion.[23]

On July 9, Lafrénière presented the Superior Council with a requisition for suppressing the Jesuit Order. Citing the actions of the

Parlement of Paris, Lafrénière demanded that the Council "proscribe for ever from this colony men who live under an Institute, the rules of which are contrary to good order, outrageous to Royal authority, perilous for the safety of our kings, and independent of all tribunals." The Council unanimously approved proceedings "to effect the dissolution of their religious community and the sale of their property for the profit of the crown."[24] A week-long auction was held to dispose of the Jesuits' property.

Jesuits in New Orleans "did not wait to be notified of the order to depart." Father Carette embarked for Santo Domingo; Father Le Roy arrived in Pensacola just as the English were taking possession, and he accompanied the Spanish governor to Vera Cruz shortly after he resumed his work in Mexico. Father le Prédour, at the Alibamu mission about 600 miles from New Orleans, received the decree some time later; he departed to Mobile, then to New Orleans, and finally to France. Father Baudoin, superior of all the missions, had lived in Louisiana for thirty-five years, twenty of them "in the midst of the forests with the Choctaw." He was seventy-two years old, infirm, and, having been born in Canada, had no relatives in France. He was granted a pension and allowed to stay in Louisiana.[25]

The courier carrying the decree to the Illinois country arrived at Fort Chartres on the night of September 23, and the decree was read to Father Watrin. Jesuit missionaries had been active in the Mississippi Valley since Father Marquette first carried the cross to the Quapaws ninety years before and established a mission at the great village of the Kaskaskias. There was no longer a mission among the Quapaws but a new church had been built at Kaskaskias in the last decade. Watrin, who had served in North America almost thirty years, described daily life at Kaskaskias:

> at sunrise the bell rang for prayer and mass; the savages said prayers in their own language, and during mass they chanted, to the air of the Roman chant, hymns and psalms, also translated into their language, with suitable prayers; at the end of mass, the missionary catechized the children. Having returned to his house, he was occupied in instructing the adult neophytes and catechumens, to prepare them for baptism and for penance, for communion or for marriage. As soon as he was free, he went through the village to arouse the believers to fervor, and to exhort unbelievers to embrace Christianity.[26]

The idyllic way of life Watrin portrayed ended that night in September. The Jesuits were ordered out of their houses. They were allowed to keep their clothes and books but all other property was confiscated. They were to be taken downriver to New Orleans and banished from the country. In late November, guarded by French troops, the Jesuits embarked in boats for the twenty-seven-day journey downriver. They had little baggage—only their bedding and clothes. They had saved some food for the journey, which they shared with forty-eight slaves, "old men, women and children," who accompanied them. "These slaves," wrote Watrin, "no longer belonged to the Jesuits, having been confiscated for the benefit of the king." The soldiers supplemented their provisions by hunting. The food situation was not helped by the presence in the boats of a score of Englishmen who had been captured by Indians some months before and delivered to the French; they were, Watrin noted, "people with good appetites."[27]

The expulsion of the Jesuits from Louisiana was part of a much larger movement. Spain suppressed the Society of Jesus in 1767 and Pope Clement XIV suppressed it throughout the world in 1773. But the Jesuits were not finished in Louisiana. After Pope Pius VII restored the order in 1814, Jesuits returned to Louisiana to resume their mission work in the 1830s.

AT ONE TIME THE DUC DE CHOISEUL had considered Louisiana the nucleus around which France might rebuild a colonial empire in America and he had hoped to people it with Canadians. In 1761 he proposed to Britain that in return for the cession of Canada, French inhabitants would receive transportation to Louisiana. The preliminaries of the Peace of Paris, drawn up in July 1762, had included such a provision.[28] But Louisiana went to Spain. French people did migrate to Louisiana as a result of the Peace of Paris, but they were exiled and dispersed Acadians looking for refuge and a place to rebuild a way of life that had been shattered by war and relocation.

The French colonized Acadia, on the northern shore of Nova Scotia along the Bay of Fundy, early in the seventeenth century. Isolated from the core of French settlement in the St. Lawrence Valley, the Acadian population grew culturally separate. As Britain and France squared off in the fight for North American hegemony, Acadia changed hands ten times between 1604 and 1710, whether by conquest or diplomatic negotiation. The fortress at Louisbourg,

Simba Run.

Vail Condominiums
1100 N. Frontage Road
Vail, Colorado 81657
1-800-SIMBA-RUN • 970-476-0344 • 970-476-0888 Fax

in particular, became a target for expeditions from New England. Nova Scotia, which included what is now New Brunswick and Prince Edward Island, was transferred to Britain at the Peace of Utrecht in 1713 and the Acadians found themselves in a precarious position: French people in English-held territory that constituted a key strategic objective for both sides.

With the outbreak of the Seven Years' War, fearing that the Acadian inhabitants might constitute a threat, authorities in Nova Scotia ordered them rounded up, detained, and dispersed. The military confiscated their lands and livestock, burned their homes, and dispatched more than 6,000 on transports into exile to the English-speaking colonies. They were to be resettled in Georgia, South Carolina, Virginia, Maryland, Pennsylvania, New York, Massachusetts, and Connecticut in groups of not more than 1,000, so that "they cannot easily collect themselves together again." In doing so, the British initiated a diaspora that scattered French Acadians across thousands of miles and produced pockets of French-speaking Catholic population in many areas of North America. Dumped on the British mainland colonies, and frequently left to fend for themselves, Acadian exiles suffered hostility, social ostracism, economic deprivation, and appalling mortality rates. About 1,500 Acadians were deported to England after Virginia refused to accept them; in the spring of 1763, the survivors—753 of them—were "repatriated" to France. More than 3,000 Acadians sought refuge in France between 1755 and 1763 but they received little or no assistance from the government, resisted assimilating into a feudal society that expected them to live as peasants, and experienced ethnic friction with the local population. They endured disease and poor living conditions and their numbers declined sharply. In the early 1760s more than 7,000 New England farmers migrated to what had been Acadia to occupy the lands from which the Acadians had been expelled.[29]

In 1763, almost 13,000 Acadian people were scattered throughout eastern North America and on both sides of the Atlantic. There were 3,500 in France; 850 in England; 2,000 in Quebec; 700 on the Bay of Chaleurs; 1,250 and maybe many more in Nova Scotia, mostly in detention centers at Halifax. About 300 lived on Prince Edward Island, where they had hid out for the duration of the war and where, in 1763, British authorities discovered about thirty families, "miserably poor, who had taken refuge in the thick of the woods." More than 1,000 Acadians lived in Massachusetts; 800 in Maryland; more than 600 in Connecticut, and several hundred in New York, Pennsylvania, Georgia, and South Carolina. About 300 Acadians lived in Louisiana.[30]

The Peace of Paris initiated another round of movements. Article 4 of the treaty, in which King Louis renounced "all pretensions" to Nova Scotia, also allowed Acadians eighteen months to leave the British colonies and "retire with all safety and freedom wherever they shall think proper."[31] Most endeavored to do so. The Acadians now became "a pawn in France's imperial designs." The Duc de Choiseul, eager to revitalize the defenses of France's battered colonial empire, regarded the exiles as a pool of potential colonists and encouraged settling them in a variety of locations. In 1763 two hundred Acadians, maybe more, were recruited for the larger French colonization effort in Cayenne (French Guiana). Without sufficient support many colonists perished in the jungle environment and most abandoned the colony and returned to France. Later in the year Louis-Antoine de Bougainville, now a captain in the French navy, engaged some Acadians to start a colony on the Falkland Islands, and larger contingents followed. But both the British and the Spanish governments were alarmed by the prospect of a French colony on the strategically located Falklands. When Spain asserted its claim to the islands in 1766, France handed them over and abandoned the Acadians. Some Acadians returned to Miquelon and St. Pierre, islands returned to France by the treaty. Others traveled to the coasts of the Gulf of St. Lawrence or Quebec. About 500 Acadians from Georgia and South Carolina and several hundred more from Pennsylvania, New York, and New England went to St. Domingue (present-day Haiti), where they were joined by 600 Acadians from Nova Scotia in 1765, and some from France in 1766. Many died from tropical diseases, scurvy, and malnutrition but others managed to integrate themselves into the island's plantation system and to intermarry with other French colonists. When the Haitian Revolution drove them out in the 1790s, most of the French refugees fled first to Santiaga de Cuba and eventually, in 1809, to New Orleans.[32]

Ironically, "the 'Frenchness' of Louisiana actually increased following its accession to Spain."[33] More French people settled in Louisiana during the Spanish era than had done so during the French era. A party of 193 Acadian refugees from detention camps in Halifax, who initially planned to sail to Saint Domingue, immediately hired another ship and sailed on to New Orleans. Forty-eight families arrived in New

Orleans in the spring of 1765, and reported that 1,000 more were on their way. Governor Aubry said Acadians were coming in such numbers that they would soon make Louisiana "a new Acadia." In September 1766 another 200 arrived at Balize from Maryland.[34]

Then came word that the new Spanish governor, Antonio de Ulloa, was eager to attract colonists, primarily to populate the Lower Mississippi Valley at strategic points against British encroachment. The Acadian migrants hoped to be reunited with relatives and to restore their communities, but Governor de Ulloa insisted on dispersing them between military posts. He regarded them as good citizen-soldiers, whose experience would make them fiercely anti-British. Seeing their hopes of reuniting dashed, some Acadians joined the New Orleans revolt in October 1768, which drove Ulloa out of the province. After Governor Alejandro O'Reilly restored order, he allowed the Acadians greater flexibility in their settlements. In Carl Brasseaux's words, "The Acadian dream was now realized, and the exiles were wedded to the Spanish regime."[35] O'Reilly encouraged immigration and colonization, assisting Acadian immigrants who were already there with land grants, food, and farm implements, and welcoming additional French migrants from the Illinois country. Acadian immigration to Louisiana continued for another twenty years. Ulloa had also encouraged Germans and Maryland Catholics to settle in Louisiana so that "the country will quickly be thickly settled with people who are irreconcilable enemies of England on account of the contempt and persecution they have suffered, and that, while the King is gaining subjects, England will be losing them."[36]

Louisiana still had a francophone population. Despite lack of assistance from the British or French governments in securing passage, Acadians in Pennsylvania, Maryland, New York, Halifax, Nova Scotia, Saint Domingue, and France sold what belongings they had to buy passage to Louisiana. Ninety percent of the Acadians in Maryland and Pennsylvania (at least 782 people) boarded English ships bound for Louisiana between 1766 and 1770. In 1785, nearly 1,600 Acadians left French ports on seven merchant vessels chartered by the Spanish government and sailed for New Orleans, the largest and the last major Acadian migration to Louisiana in the eighteenth century, although more would arrive in the massive influx of refugees from Saint Domingue in 1809.[37]

In Louisiana the Acadians, "the sport of fortune," tried to rebuild the world they had lost. They established settlements on both sides of the

Mississippi, close to German communities and close to the villages of the Houmas, Alibamons, and Chitchimachas, all of whom had been greatly reduced in number over the course of the last eighty years or so.[38] The migrants usually arrived in family units and they established settlement patterns that have endured. They engaged in a variety of agricultural production, raised hogs and chickens, and ranched cattle on southern Louisiana's grasslands. They also operated a lucrative contraband trade, selling their produce to British across the Mississippi. They brought with them, and adapted, Acadian styles of clothing and architecture. They also adapted Acadian cuisine to Louisiana's agricultural products, boiling and frying various foods, and incorporating elements from Indian and African cultures, to produce new, Cajun, cooking.[39]

Not until the end of the century did the Acadians find relief from the winds of international conflicts in refuges where they were free to pursue their agrarian way of life. By 1800, their diaspora began to stabilize. More than 8,000 lived in the Maritime Provinces, another 8,000 in Quebec. About 1,000 lived in France, another 1,000 in the United States, and perhaps 1,000 were scattered in other locations. About 4,000 lived in Louisiana.[40] A French-speaking community remained in Louisiana when the United States bought it in 1803. According to Thomas Jefferson, not one in fifty of the Louisiana Creoles understood the English language.[41] The Acadians had made adjustments to their new environment but, "in the mainstream, Acadian culture differed only cosmetically from its pre-dispersal counterpart."[42]

North America in 1763 was on the move. Scots and Scots-Irish arrived in unprecedented numbers and most funneled south and west from Philadelphia; French settlers crossed the Mississippi from Illinois; Spanish colonists evacuated Florida and relocated to Cuba; British colonists—and their slaves—moved into West Florida; Jesuits were expelled from Louisiana; displaced Acadians regrouped in Louisiana, and Indians moved in response to increasing pressures from settlers, developments in the fur trade, and changes in the imperial order in North America. In a year of peace, people were still being driven by the winds of war. Colonial governments struggled to regulate their empires. In some cases that meant encouraging settlement and relocating people; in others it meant demarking boundaries and trying to rein in subjects. The events of 1763 not only redrew the political map of North America, but they also changed its human geography.

Epilogue:
A Tale of Two Treaties

*A*S THE ROOTS OF THE SECOND WORLD WAR can be found in the Versailles Peace Settlement of 1918, so in the 1763 Peace of Paris can be found the roots of the American Revolution, the Peace of Paris in 1783, and the American national empire that followed. Looking back, the road from victory in 1763 to revolution in 1775 seems clear, and the British government's missteps and misjudgments with regard to taxing the colonists seem obvious. But Britons, on whichever side of the Atlantic they lived, did not see things so clearly in 1763. They were entering uncharted territory, sometimes literally. Never before had Britons enjoyed such power, imagined such possibilities, or confronted such challenges. The path to revolution was only one of many stories unfolding that year.

At the Peace of Paris in 1763, France handed over to Great Britain all its North American territories east of the Mississippi. It transferred Louisiana to Spain, and Spain transferred Florida to Britain. Twenty years later, at another Peace of Paris, Britain recognized the independence of thirteen former colonies and transferred to the new United States all its territory south of the Great Lakes, north of the Floridas, and east of the Mississippi. It returned Florida to Spain, and the British inhabitants of St. Augustine packed up and left, just as the Spanish inhabitants had done in 1763. In 1783 as in 1763, the ministry that concluded the Peace of Paris was not the same ministry that had conducted the war.

During the debates in England over whether to give up Canada or Guadeloupe at the 1763 peace settlement, William Burke, a relative of the renowned statesman Edmund Burke, had argued that Canada

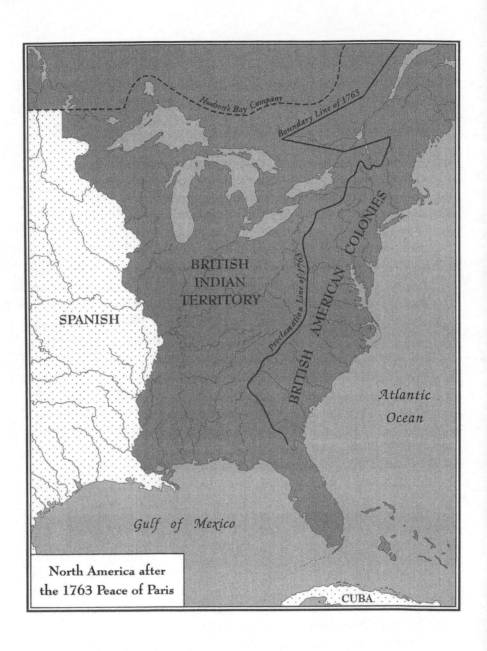

North America after
the 1763 Peace of Paris

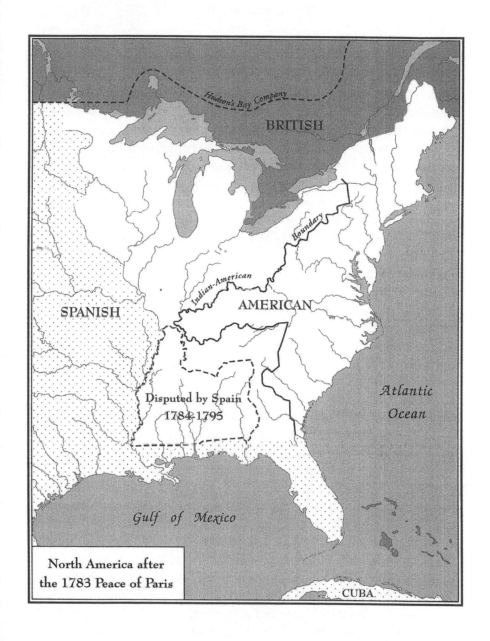

North America after
the 1783 Peace of Paris

should be left in French hands as a way of binding the North American colonies to Britain: "A neighbor that keeps us in some awe is not always the worst of neighbors," he explained; removing French Canada would free the original thirteen colonies to separate from the mother country. "By eagerly grasping at extensive territory," he warned, "we may run the risqué, and that perhaps in no very distant period, of losing what we now possess."[1] As Canadian historian William Eccles pointed out, the Duc de Choiseul not only predicted the American Revolution, but "was counting on it." For Choiseul, 1763 gave France the peace it needed to rebuild for war. He started rebuilding the navy even before the treaty was signed, and the ink was barely dry before the French were surveying the English coasts to formulate revised invasion plans. France restored its overseas trade, implemented reforms in its army and navy, and strengthened its economy, while at the same time keeping Britain diplomatically isolated in Europe. When, as Choiseul knew they would, the American colonies revolted, France had the power to make the difference. During the War of Independence Britain found itself in the same position France had been during the Seven Years' War—bogged down in a protracted land war while the enemy took full advantage of its renewed sea power. The British navy momentarily lost command of the seas to France, and Lord Cornwallis lost his army.[2] Louis-Antoine de Bougainville, who had carried the articles of Montreal's surrender to the British in 1760, was present when the British surrendered at Yorktown in 1781.

Looking back over the course of events from 1763 to 1783, Henry Ellis explained the connection between the two treaties. "What did Britain gain by the most glorious and successful war on which she ever engaged?" he asked. "A height of Glory which excited the Envy of the surrounding nations and united them in the late unnatural contest with our revolted colonies—an extent of empire we were equally unable to maintain, defend or govern—the final independence of those colonies which the dispossession of the French from Canada necessarily tended to promote and accelerate, and the enormous debt of two hundred and fifty millions."[3] Faced with a huge new territorial empire in North America in 1763, the British tried to defend it, administer it, and finance it. Instead they lost it. They turned to the kind of empire they did best—an ocean-based commercial empire.[4]

France exacted revenge for the humiliation of 1763 but achieved little else. American negotiators signed the preliminary articles of peace with Britain in 1783 without informing the French. France did not replace Britain as America's trading partner and was unable to shape the direction of American expansion. The French minister, Vergennes, wanted the old Proclamation Line of 1763 to mark the western territorial limits of the new United States, with the lands between the Appalachians and the Mississippi reserved as Indian country. The Earl of Shelburne, now Secretary of State, recognized that American settlements in the West would gravitate to British trade and envisaged joint British participation in the commercial development of the Mississippi Valley. Britain sold out its Indian allies and handed their lands to the United States. "It is rather ironic," notes William Eccles, "that the British government here insisted on giving away what France had once sought to deny to Britain but now desperately wanted Britain to retain."[5]

Neither the Peace of 1763 nor the Peace of 1783 made any mention of the Indian peoples who inhabited the territories being transferred. In both cases, Indian interests were sacrificed to imperial agendas. As in 1763, Indians in 1783 were "thunderstruck" by the terms of a treaty that did not include them. As in 1763, they complained that a foreign king had no right to transfer lands and rights they had had never given up, let alone breach treaties previously made in solemn council. No such cession could "be binding without their Express Concurrence & Consent." A Cherokee chief, Little Turkey, said "the peacemakers and our Enemies have talked away our lands at a Rum Drinking."[6] As in 1763, the victors looked west across vast territories transferred to them in Paris and wondered how to make them into an empire. As in 1763, they believed for a time that they could dispense with the protocols of doing business in Indian country and could dictate to the Indians from a position of strength. As in 1763, they learned their mistake.

Pontiac's war was not the last Indian war for independence. States and nation encroached on Indian lands and life even more aggressively than had colonies and empire. Multi-tribal coalitions resisted American occupation of the lands ceded by Britain in 1783 just as they had resisted British occupation of the lands ceded by France in 1763. During the 1780s and 1790s, and again in the first decade of the nineteenth century, multi-tribal coalitions stalled American advance into the West and mounted formidable opposition to American expansion that sought to gobble up tribal lands piecemeal.

The United States learned from some of Britain's mistakes. It bound its new territories to it by interest rather than by imperial administration. In the Northwest Ordinance of 1787, the Confederation Congress laid out the provisions by which western territories could enter the union as equal states. In so doing it established a blueprint for perpetual nation-building rather than eventual separation. In Jefferson's "empire of liberty," the citizens of the nation shared the fruits of its expansion.

Napoleon Bonaparte had dreams of a revived French empire in America, certainly of a revived French sugar empire in the Caribbean. "I know the full value of Louisiana," he said, "and I have been desirous of repairing the fault of the French negotiator who abandoned it in 1763."[7] On October 1, 1800, at the Treaty of San Ildefonso, Spain secretly ceded Louisiana back to France. Thomas Jefferson understood the value of Louisiana too. The threat of an aggressive (rather than a weak) European power having a stranglehold on New Orleans sent a chill down his spine. It looked as if France was to be the United States' "natural enemy." But a French Caribbean empire was not viable so long as British sea power remained intact and the slave revolt of Toussaint l'Ouverture remained defiant in Saint Domingue. Napoleon had to defeat them both. He could do neither. Yellow fever decimated his army in Saint Domingue and Horatio Nelson destroyed his fleet at Trafalgar. The French emperor needed money to wage war against England. He decided to cut his American losses and unload Louisiana. Louisiana, ceded to Spain in 1763, was French again for less than three years. In the spring of 1803, Robert Livingston and James Monroe, special ministers to Paris, concluded negotiations with Charles Maurice de Talleyrand. For $15 million (80 million francs), the 900,000 square miles of Louisiana became American territory. Passed back and forth like an unwanted stepchild since the Peace of Paris in 1763, Louisiana changed hands one more time in Paris in 1803. The events initiated in 1763 finally played themselves out. The empire in the West would not be French, Spanish, or British; it would be American.

Western lands—those between the Appalachians and the Mississippi that passed from French to British hands in 1763 and then from British to American hands in 1783, and those between the Mississippi and the Rockies that passed from French to Spanish hands in 1763, briefly back to France, and then to the United States in 1803—allowed an empire of slavery as well as an empire of liberty to expand.[8] Should the western territories and the new states formed from them be slave or free? The question proved to be volatile and, despite repeated attempts at compromise, defied resolution. The West split the British Empire after 1763. Less than a century later it split the United States. The Revolution severed the relationship between the thirteen colonies and the empire, but it took another revolution to settle the relationship between the states and the union. The relationship between the people who were the citizens of the new nation and peoples who were not continued to contradict the ideals expressed to justify the nation's birth.

The Peace of 1763 transferred huge stretches of territory and transformed America. The contest for North American dominance that had raged between France and Britain for close to 100 years was settled once and, with the exception of a brief Napoleonic dream, for all. But the Peace brought little peace and much turmoil to North America. In wrapping up one round of conflicts, it ushered in others. One peace led to another. Territories that had changed hands in Paris in 1763 changed hands again in Paris in 1783. Twenty years later Louisiana changed hands, again in Paris. A new American nation emerged and built a single empire on the lands of numerous Indian nations transferred among three European nations in 1763.

Like King Midas, eighteenth-century Britons perhaps had wished for something too much in America. As happened in 1861, 1914, and 2003, people in 1763 responded to problems whose consequences they could see but not accept by initiating actions whose consequences they could not clearly foresee. In doing so, they set in motion events that changed forever the America they had known.

Notes

The following abbreviations appear throughout the notes:

MPHC *Collections of the Michigan Pioneer and Historical Society.* 40 vols., 1874–1929.

NYCD E. B. O'Callaghan and Berthold Fernow, eds., *Documents Relative to the Colonial History of the State of New York.* 15 vols. (Albany: Weed, Parsons, 1853–87).

WJP James Sullivan et al., eds., *The Papers of Sir William Johnson.* 15 vols. (Albany: State University of New York Press, 1921–1965).

INTRODUCTION

1. Frederick A. Pottle, ed., *Boswell's London Journal, 1762–1763* (New York: McGraw-Hill, 1950), 161, 260, 304.

2. *Pennsylvania Archives,* 1st series, 3 (1853), 539.

3. Michael N. McConnell, *A Country Between: The Upper Ohio Valley and Its Peoples, 1724–1774* (Lincoln: University of Nebraska Press, 1992), chs. 1–5; Richard White, *The Middle Ground: Indians, Empires, and Republics in the Great Lakes Region, 1650–1815* (Cambridge: Cambridge University Press, 1991), ch. 5.

4. French documents relating to Washington's expedition, including the terms of surrender, are reproduced in Joseph L. Peyser, trans. and ed., *Letters from New France: The Upper Country 1686–1783* (Urbana: University of Illinois, 1992), 196–210; the terms of surrender, plus a plan of Fort Duquesne in 1754, are also in *Pennsylvania Archives,* 1st series, 2 (1853), 146–47.

5. Charles Henry Lincoln, ed., *Manuscript Records of the French and Indian War in the Library of the American Antiquarian Society* (1909; reprinted Bowie, Md.: Heritage Books, 1992), 174–77. Fred Anderson, *Crucible of War: The Seven Years' War and the Fate of Empire in British North America, 1754–1766* (New York: Knopf, 2000), 94–97, provides an account of the battle. Sources relating to the campaign are available in Winthrop Sargent, *The History of an expedition against Fort Du Quesne, in 1755; under Major-General Edward Braddock ... Edited from the original manuscripts* (Philadelphia, Lippincott, Grambo, for the Historical Society of Pennsylvania, 1855) and Paul E.

Kopperman, *Braddock at the Monongahela* (Pittsburgh: University of Pittsburgh Press, 1977).

6. *Pennsylvania Archives*, 1st series, 2 (1853), 443–45, 450, 475–76, 494, 528, 548.

7. Stephen Brumwell, *Redcoats: The British Soldier and War in the Americas, 1755–1763* (Cambridge: Cambridge University Press, 2002).

8. Alfred Proctor James, ed., *Writings of General John Forbes Relating to His Service in North America* (Menasha, Wis.: Collegiate Press, 1938).

9. *Pennsylvania Archives*, 1st series, 3, 744–52; 4 (1853), 48–49; Sylvester K. Stevens et al., eds., *The Papers of Henry Bouquet*. 6 vols. (Pennsylvania Historical and Museum Commission, 1951–94), 5: 150–56; "George Croghan's Journal, 1760–61," in Reuben G. Thwaites, ed., *Early Western Travels, 1746–1846* (Cleveland: Arthur H. Clark Co., 1904–07) 1: 104 (full journal 100–25). Jon William Parmenter, "Pontiac's War: Forging New Links in the Anglo-Iroquois Covenant Chain, 1758–1766," *Ethnohistory* 44 (1997), 617–54, traces the diplomatic efforts and achievements of the western tribes. Frank McLynn, *1759* (New York: Atlantic Monthly Press, 2004).

10. Anderson, *Crucible of War*, 344–68, sees the victory as the fortuitous outcome of Wolfe's wish for a heroic death rather than a brilliantly planned and executed assault.

11. Arthur Herman, *To Rule the Waves: How the British Navy Shaped the Modern World* (New York: HarperCollins, 2004), ch. 12; Peter Cunningham, ed., *The Letters of Horace Walpole, Earl of Orford*. 9 vols. (London: Bickers and Son, 1880) 3: 259.

12. J. Clarence Webster, ed., *The Journal of Jeffery Amherst* (Toronto: Ryerson Press, 1931), 247.

13. D. Peter Macleod, *The Canadian Iroquois and the Seven Years' War* (Toronto: Dundurn Press, 1996), 177–79; Jean-Pierre Sawaya, *Alliance et Dépendence: Comment la couronne britannique a obtenu la collaboration des Indians de la vallée du Saint-Laurent entre 1760 et 1764* (Sillery, Que: Les Editions Septentrion, 2002), ch. 1; *WJP* 13: 163–66. The St. Lawrence Indians comprised eight villages: Kahnawake (Iroquois); Kanasatake (Iroquois, Algonquin, and Nipissing); Akwesasne (Iroquois); Oswegatchie (Iroquois); Wendake (Huron); Odanak (Abenaki); Wolinak (Abenaki), and Pointe-du-Lac (Algonquin). From fall 1763, they associated as the Seven Nations of Canada. The Iroquois of Oswegatchie were not part of the Seven Nations; they dealt with Onondaga, not Kahnawake; Sawaya, 54n.

14. Edward P. Hamilton, ed., *Adventure in the Wilderness: The American Journals of Louis Antoine de Bougainville, 1756–1760* (Norman: University of Oklahoma Press, 1964, 1990), quote at 222.

15. Stanley J. Stein and Barbara H. Stein, *Apogee of Empire: Spain and New Spain in the Age of Charles III, 1759–1789* (Baltimore: Johns Hopkins University Press, 2003), 11–13; J. Leitch Wright, Jr., *Anglo-Spanish Rivalry in North America* (Athens: University of Georgia Press, 1971), 107.

16. Stein and Stein, *Apogee of Empire*, 51–55 (British forces at 54, quotes at 55); Henry Kamen, *Empire: How Spain Became a World Power, 1492–1763* (New York: HarperCollins, 2003), 481–82, gives slightly different figures on the British forces.

17. Quoted in Francis Parkman, *Montcalm and Wolfe: The French and Indian War* (New York: Da Capo Press, 1995), 535.

18. D. W. Meinig, *The Shaping of America: A Geographical Perspective on 500 Years of History*. Vol. 1: *Atlantic America, 1492–1800* (New Haven: Yale University Press, 1986), 269.

19. Philip Lawson, *The Imperial Challenge: Quebec and Britain in the Age of the American Revolution* (Montreal: McGill-Queens University Press, 1989), ch. 1, for the role of Quebec in the peace negotiations; quote in Guy Frégault, *Canada: The War of the Conquest* (Toronto: Oxford University Press, 1969), 299.

20. Mark Kurlansky, *Cod: A Biography of the Fish That Changed the World* (New York: Penguin, 1998), 43–44, 87.

21. Quoted in J. H. Plumb, *England in the Eighteenth Century* (New York: Penguin, 1950), 114.

22. *The North Briton*, No. 45: 156a–b. *The Gentleman's Magazine* 33 (1763), 239–46, contained a narrative of the proceedings for and against John Wilkes.

23. Lord John Russell, ed., *Correspondence of John, Fourth Duke of Bedford.* 3 vols. (London: Longman, Brown, Green, and Longmans, 1846), 3: 230.

24. *The Annual Register for 1763* (London: J. Dodsley, 1796), 18–19.

25. Thomas Mante, *The History of the Late War in North-America, and the Islands of the West-Indies* (London, 1772; New York: Research Reprints Inc., 1970), 478. Mante also tried his hand at sheep farming and wrote a book on raising sheep in France; Richard Cargill Cole, *Thomas Mante: Writer, Soldier, Adventurer* (New York: Peter Lang, 1993).

26. Russell, ed., *Correspondence of John, Fourth Duke of Bedford*, 3: 200.

27. H. T. Dickinson, *Caricatures and the Constitution, 1760–1832* (Cambridge: Chadwyck-Healey, 1986), 46–56; Philo-Britannicus "Letter from Scots Sawney the Barber, to Mr. Wilkes an English Parliameneter," (London, 1763).

28. *NYCD* 7: 592.

29. John Shy, "The American Colonies in War and Revolution, 1748–1783," in P. J. Marshall, ed., *The Oxford History of the British Empire: The Eighteenth Century* (New York: Oxford University Press, 1998), 308.

30. "Rev. Thomas Barnard Looks to Future Glories, 1763," in Richard D. Brown, ed., *Major Problems in the Era of the American Revolution, 1761–1791.* 2nd ed. (Boston: Houghton Mifflin, 2000), 77–78.

31. Linda Colley, *Britons: Forging the Nation 1707–1837* (New Haven: Yale University Press, 1992), 101–3.

32. Jack M. Sosin, *Whitehall and the Wilderness: The Middle West in British Colonial Policy, 1760–1775* (Lincoln: University of Nebraska Press, 1961), 25.

33. Stephen J. Hornsby, *British Atlantic, American Frontier: Spaces of Power in Early Modern British America* (Hanover: University Press of New England, 2004); Peggy K. Liss, *Atlantic Empires: The Network of Trade and Revolution, 1713–1826* (Baltimore: Johns Hopkins University Press, 1983).

34. Shy, "The American Colonies in War and Revolution, 1748–1783," 307–8.

35. Robert Middlekauff, *The Glorious Cause: The American Revolution, 1763–1789* (New York: Oxford University Press, 1982), 57 (Jan. 5 figures); Shy, "The American Colonies in War and Revolution, 1748–1783," 327; Sosin, *Whitehall and the Wilderness*, 82–83; Alan Taylor, *American Colonies*

(New York: Penguin, 2001), 433; Walter S. Dunn, Jr., *The New Imperial Economy: The British Army and the American Frontier, 1764–1768* (Westport, Conn.: Praeger, 2001), 4, 15–16.

36. Jack P. Greene, "Convergence: Development of an American Society, 1720–80," in Philip D. Morgan, ed., *Diversity and Unity in Early North America* (New York: Routledge, 1993), 62.

37. *The New Hampshire Gazette and Historical Chronicle*, March 12, 1763. Thanks to my colleague, Jere Daniell, *Colonial New Hampshire: A History* (Millwood, N.Y.: KTO Press, 1981), 170–71, for this reference.

38. Lawrence Henry Gipson, *The British Empire Before the American Revolution*. 15 vols. (New York: Knopf, 1936–1970), 10: 204–22; Edmund S. Morgan and Helen M. Morgan, *The Stamp Act Crisis: Prologue to Revolution* (Chapel Hill: University of North Carolina Press, 1953), 29–33; "The Fitch Papers: Correspondence and Documents during Thomas Fitch's Governorship of the Colony of Connecticut, 1754–1766," *Collections of the Connecticut Historical Society* 18 (1920), 261–73, 277–79, 284–85 ("mortal Wound" at 261).

39. Gary B. Nash, *The Urban Crucible: The Northern Seaports and the Origins of the American Revolution* (Cambridge: Harvard University Press, 1986), ch. 5.

40. Morgan and Morgan, *The Stamp Act Crisis*, 5–6; Harry M. Ward, *The American Revolution: Nationhood Achieved, 1763–1788* (New York: St. Martin's Press, 1995), 12.

41. Norman K. Risjord, *Jefferson's America, 1760–1815* (Madison, Wis.: Madison House Publishers, 1991), 55.

42. Sosin, *Whitehall and the Wilderness*, ch. 4.

43. Simon Schama, *A History of Britain*. Vol. 2. *The Wars of the British, 1603–1776* (New York: Hyperion, 2001), 464.

44. *Journals of the House of Representatives of Massachusetts*, Vol. 40: 1763–1764 (Boston: Massachusetts Historical Society, 1970), vii, 9–10; His Excellency Francis Barnard, *A Proclamation for Public Thanksgiving* (Boston, 1763).

45. "Governor Francis Bernard Describes the Boston Riot, 1765," in Richard Brown, ed., *Major Problems in the Era of the American Revolution, 1761–1791*. 2nd ed. (Boston: Houghton Mifflin, 2000), 100–102.

46. For example: Christopher Lee, *1603* (New York: St. Martin's Press, 2003); Stephen Saunders Webb, *1676: The End of American Independence* (New York: Alfred A. Knopf, 1984); John E. Willis, Jr., *1688: A Global History* (New York: W. W. Norton, 2001); McLynn, *1759*; David G. McCullough, *1776* (New York: Simon & Schuster, 2005); C. Edward Skeen, *1816: America Rising* (Lexington: University Press of Kentucky, 2003); Louis P. Masur, *1831: Year of Eclipse* (New York: Hill and Wang, 2001); Bernard De Voto, *The Year of Decision: 1846* (Boston: Houghton Mifflin, 1942); Mark Kurlansky, *1968: The Year That Rocked the World* (New York: Ballantine, 2003).

47. Max Savelle, *Empires to Nations: Expansion in North America, 1713–1824* (Minneapolis: University of Minnesota Press, 1974), 149; Parkman, *Montcalm and Wolfe: The French and Indian War*, 526.

48. Meinig, *The Shaping of America: A Geographical Perspective on 500 Years of History*. Vol. 1: *Atlantic America, 1492–1800*, 279, 280, 283.

49. David J. Weber, *The Spanish Frontier in North America* (New Haven: Yale University Press, 1992), 198.

50. Colin G. Calloway, *The Western Abenakis of Vermont: War, Migration, and the*

Survival of an Indian People (Norman: University of Oklahoma Press, 1990), ch. 9; Jane T. Merritt, *At the Crossroads: Indians and Empires on a Mid-Atlantic Frontier, 1700–1763* (Chapel Hill: University of North Carolina Press, 2003), ch. 5; James Drake, *King Philip's War: Civil War in New England* (Amherst: University of Massachusetts Press, 1999).

51. Daniel Richter, *Facing East from Indian Country* (Cambridge, Mass.: Harvard University Press, 2001), 190, 207–8. See also James H. Merrell, *Into the American Woods: Negotiators on the Pennsylvania Frontier* (New York: Knopf, 1999) and Merritt, *At the Crossroads*.

52. Stanley Pargellis, ed., *Military Affairs in North America 1748–1765; Selected Documents from the Cumberland Papers in Windsor Castle* (New York: Appleton-Century, 1933), 461.

CHAPTER 1: AMERICA AND AMERICANS IN 1763

1. J. Clarence Webster, ed., *The Journal of Jeffery Amherst* (Toronto: Ryerson Press, 1931), 303; Philip M. Hamer, ed., *The Papers of Henry Laurens*. 16 vols. (Columbia: University of South Carolina Press, 1968–), 4: xvii.

2. George Reese, ed., *The Official Papers of Francis Fauquier, Lieutenant Governor of Virginia, 1758–1768*. 3 vols. (Charlottesville: University Press of Virginia, 1980–83), 2: 917, 1002–3, 1043, 1046; William L. Saunders and Walter Clark, eds., *The Colonial and State Records of North Carolina*. 30 vols. (Raleigh: Secretary of State, 1886–1914), 6: 973.

3. "Aubry's Account of the Illinois Country, 1763," in Clarence Walworth Alvord and Clarence Edwin Carter, eds., *The Critical Period 1763–1765 in Collections of the Illinois State Historical Library* 10 (1915), 2.

4. Lawrence Henry Gipson, *The British Empire before the American Revolution*. 15 vols. (New York: Knopf, 1936–1970), 10: 9–11.

5. I am grateful to my colleagues Peter Carini, Joseph Cullon, and Jere Daniell for their insights on papermaking in the colonies.

6. Peter Linebaugh and Marcus Rediker, *The Many-Headed Hydra: Sailors, Slaves, Commoners, and the Hidden History of the Revolutionary Atlantic* (Boston: Beacon Press, 2000).

7. Grace Steele Woodward, *The Cherokees* (Norman: University of Oklahoma Press, 1963), 80–82.

8. Quoted in J. Russell Snapp, *John Stuart and the Struggle for Empire on the Southern Frontier* (Baton Rouge: Louisiana State University Press, 1996), 87.

9. "Journal of Captain Morris, 1764," in Reuben G. Thwaites, ed., *Early Western Travels, 1748–1846*. 32 vols. (Cleveland: Arthur H. Clark, 1904–07), 1: 308, 312.

10. Robert V. Wells, *The Population of the British Colonies in America before 1776: A Survey of Census Data* (Princeton: Princeton University Press, 1975), 64–65, 79, 89, 146, 260. Gipson, *The British Empire before the American Revolution*, 10: 12–13. According to estimates provided by Governor Wright, the population of Georgia numbered 6,800 white and 4,500 black people in 1762; Louis De Vorsey, *The Indian Boundary in the Southern Colonies, 1763–1775* (Chapel Hill: University of North Carolina Press, 1966), 148.

11. For example, William M. Denevan, *The Native Population of the Americas in 1492*. 2nd ed. (Madison: University of Wisconsin Press, 1992), xxvii–xxix;

Russell Thornton, *American Indian Holocaust and Survival: A Population History since 1492* (Norman: University of Oklahoma Press, 1987), 90.

12. W. W. Abbot and Dorothy Twohig, eds., *The Papers of George Washington: Colonial Series.* 10 vols. (Charlottesville: University Press of Virginia, 1983–1995), 7: 180–81, 186–87, 205–7, 226.

13. Webster, ed., *The Journal of Jeffery Amherst*, 17.

14. Gail D. Danvers, "Gendered Encounters: Warriors, Women, and William Johnson," *Journal of American Studies* 35 (2001), 187–202.

15. *NYCD* 6: 741.

16. Fred Anderson, *Crucible of War: The Seven Years' War and the Fate of Empire in British North America, 1754–1766* (New York: Alfred Knopf, 2000), 593–94; John C. Fitzpatrick, *The Writings of George Washington.* 39 vols. (Washington, D. C.: Govt. Printing Office, 1931–44), 2: 396–97; Abbot and Twohig, eds., *Papers of George Washington*, 7: 205–7. On Martha Dandridge see Henry Wiencek, *An Imperfect God: George Washington, His Slaves, and the Creation of America* (New York: Farrar, Straus and Giroux, 2003), 84, 282–83. On surveying and speculating: Andro Linklater, *Measuring America: How the United States Was Shaped by the Greatest Land Sale in History* (New York: Penguin/Plume, 2003), 39, 44–45.

17. Fred Anderson points out parallels between the conflict called Pontiac's War and colonial protests against the Stamp Act in 1766, both representing efforts to defend local autonomy within the empire. Anderson, *Crucible of War*, xx–xxi.

18. Milo Milton Quaife, ed., *The Siege of Detroit in 1763: The Journal of Pontiac's Conspiracy and John Rutherfurd's Narrative of a Captivity* (Chicago: R. R. Donnelley and Sons, 1958), 3.

19. Francis Parkman, *The Conspiracy of Pontiac.* 2 vols. (1851; New York: E. P. Dutton, 1908), 1: 132, 159, 168, 171, 187.

20. "George Croghan's Journal, 1765," in Thwaites, ed., *Early Western Travels*, 1: 126–73; quotes at 157, 170; *WJP* 4: 743. "Journal of a Detachment of the 42nd Regiment from Fort Pitt down the Ohio to the Country of the Illenoise," National Archives of Scotland, GD298/196: 135, 144–46.

21. Clarence Edwin Carter, ed., *Correspondence of General Thomas Gage.* 2 vols. (New Haven: Yale University Press, 1931–33), 1: 25–26.

22. Carl A. Brasseaux, trans. and ed., "The D'Abbadie Journal [1763–64]" in *A Comparative View of French Louisiana, 1699 and 1762: The Journals of Pierre Le Moyne d'Iberville and Jean-Jacques Blaise d'Abbadie.* Rev. ed. (Lafayette: University of Southwestern Louisiana Center for Louisiana Studies, 1981), 84–87.

23. James Dow McCallum, ed., *The Letters of Eleazar Wheelock's Indians* (Hanover, N.H.: Dartmouth College Publications, 1932), 254, 265. On Indian students in English schools see Margaret Connell Szasz, *Indian Education in the American Colonies, 1607–1783* (Albuquerque: University of New Mexico Press, 1985); Hannah Garret at 226.

24. *WJP* 4: 84, 147.

25. *Journals of the House of Representatives of Massachusetts 29: 1762–1763* (Boston: Massachusetts Historical Society, 1969), 176, 184, 271.

26. Jean B. Lee, *The Price of Nationhood: The American Revolution in Charles County* (New York: W. W. Norton, 1994), 44.

27. Gwendolyn Mildo Hall, *Africans in Colonial Louisiana: The Development of Afro-Creole Culture in the Eighteenth Century* (Baton Rouge: Louisiana State University Press, 1992), tables at 10 and 279; John Shy, "The American Colonies in War and Revolution, 1748–1783" in P. J. Marshall, ed., *The Oxford History of the British Empire: The Eighteenth* Century (New York: Oxford University Press, 1998), 310; Gipson, *The British Empire before the American Revolution,* 10; 26; Philip D. Morgan, *Slave Counterpoint: Black Culture in the Eighteenth-Century Chesapeake and Low Country* (Chapel Hill: University of North Carolina Press, 1998), quotes at xv. Ira Berlin, "Time, Space, and the Evolution of Afro-American Society on British Mainland North America," in Philip D. Morgan, ed., *Diversity and Unity in Early North America* (New York: Routledge, 1993), 113–46, surveys the regionally different systems of slavery and the differences in the African American societies that developed.

28. "Letter Book of John Watts, Merchant and Councillor of New York, 1762–1765," *Collections of the New-York Historical Society,* 61 (1928), 127.

29. Hamer et al., eds., *The Papers of Henry Laurens* 3: 539; 4: 31, 44.

30. Hamer et al., eds., *The Papers of Henry Laurens* 3: 203, 205.

31. John Wood Sweet, *Bodies Politic: Negotiating Race in the American North, 1730–1830* (Baltimore: Johns Hopkins University Press, 2003), 169

32. *New Hampshire Gazette and Historical Chronicle,* March 11, March 25, June 10, 1763.

33. Billy G. Smith and Richard Wojtowicz, eds., *Blacks Who Stole Themselves: Advertisements for Runaways in the Pennsylvania Gazette, 1728–1790* (Philadelphia: University of Pennsylvania Press, 1989), 62–66.

34. Reese, ed., *The Official Papers of Francis Fauquier,* 2: 998.

35. Gary B. Nash, *The Urban Crucible: The Northern Seaports and the Origins of the American Revolution* (Cambridge: Harvard University Press, 1986), ix.

36. Billy G. Smith, *The "Lower Sort": Philadelphia's Laboring People, 1750–1800* (Ithaca: Cornell University Press, 1990), 7, 43, 206; Gipson, *The British Empire before the American Revolution,* 10: 12–14. Norman K. Risjord, *Jefferson's America, 1760–1815* (Madison, Wis.: Madison House Publishers, 1991), 3, 34.

37. John Demos, "The High Place: Potosi," *Common-Place (www.common-place.org),* vol. 3, no. 4 (July 2003): Special Issue "Early Cities of the Americas."

38. R. Cole Harris, ed., *Historical Atlas of Canada,* Vol. 1: *From the Beginning to 1800* (Toronto: University of Toronto Press, 1987), plate 50; Wells, *The Population of the British Colonies in America before 1776,* 65.

39. "Enumeration of Indians within the Northern Department," *NYCD* 7: 582; *WJP* 10: 878.

40. Lord Adam Gordon, "Journal of an Officer who Travelled in America and the West Indies in 1764 and 1765," in Newton D. Mereness, ed., *Travels in the American Colonies* (New York: Macmillan, 1961), 398; population figures from "Pelatiah Webster Describes the Uniqueness of Charleston, 1765," in Karen Ordahl Kupperman, ed., *Major Problems in American Colonial History* (Lexington, Mass.: D. C. Heath, 1993), 549–50; sanded streets in David S. Shields, "Mean Streets, Mannered Streets: Charleston," *Common-Place (www.common-place.org),* vol. 3, no. 4 (July 2003).

41. Joshua Piker, *Okfuskee, a Creek Indian Town in Colonial America* (Cambridge: Harvard University Press, 2004), 6–7.

42. Thornton, *American Indian Holocaust and Survival,* 79, Thornton, *The Cherokees: A Population History* (Lincoln: University of Nebraska Press, 1990), 31–32.

43. Colin G. Calloway, "Chota: Cherokee Beloved Town in a World at War," in *The American Revolution in Indian Country* (Cambridge: Cambridge University Press, 1995), ch. 7; *The Memoirs of Lieutenant Henry Timberlake* (London, 1765), frontispiece; Public Record Office, Colonial Office Records, C. O. 323/17: 233; Tom Hatley, *The Dividing Paths: Cherokees and South Carolinians through the Era of Revolution* (New York: Oxford University Press, 1993), 163 (Ostenaco quote).

44. "Robertson's Report of Florida in 1763," in James W. Covington, ed., *The British Meet the Seminoles* (Gainesville: University of Florida Press, 1961), 5; Gordon, "Journal of an Officer," in Mereness, ed., *Travels in the American Colonies,* 394.

45. Brian Leigh Dunnigan, ed., "Fortress Detroit, 1701–1826," in David Curtis Skaggs and Larry L. Nelson, eds., *The Sixty Years' War for the Great Lakes, 1754–1814* (East Lansing: Michigan State University Press, 2001), 167–85; Harris, ed., *Historical Atlas of Canada,* vol. 1, plate 41.

46. On the French longlot settlement pattern in North America, see Carl J. Ekberg, *French Roots in the Illinois Country: The Mississippi Frontier in Colonial Times* (Urbana: University of Illinois Press, 1998), ch. 1.

47. "Enumeration of Indians within the Northern Department, *NYCD* 7: 583; "Bouquet Papers," *MPHC,* 19 (1892), 48; Parkman, *Conspiracy of Pontiac,* 155, 158.

48. Jay Gitlin, "Constructing the House of Choteau," *Common-Place (www.common-place.org),* vol. 3, no. 4 (July 2003).

49. Daniel H. Usner, Jr., *Indians, Settlers, and Slaves in a Frontier Exchange Economy: The Lower Mississippi Valley before 1783* (Chapel Hill: University of North Carolina Press, 1992), 108; cf. Captain Philip Pittman, *The Present State of the European Settlements on the Mississippi* (Cleveland: Arthur H. Clark, 1906), 43, estimate of 7,000 inhabitants around the middle of the decade, "exclusive of the slaves."

50. John Robert McNeill, *Atlantic Empires of France and Spain: Louisbourg and Havana, 1700–1763* (Chapel Hill: University of North Carolina Press, 1985); Stanley J. Stein and Barbara H. Stein, *Apogee of Empire: Spain and New Spain in the Age of Charles III, 1759–1789* (Baltimore: Johns Hopkins University Press, 2003), 53.

51. W. Raymond Wood and Thomas D. Thiessen, eds., *Early Fur Trade on the Northern Plains: Canadian Traders among the Mandans and Hidatsas 1738–1818* (Norman: University of Oklahoma Press, 1985).

52. "Journal of Col. James Gordon," *William and Mary Quarterly,* 1st series, 11 (1902–03), 217–6 (death of Sally at 236); 12 (1903–04), 1–12 (Nancy's recovery and neighbor's affair at 1; Scipio at 2–3).

53. Jack P. Greene, ed., *The Diary of Colonel Landon Carter of Sabine Hall, 1752–1778.* 2 vols. (Charlottesville: University Press of Virginia, 1965), 1: 242–44.

54. Cf. Robert V. Wells, *Facing the "King of Terrors": Death and Society in an*

American Community, 1750–1990 (Cambridge: Cambridge University Press, 2000), chs. 1–2.

55. Quoted in Ben Mutschler, "The Province of Affliction: Illness in New England, 1690–1820," Ph.D. diss., Columbia University, 2000, 31.

56. George Francis Dow, ed., *The Holyoke Diaries 1709–1856* (Salem, Mass.: The Essex Institute, 1911), 58–60. ("Polly" was also called Mary, 55).

57. Letter Book, by Nathaniel Whitaker, Rauner Special Collections and Rare Book Library, Dartmouth College, 3. For the commonality of such health concerns in the lives of eighteenth-century families and communities, see Mutschler, "The Province of Affliction."

58. John Duffy, *Epidemics in Colonial America* (Baton Rouge: Louisiana State University Press, 1953), 127; Smith, *The "Lower Sort,"* 48–49, 206, 211.

59. Hamer, ed., *Papers of Henry Laurens,* 3: 205–6, 208, 217, 237; 4: 85.

60. Reese, ed., *The Official Papers of Francis Fauquier,* 2: 984–85.

61. Allen D. Chandler et al., eds., *The Colonial Records of the State of Georgia.* 32 vols. (Atlanta: State Printer, 1904–1989), 9: 18–20, 67–69.

62. Julian P. Boyd, ed., *Papers of Thomas Jefferson.* 30 vols. (Princeton: Princeton University Press, 1950–), 1: 8.

63. Patricia Kay Galloway, Dunbar Rowland, and A. G. Sanders, eds., *Mississippi Provincial Archives,* Vol. 5: *French Dominion, 1749–1763* (Baton Rouge: Louisiana State University Press, 1984), 288.

64. *Pennsylvania Archives,* 1st series, 4 (1853), 140, 144.

65. Letter Book, by Nathaniel Whitaker, 3.

66. Dow, ed., *The Holyoke Diaries,* 60–61; *Journals of the House of Representatives of Massachusetts,* vol. 40: 1763–1764 (Boston: Massachusetts Historical Society, 1970), 197–98, 213, 228–29.

67. Daniel R. Mandell, *Behind the Frontier: Indians in Eighteenth-Century Eastern Massachusetts* (Lincoln: University of Nebraska Press, 1996), 182; Elizabeth Little, "The Nantucket Indian Sickness," in William Cowen, ed., *Papers of the Twenty-First Algonquian Conference* (Ottawa: Carleton University, 1990), 181–96.

68. Matthew C. Ward, "The Microbes of War: The British Army and Epidemic Disease among the Ohio Indians, 1758–1765," in Skaggs and Nelson, eds., *The Sixty Years' War for the Great Lakes,* 63–78. Figures and Johnson quoted in McNeill, *Atlantic Empires,* 104; Donald Greene, ed., *Samuel Johnson: Political Writings.* Vol. 10 of the Yale Edition of *The Works of Samuel Johnson* (New Haven: Yale University Press, 1977), 374.

Chapter 2: Contested Lands

1. Adam Shortt and Arthur G. Doughty, eds., *Documents relating to the Constitutional History of Canada, 1759–1791.* 2 vols. (Ottawa: Historical Documents Publication Board, 1918), 1: 132–47, quote at 137.

2. *NYCD* 7: 575.

3. D. Peter MacLeod, "Microbes and Muskets: Smallpox and the Participation of the Amerindian Allies of New France in the Seven Years' War," *Ethnohistory* 39 (1992), 45, fig. 1; Edward P. Hamilton, ed., *Adventure in the Wilderness: The American Journals of Louis Antoine de Bougainville, 1756–1760* (Norman: University of Oklahoma Press,

1964, 1990), 150; *NYCD* 10: 607–8, 610. On the experiences of the Iroquois from the St. Lawrence communities see Peter MacLeod, *The Canadian Iroquois in the Seven Years War* (Toronto: Dundurn Press, 1996).

4. Quoted in *The Journal of Major George Washington* (Williamsburg, 1754; reprinted 1959), 7; also in Donald H. Kent, ed., *Pennsylvania Treaties, 1737–1756* (Frederick, Md.: University Publications of America, 1984), 309. See also Lois Mulkearn, ed., *George Mercer Papers relating to the Ohio Company of Virginia* (Pittsburgh: University of Pittsburgh Press, 1954), 76.

5. Mulkearn, ed., *Mercer Papers*, 96.

6. *NYCD* 7: 18; Samuel Johnson, "Observations on the Present State of Affairs, 1756," in Donald J. Greene, ed., *Samuel Johnson: Political Writings* (The Yale Edition of the Works of Samuel Johnson, vol. 10; New Haven: Yale University Press, 1977), 188. I am grateful to Elijah Gould for bringing this quotation to my attention.

7. Brian Leigh Dunnigan, ed., *Memoir on the Late War in North America between France and England by Pierre Pouchot.* Trans. by Michael Cardy (Youngstown, N.Y.: Old Fort Niagara Association, 1994), 57.

8. *Pennsylvania Archives,* 1st series, 3 (1853), 534–35; "Journal of Christian Frederick Post," in Reuben G. Thwaites, ed., *Early Western Travels, 1748–1846.* 32 vols. (Cleveland: Arthur H. Clark, 1904–7), 1: 214–16; the Delawares' speech is reproduced in Colin G. Calloway, ed., *The World Turned Upside Down: Indian Voices from Early America* (Boston: Bedford Books, 1994), 133–34.

9. *WJP* 4: 308.

10. Clarence Walworth Alvord and Clarence Edwin Carter, eds., *The Critical Period, 1763–1765* (Springfield: Collections of the Illinois State Historical Library, 10, 1915), 257–58.

11. Richard Aquila, *The Iroquois Restoration: Iroquois Diplomacy on the Colonial Frontier, 1701–1754* (Detroit: Wayne State University Press, 1983).

12. Colin G. Calloway, *The Western Abenakis of Vermont, 1600–1800: War, Migration, and the Survival of an Indian People* (Norman: University of Oklahoma Press, 1990), ch. 10.

13. Geoffrey Plank, *An Unsettled Conquest: The British Campaign against the Peoples of Acadia* (Philadelphia: University of Pennsylvania Press, 2001), 162–63.

14. Julian P. Boyd, ed., *The Susquehannah Company Papers.* 11 vols. (Ithaca, N. Y.: Cornell University Press for the Wyoming Historical and Genealogical Society, 1962), 2: 175.

15. Patrick Frazier, *The Mohicans of Stockbridge* (Lincoln: University of Nebraska Press, 1992), 152–56.

16. The Southhold, New York (Long Island) Papers are in the Manuscript Department of the New-York Historical Society, New York. I am grateful to Anna Fleder for locating and copying these papers.

17. Jack Campisi, *The Mashpee Indians: Tribe on Trial* (Syracuse: Syracuse University Press, 1991), 83–87, quotes at 85–86; Daniel R. Mandell, "'We, as a tribe, will rule ourselves': Mashpee's Struggle for Autonomy, 1746–1840," in Colin G. Calloway and Neal Salisbury, eds., *Reinterpreting New England Indians and the Colonial Experience* (Boston: Colonial Society of Massachusetts, 2003), 299–340. The "humble Petition of Reuben Cognehew" is in Massachusetts State Archives, Boston, *Massachusetts Archives*, 33: 146–48.

18. William S. Simmons and Cheryl L. Simmons, eds., *Old Light on Separate Ways: The Narragansett Diary of Joseph Fish, 1765–1776* (Hanover, N.H.: University Press of New England, 1982), xxxii–xxxv, 35–39, 46–47; James Dow McCallum, ed., *The Letters of Eleazar Wheelock's Indians* (Hanover, N.H.: Dartmouth College Publications, 1932), 208, 213; *WJP* 4: 152–60, 587–95; 5: 491, 497–98, 683; 9: 237–38, 405–140, 639, 961–62; 12: 349–50; John Russell Bartlett, ed., *Records of the Colony of Rhode Island and Providence, 1757–1769*. 10 vols. (Providence: State Printers, 1856–65), 6: 221, 357, 401–2, 530, 533, 564.

19. Boyd, ed., *The Susquehannah Company Papers*, 2: 175–300; esp. 180–83 (conference with governor); 217 (Onondaga alarm and fatal consequences); 299 (did not understand); "The Fitch Papers: Correspondence and Documents during Thomas Fitch's Governorship of the Colony of Connecticut, 1754–1766," *Collections of the Connecticut Historical Society*, 18 (1920), 224–27 (horrors of Indian war at 225), 229–334 ("Thousand Families" at 230), 237–40.

20. Boyd, ed., *The Susquehannah Company Papers*, 2: 237 (grievous news); 248 (dignity of oratory); Anthony F. C. Wallace, *King of the Delawares: Teedyuscung, 1700–1763* (1949; reprinted Syracuse: Syracuse University Press, 1990), 258–61; *Pennsylvania Archives*, 1st series, 4 (1853), 127; Jane T. Merritt, *At the Crossroads: Indians and Empires on a Mid-Atlantic Frontier, 1700–1763* (Chapel Hill: University of North Carolina Press, 2003), 275–77; Arman Francis Lucier, comp., *Pontiac's Conspiracy and Other Indian Affairs: Notices Abstracted from Colonial Newspapers, 1763–1765* (Bowie, Md.: Heritage Books, 2000), 11–13; "Fitch Papers," 250, 258.

21. Fred Anderson, *Crucible of War: The Seven Years' War and the Fate of Empire in British North America, 1754–1766* (New York: Alfred Knopf, 2000), 284–85, 328–29; Michael N. McConnell, *A Country Between: The Upper Ohio Valley and Its Peoples, 1724–1774* (Lincoln: University of Nebraska Press, 1992), 166–67. On Fort Pitt see Charles Morse Stotz, *Outposts of the War for Empire* (Pittsburgh: University of Pittsburgh Press, 1985), 127–40; J. Clarence Webster, *The Journal of Jeffery Amherst* (Toronto: The Ryerson Press, 1931), 302 (flooding).

22. *WJP* 10: 891.

23. *WJP* 10: 680; *The Annual Register for 1763* (London: J. Dodsley, 1796), 22 ("germ" quote).

24. Thwaites, ed., *Early Western Travels*, 1: 274, 278; Randolph C. Downes,

Council Fires on the Upper Ohio: A Narrative of Indian Affairs in the Upper Ohio Valley until 1795 (Pittsburgh: University of Pittsburgh Press, 1940), 93–95.

25. Alfred Proctor James, ed., *Writings of General John Forbes Relating to His Service in North America* (Menasha, Wis.: Collegiate Press, 1938), 275, 277, 283–84, quote at 290.

26. *WJP* 4: 95; *NYCD* 7: 577.

27. *WJP* 10: 690; Gregory Evans Dowd, *War under Heaven: Pontiac, the Indian Nations, and the British Empire* (Baltimore: Johns Hopkins University Press, 2002), 65, 83. The woman was identified as a "Panis" but was not necessarily a Pawnee as the term was commonly applied in French America to any Indian slaves from beyond the Mississippi.

28. *WJP* 4: 95.

29. Armand Francis Lucier, comp., *French and Indian War Aftermath: Notices from Colonial Newspapers, January 1, 1761–January 17, 1763* (Bowie, Md.: Heritage Books, 2000), 339.

30. D. W. Meinig, *The Shaping of America: A Geographical Perspective on 500 Years of History.* Vol. 1: *Atlantic America, 1492–1800* (New Haven: Yale University Press, 1986), 294; Robert V. Wells, *The Population of the British Colonies in America before 1776: A Survey of Census Data* (Princeton: Princeton University Press, 1975), 29–32.

31. Bernard Bailyn, *Voyagers to the West: A Passage in the Peopling of America on the Eve of the Revolution* (New York: Vintage, 1988), 26.

32. Colin G. Calloway, Gerd Gemünden, and Susanne Zantop, eds., *Germans and Indians: Fantasies, Encounters, Projections* (Lincoln: University of Nebraska Press, 2002), 47–50; Leonard W. Labaree, ed., *The Papers of Benjamin Franklin.* 35 vols. (New Haven: Yale University Press, 1959–99), 4: 234, 484–85.

33. Barbara DeWolfe, ed., *Personal Accounts of British Emigrants to North America during the Revolutionary Era* (Cambridge: Cambridge University Press, 1997), 3; James Webb, *Born Fighting: How the Scots-Irish Shaped America* (New York: Broadway Books, 2004); Patrick Griffen, *The People with No Name: Ireland's Ulster Scots, America's Scots Irish, and the Creation of a British Atlantic World, 1689–1764* (Princeton: Princeton University Press, 2001).

34. James Horn, "British Diaspora: Emigration from Britain, 1680–1815," in P. J. Marshall, ed., *The Oxford History of the British Empire: The Eighteenth Century* (New York: Oxford University Press, 1998), 41, 44; Eric Richards, "Scotland and the Uses of the Atlantic Empire," in Bernard Bailyn and Philip D. Morgan, eds., *Strangers within the Realm: Cultural Margins of the First British Empire* (Chapel Hill: University of North Carolina Press, 1991), 67–114; T. C. Smout, N. C. Landsman, and T. M. Devine, "Scottish Emigration in the Seventeenth and Eighteenth Centuries," in Nicholas Canny, ed., *Europeans on the Move: Studies on*

European Migration, 1500–1800 (Oxford: Clarendon Press, 1994), 76–112; Bailyn, *Voyagers to the West*, 36–49; J. M. Bumsted, *The People's Clearance: Highland Emigration to British North America, 1770–1815* (Edinburgh: Edinburgh University Press, 1982), ch. 1.

35. Andrew Mackillop, *"More Fruitful than the Soil": Army, Empire and the Scottish Highlands, 1715–1815* (East Linton, Scotland: Tuckwell Press, 2000), 185–86; Jenni Calder, *Scots in Canada* (Edinburgh: Luath Press, 2003), 26 (Fraser's Highlanders).

36. Michael Fry, *The Scottish Empire* (Edinburgh: Birlinn Ltd, 2002), 101.

37. Bailyn, *Voyagers*, 8.

38. Bailyn, *Voyagers*, 10–12; Calloway, *The Western Abenakis of Vermont*, ch. 10; David Jaffee, *People of the Wachusett: Greater New England in History and Memory, 1630–1860* (Ithaca: Cornell University Press, 1999), part 3.

39. Labaree, ed., *The Papers of Benjamin Franklin*, 10: 429–30.

40. Bailyn, *Voyagers*, 12–14.

41. Bailyn, *Voyagers*, 14–15, 18–20.

42. David Hackett Fischer, *Albion's Seed: Four British Folkways in America* (New York: Oxford University Press, 1989), 605–782; Webb, *Born Fighting*.

43. Bailyn, *Voyagers*, 7–8, 20.

44. Woody Holton, *Forced Founders: Indians, Debtors, Slaves, and the Making of the American Revolution in Virginia* (Chapel Hill: University of North Carolina Press, 1999), 7–8.

45. Boyd, ed., *The Susquehannah Company Papers*, 2: 175–300.

46. Jack Sosin, *Whitehall and the Wilderness: The Middle West in British Colonial Policy, 1760–1775* (Lincoln: University of Nebraska Press, 1961), 50, 136–38; Memorial and Articles of the Mississippi Company reprinted in Clarence Edwin Carter, ed., *Great Britain and the Illinois Country, 1763–1774* (Washington D. C.: The American Historical Association, 1910), 165–71, and Alvord and Carter, eds., *The Critical Period, 1763–1765*, 19–29; W. W. Abbot and Dorothy Twohig, eds., *The Papers of George Washington: Colonial Series*. 10 vols. (Charlottesville: University Press of Virginia, 1980–1995), 7: 219–25, 242–46, 269–70.

47. Jean B. Lee, *The Price of Nationhood: The American Revolution in Charles County* (New York: W. W. Norton, 1994), 39–40.

48. Abbot and Twohig, eds., *Papers of George Washington*, 7: 191–97; John C. Fitzpatrick, ed., *The Writings of George Washington*. 39 vols. (Washington, D.C.: Govt. Printing Office, 1931–44), 2: 392–95, 414–20.

49. Fitzpatrick, ed., *Writings of George Washington*, 2: 398, 407.

50. Fitzpatrick, ed., *Writings of George Washington*, 2: 352, 395–96, 420–21; Abbot and Twohig, *Papers of George Washington*, 7: 201–2.

51. David Hackett Fischer and James C. Kelly, *Bound Away: Virginia and*

the Westward Movement (Charlottesville: University Press of Virginia, 2000).

52. *WJP* 10: 674–75.
53. Anderson, *Crucible of War,* 332.
54. *WJP* 4: 40.
55. *WJP* 4: 283; 10: 662
56. *WJP* 13: 282; Fuller's account for the work done at Johnson Hall is in *WJP* 13: 303–17.
57. *WJP* 13: 303.
58. *WJP* 1: 229–30.
59. Michael J. Mullin, "Personal Politics: William Johnson and the Mohawks," *American Indian Quarterly* 17 (1993), 350–58; *NYCD* 6: 740–41.
60. *WJP* 4: 370, 10: 370.
61. Robert Rogers, *Ponteach, or the Savages of America: A Tragedy* (London, 1766; reprinted with an intro. by Allan Nevins, Chicago: The Caxton Club, 1914), 180.
62. *NYCD* 7: 579.
63. Francis Jennings, *Empire of Fortune: Crowns, Colonies and Tribes in the Seven Years War in America* (New York: W. W. Norton, 1988), 452.

CHAPTER 3: THE FIRST WAR OF INDEPENDENCE

1. Netawatwees quoted in "Journal of James Kenny, 1761–1763," *The Pennsylvania Magazine of History and Biography* 37 (1913), 187. "Bouquet Papers," *MPHC* 19 (1892), 183–84; *WJP* 10: 659–60.
2. Minavana's speech is in Colin G. Calloway, ed., *The World Turned Upside Down: Indian Voices from Early America* (Boston: Bedford/St. Martin's, 1994), 136; Armand Francis Lucier, comp., *Pontiac's Conspiracy and Other Indian Affairs: Notices Abstracted from Colonial Newspapers, 1763–1765* (Bowie, Md.: Heritage Books, 2000), 93; Johnson in *NYCD* 7: 665.
3. For studies of Pontiac's War see Gregory Evans Dowd, *War under Heaven: Pontiac, the Indian Nations and the British Empire* (Baltimore: Johns Hopkins University Press, 2002); David Dixon, *Never Come to Peace Again: Pontiac's Uprising and the Fate of the British Empire in North America* (Norman: University of Oklahoma Press, 2005); William R. Nester, *"Haughty Conquerors": Amherst and the Great Indian Uprising of 1763* (Westport, Conn.: Praeger, 2000); Jon William Parmenter, "Pontiac's War: Forging New Links in the Anglo-Iroquois Covenant Chain, 1758–1766," *Ethnohistory* 44 (1997), 617–54, and Richard White, *The Middle Ground: Indians, Empires, and Republics in the Great Lakes Region, 1650–1815* (Cambridge: Cambridge University Press, 1991), ch. 7. Older studies include Howard H. Peckham, *Pontiac and the Indian Uprising* (Princeton: Princeton University Press, 1947), and Francis Parkman, *The Conspiracy of Pontiac.* 2 vols. (1851; New York: E. P. Dutton, 1908).
4. Dowd, *War under Heaven,* 175.
5. Leonard W. Labaree, ed., *The Papers of Benjamin Franklin.* 35 vols. (New Haven: Yale University Press, 1959–99), 10: 21, 273–74.

6. Dowd, *War under Heaven*; Croghan to Bouquet December 10, 1762, Sir Jeffery, First Baron Amherst. Official Papers and Correspondence, 1740–1783. 202 reels. London: World Microfilm Publications, 1979 (hereafter Amherst Papers), reel 30: 216–17.

7. Nester, *"Haughty Conquerors,"* 50–52; Wilbur R. Jacobs, *Wilderness Politics and Indian Gifts: The Northern Colonial Frontier, 1748–1763* (1950; reprint, Lincoln: University of Nebraska Press, 1966), 180–85; White, *The Middle Ground*, 256–68; Eric Hinderaker, *Elusive Empires: Constructing Colonialism in the Ohio Valley, 1673–1800* (Cambridge: Cambridge University Press, 1997), 147–49; *WJP* 3: 185–86, 345, 530–31, 733; Amherst, Johnson, and Onondaga quotes at *WJP* 10: 649, 652, 657. See, generally, Amherst Papers.

8. *The Annual Register for 1763* (London: J. Dodsley, 1796), 22.

9. *WJP* 10: 521–29.

10. "Bouquet Papers," *MPHC* 19 (1892), 77–79, 83, 86–88; McConnell, *A Country Between*, 171–75; Thomas S. Abler, "Guyasuta," *American National Biography* (American Council of Learned Societies and Oxford University Press, 1999), 5: 750–51; Parmenter, "Pontiac's War," 624.

11. Johnson to Colden, July 25, 1763, "The Letters and Papers of Cadwallader Colden. Volume 6: 1761–1764," *Collections of the New-York Historical Society*, 55 (1922), 228.

12. Gregory Evans Dowd, *A Spirited Resistance: The North American Indian Struggle for Unity* (Baltimore: Johns Hopkins University Press, 1992), 33–36; Dowd, "Thinking and Believing: Nativism and Unity in the Ages of Pontiac and Tecumseh," *American Indian Quarterly* 16 (1992), 309–35. Wolf's speech in Milo M. Quaife, ed., *The Siege of Detroit in 1763: The Journal of Pontiac's Conspiracy and John Rutherfurd's Narrative of a Captivity* (Chicago: R. R. Donnelley and Sons, 1958), 8–16; living "without any Trade or Connections" quote in "Journal of James Kenny," 171; "vision of Heaven," 175.

13. Quaife, ed., *The Siege of Detroit in 1763*, 22.

14. *WJP* 10: 965.

15. "Bouquet Papers," *MPHC* 19 (1892), 196–97; Amherst to Murray, June 24, 1763, James Murray Papers, National Archives of Canada, MG A-1992, reel 1; Quaife, ed., *The Siege of Detroit in 1763*, 58. Peckham, *Pontiac and the Indian Uprising*, 121–25, discusses the various sources for Gladwin's information (Gladwin's quote at 121) and Helen F. Humphrey considers "The Identity of Major Gladwin's Informant," *Mississippi Valley Historical Review* 21 (1934), 147–62. According to the Amherst Papers, reel 33: 103, the major simply got warning "the Night before."

16. Amherst Papers, reel 33: 103.

17. Matthew C. Ward, "'The Indians Our Real Friends': The British Army and the Ohio Indians, 1758–1772," in Daniel P. Barr, ed., *The Boundaries between Us: Natives and Newcomers along the Frontiers of the Old Northwest Territory* (forthcoming, Kent State University Press); *WJP* 10: 731–32.

18. "Bouquet Papers," *MPHC* 19 (1892), 209–18; "Gladwin Manuscripts," *MPHC* 27 (1897), 636–39, 668–69; Charles Morse Stotz, *Outposts of the War for Empire* (Pittsburgh: University of Pittsburgh Press, 1985), 52. The circumstances of the capture of Michilimackinac were related by trader Alexander Henry who survived the attack and by William Warren who

"learned [it] verbally from the old French traders and half-breeds, who learned it from the lips of those who were present." William Warren, *History of the Ojibway People* (1885; reprinted St. Paul: Minnesota Historical Society Press, 1984), 201–9; Amherst Papers, reel 33: 101 (Amherst's warning).

19. "Bouquet Papers," *MPHC* 19: 21; *NYCD* 7: 532; Amherst to Murray, July 18, 1763, James Murray Papers, National Archives of Canada, MG A-1992, reel 1.

20. Lucier, comp., *Pontiac's Conspiracy and Other Indian Affairs,* 143; Sylvester K. Stevens et al., eds., *The Papers of Henry Bouquet.* 6 vols. (Pennsylvania Historical Museum Commission, 1951–), 6: 261–62; also quoted in Parkman, *The Conspiracy of Pontiac,* 2: 15.

21. William Smith, *An Historical Account of the Expedition against the Ohio Indians in the Year 1764 under the Command of Henry Bouquet* (Dublin: John Milliken, 1769), vi.

22. J. Clarence Webster, ed., *The Journal of Jeffery Amherst* (Chicago: University of Chicago Press, 1931), 311; Amherst Papers, reel 76, pt. 1: 172, 178–79, 185–89; pt. 2: 3.

23. *Journals of the House of Representatives of Massachusetts,* Vol. 40: *1763–1764,* x, 118–21, 151; "The Fitch Papers: Correspondence and Documents during Thomas Fitch's Governorship of the Colony of Connecticut, 1754–1766," *Collections of the Connecticut Historical Society,* 18 (1920), 274–75.

24. Larry L. Nelson, *A Man of Distinction among Them: Alexander McKee and the Ohio Country Frontier, 1754–1799* (Kent, Ohio: Kent State University Press, 1999), 44–47.

25. *WJP* 4: 348, 365, 367–72; *NYCD* 7: 526; Parmenter, "Pontiac's War: Forging New Links in the Anglo-Iroquois Covenant Chain, 1758–1766," 624–25.

26. *WJP* 11: 69, 113; *NYCD* 7: 534; Amherst Papers, reel 76, pt. 2: 40, 133.

27. Nester, *"Haughty Conquerors,"* 114–17; *WJP* 10: 733; "Bouquet Papers," *MPHC* 19: 203; Amherst Papers, reel 33: 110; reel 76, pt. 2: 69–70.

28. Clarence Edwin Carter, ed., *The Correspondence of General Thomas Gage.* 2 vols. (New Haven: Yale University Press, 1931–33), 1: 3.

29. "Journal of William Trent," in John W. Harpster, ed., *Pen Pictures of Early Western Pennsylvania* (Pittsburgh: University of Pittsburgh Press, 1938), 103–4; Bernard Knollenberg, "General Amherst and Germ Warfare," *Mississippi Valley Historical Review* 41 (1954–55), 489–94, and Donald K. Kent's rejoinder, ibid., 762–63. Elizabeth A. Fenn, "Biological Warfare in Eighteenth-Century North America: Beyond Jeffery Amherst," *Journal of American History* 86 (2000), 1552–80, weighs the evidence against Amherst, traces the long-standing debate about whether he ordered germ warfare, considers the broader context for the application of such tactics, and reproduces the invoice at 1554. Philip Ranlet, "The British, the Indians, and Smallpox: What Actually Happened at Fort Pitt in 1763," *Pennsylvania History* 67 (2000), 427–41, and Ron Welburn, "Amherst and Indians; Then and Today: A Cautionary Review," in his *Roanoke and Wampum: Topics in Native American Heritage and Literatures* (New York: Peter Lang, 2001), 35–50, also review the evidence. An escaped captive, Gorsham Hicks, reported that smallpox was widespread among the Indians after the spring of 1763; "Bouquet Papers," *MPHC* 19: 254.

30. Amherst Papers, reel 76, pt. 1: 70–71; "Letter Book of John Watts, Merchant

and Councillor of New York, 1762–1765," *Collections of the New-York Historical Society*, 61 (1928), 159, 181.

31. "Bouquet Papers," *MPHC* 19 (1892), 219–22.

32. "Bouquet Papers," *MPHC* 19 (1892), 237; Lucier, comp., *Pontiac's Conspiracy and Other Indian Affairs*, 79–82.

33. Michael N. McConnell, *Army and Empire: British Soldiers on the American Frontier, 1758–1775* (Lincoln: University of Nebraska Press, 2004), 130. McConnell notes that one of the survivors was "the improbably named Noah Flood."

34. Jean-Pierre Sawaya, *Alliance et Dépendence* (Sillery: Septentrion, 2002), chs. 1–2; *WJP* 10: 792–94; 843, 856; 11: 67; *NYCD* 7: 554–59.

35. [No Author], *Pontiac's War, 1763–1764: An Exhibition of Source Materials in the William L. Clements Library* (Ann Arbor: University of Michigan, 1963), 14–15.

36. *WJP* 4: 466–81; Lucier, comp., *Pontiac's Conspiracy and Other Indian Affairs*, 195–98; Carter, ed., *Correspondence of General Thomas Gage*, 2: 19; Nester, *"Haughty Conquerors,"* 190–93.

37. Smith, *An Historical Account of the Expedition against the Ohio Indians*, 2.

38. Smith, *An Historical Account of the Expedition against the Ohio Indians*, 17–21; "Bouquet Papers," *MPHC* 19 (1892), 279–82; "Journal of John Bremner, 1756–1764," New-York Historical Society, Manuscript Department (typescript), 52–77.

39. Smith, *An Historical Account of the Expedition against the Ohio Indians*, 25–37; Carter ed., *Correspondence of General Thomas Gage*, 1: 45–46. Ohio Indians captured hundreds of colonists in the war years; Matthew C. Ward, "Redeeming the Captives: Pennsylvania Captives among the Ohio Indians, 1755–1765," *Pennsylvania Magazine of History and Biography* 125 (2001), 161–89.

40. Joseph L. Peyser, trans. and ed., *Letters from New France: The Upper Country 1686–1783* (Urbana: University of Illinois Press, 1992), 214.

41. Peckham, *Pontiac and the Indian Uprising*, 267–68, 274–75; White, *Middle Ground*, 301–5.

42. "Journal of Captain Morris, 1764," in Reuben G. Thwaites, ed., *Early Western Travels, 1748–1846.* 32 vols. (Cleveland: Arthur H. Clarke, 1904), 1: 308–12.

43. "George Croghan's Journal, 1765," in Thwaites, ed., *Early Western Travels*, 1: 126–73; *WJP* 4: 848; 11: 577, 629, 839, 889–901; *NYCD* 7: 787–78, 854–67 (Johnson's meeting with Pontiac); Parmenter, "Pontiac's War," 636–39.

44. White, *Middle Ground*, 305–6; Dowd, *War under Heaven*, ch. 7.

45. Matthew C. Ward, *Breaking the Backcountry: The Seven Years' War in Virginia and Pennsylvania, 1754–1764* (Pittsburgh: University of Pittsburgh Press, 2003), chs. 2–3.

46. "Letter Book of John Watts," 153.

47. *The Annual Register for 1763* (London: J. Dodsley, 1796), 23 ("hopeful settlements"); Lucier, comp, *Pontiac's Conspiracy and Other Indian Affairs*, 37.

48. Paul A. W. Wallace, ed., *Thirty Thousand Miles with John Heckewelder or Travels among the Indians of Pennsylvania, New York and Ohio in the 18th*

Century (1958; reprinted Lewisburg, Penn.: Wennawoods Publishing, 1998), 71.

49. Wallace, *Thirty Thousand Miles*, 72–77.

50. Penn in "The Letters and Papers of Cadwallader Colden, Vol. 6: 1761–164," *Collections of the New-York Historical Society*, 55 (1922), 274.

51. On the Paxton Boys' massacre see James H. Merrell, *Into the American Woods: Negotiators on the Pennsylvania Frontier* (New York: W. W. Norton, 1999), 285–88; Jane T. Merritt, *At the Crossroads: Indians and Empires on a Mid-Atlantic Frontier, 1700–1763* (Chapel Hill: University of North Carolina Press, 2003), 283–94; *Pennsylvania Archives*, 1st series, 4 (1853), 147–49, 151–55, 160–62; Lucier, comp., *Pontiac's Conspiracy and Other Indian Affairs*, 138–39, 164–73, 176–85, and Labaree, ed., *The Papers of Benjamin Franklin*, 11: 22–30, 42–44.

52. Parkman, *The Conspiracy of Pontiac*, 2: 251.

53. Benjamin Franklin, "A Narrative of the Late Massacres in Lancaster County," (1764), reprinted in Labaree, ed., *The Papers of Benjamin Franklin*, 11: 47–69 (names at 48–49; red hair quote at 55); Paxton retort quoted in Merritt, *At the Crossroads*, 290. See also Alison Olson, "The Pamphlet War over the Paxton Boys," *Pennsylvania Magazine of History and Biography* 123 (1999), 31–55.

54. Merrell, *Into the American Woods*, 287.

55. "Bouquet Papers," *MPHC* 19 (1892), 294.

56. "Bouquet Papers," *MPHC* 19: 268.

57. Charles Pettit to Joseph Reed, December 17, 1763, and letter from a friend to Joseph Reed, March 22, 1764, Joseph Reed Papers, New-York Historical Society. Thanks to Anna Fleder for these documents.

58. Labaree, ed., *The Papers of Benjamin Franklin*, 10: 105.

59. Marjolene Kars, *Breaking Loose Together: The Regulator Rebellion in Pre-Revolutionary North Carolina* (Chapel Hill: University of North Carolina Press, 2002).

60. "Information Concerning White Captives," *WJP* 4: 495.

61. Johnson to Colden, January 12, 1764, "The Letters and Papers of Cadwallader Colden. Volume 6: 1761–1764," *Collections of the New-York Historical Society*, 55 (1922), 277.

62. June Namias, ed., *A Narrative of the Life of Mary Jemison by James E. Seaver* (Norman: University of Oklahoma Press, 1992), 15–16, 80, 83–84. Namias implies that the incident at Fort Pitt occurred at the end of the war, but this is unlikely since Jemison said she had been with the Indians only about a year at the time.

63. Smith, *An Historical Account of the Expedition against the Ohio Indians in the year 1764, under the Command of Henry Bouquet*, 16; "Bouquet Papers," *MPHC* 19: 281.

64. Labaree, ed., *Papers of Benjamin Franklin*, 11: 173–74; Merritt, *At the Crossroads*, 299.

65. Merrell, *Into the American Woods*, 38.

66. Cf. Peter C. Mancall, *Valley of Opportunity: Economic Culture along the Upper Susquehanna, 1700–1800* (Ithaca: Cornell University Press, 1991), ch. 4.

67. On British regulars in the Seven Years' War see Stephen Brumwell, *Redcoats:*

The British Soldier and War in the Americas, 1755–1763 (Cambridge: Cambridge University Press, 2002), and McConnell, *Army and Empire;* more generally see Richard Holmes, *Redcoat: The British Soldier in the Age of Horse and Musket* (New York: W. W. Norton, 2002).

68. "Letter Book of John Watts," 155.
69. "Gladwin Manuscripts," *MPHC* 27: 636.
70. Peter Way, "The Cutting Edge of Culture: British Soldiers Encounter Native Americans in the French and Indian War," in Martin Daunton and Rick Halpern, eds., *Empire and Others: British Encounters with Indigenous Peoples, 1600–1850* (Philadelphia: University of Pennsylvania Press, 1999), 123–48 ("decentering"); Ward, *Breaking the Backcountry,* 42–3, 55 (psychological warfare and British regulars).
71. Thomas Mante, *The History of the Late War in North-America, and the Islands of the West-Indies* (London, 1772; New York: Research Reprints Inc, 1970), 485; "Letter Book of John Watts," 84; "Letter from a Gentleman in New York," in *Gentleman's Magazine* 33 (1763), 88; Brumwell, *Redcoats,* 267–68; Archibald Forbes, *The Black Watch: The Record of an Historic Regiment* (Reprint, Bowie, Md.: Heritage Books, 2002), 88 ("mere skeleton"); Andrew Mackillop, *"More Fruitful than the Soil": Army, Empire and the Scottish Highlands, 1715–1815* (East Linton, Scotland: Tuckwell Press, 2000), 186 (land grants); Samuel Johnson, *A Journey to the Western Islands of Scotland* (New York: Penguin, 1984), 104. On the condition of the troops encamped on Staten Island see Amherst Papers, reel 74: 21, 64–65, 68, 202, 207–8, 211–12, 214–15; reel 75: 117; reel 76, pt. 1: 47, 172, 178–79, 185–89, 191.
72. Brumwell, *Redcoats,* 137–38; "Journal of a Detachment of the 42nd Regiment from Fort Pitt down the Ohio to the Country of the Illenoise," National Archives of Scotland, GD298/196.
73. *The Annual Register for 1763,* 28; Amherst to Murray, July 30, 1763, and August 1, 1763, James Murray Papers, National Archives of Canada, MG A-1992, reel 1; Peter Way, "Rebellion of the Regulars: Working Soldiers and the Mutiny of 1763–1764," *William and Mary Quarterly* 3rd series, 57 (2000), 761–92; complaint re: 4 pence for provisions is in Webster, ed., *The Journal of Jeffery Amherst,* 324. *The Annual Register for 1763,* 159–60, printed an account of the mutiny at Quebec written by an officer of the garrison.
74. Dunbar Rowland, ed., *Mississippi Provincial Archives: English Dominion, 1763–1766* (Nashville: Barton Printing Company, 1911), 1: 141.
75. Rowland, ed., *Mississippi Provincial Archives: English Dominion* 1: 39.
76. Michael N. McConnell, *A Country Between: The Upper Ohio Valley and Its Peoples, 1724–1774* (Lincoln: University of Nebraska Press, 1992), 148.
77. Mark Boyd, ed. "From a Remote Frontier: Letters and Documents pertaining to San Marcos de Apalache, 1763–1769," *Florida Historical Quarterly* 19 (1941), 405, 408, 410.
78. *WJP* 3: 958; 4: 314, 319, 329, 367, 377, 438, 485; 11: 217, 318.
79. "Bouquet Papers," *MPHC* 19: 182–83.
80. "Bouquet Papers," *MPHC* 19: 139, 153–54 .
81. "Bouquet Papers," *MPHC* 19: 212–18; *WJP* 10: 744; 13: 296
82. Lucier, comp., *Pontiac's Conspiracy and Other Indian Affairs,* 47; Quaife, ed., *The Siege of Detroit in 1763,* 53–58, 158–59, 175–76; *New Hampshire Gazette and Historical Chronicle,* August 19, 1763.

83. "Letter Book of John Watts," 169.
84. "Bouquet Papers," *MPHC* 19: 218.
85. Anonymous letter reprinted in Parkman, *The Conspiracy of Pontiac*, 1: 180; "Journal of John Bremner, 1756–1764," New-York Historical Society, Manuscript Division (typescript), 41; "Bouquet Papers," *MPHC* 19: 252.
86. October 7, 1763, original in Burton Historical Collection, Detroit Public Library, quoted in Peckham, *Pontiac and the Indian Uprising*, 233.
87. Gladwin to Bouquet, November 1, 1763, "Gladwin Manuscripts," *MPHC* 27: 680.
88. Gladwin to Gage, February 24, 1774, "Gladwin Manuscripts," *MPHC* 27: 677.
89. Charles E. Brodine, Jr., "Henry Bouquet and British Infantry Tactics on the Ohio Frontier, 1758–1764," in David Curtis Skaggs and Larry L. Nelson, eds., *The Sixty Years' War for the Great Lakes, 1754–1814* (East Lansing: Michigan State University Press, 2001), 43–61; "dogs" quote at 51; "Bouquet Papers," *MPHC* 19: 201, 262.
90. Lawrence Henry Gipson, *The British Empire before the American Revolution.* 15 vols. (New York: Alfred A. Knopf, 1936–1970), 9: 90; Lois Mulkearn, ed., *George Mercer Papers Relating to the Ohio Company of Virginia* (Pittsburgh: University of Pittsburgh Press, 1954), 614–15.
91. *NYCD* 7: 541.
92. Letter from Bouquet, Camp at Edge Hill, August 5, 1763, Stevens et al., eds., *The Papers of Henry Bouquet*, 6: 338–40; "Bouquet Papers," *MPHC* 19: 219–23; reprinted in *The Gentleman's Magazine* for 1763: 487–88, and in Parkman, *Conspiracy of Pontiac*, 235–37; Brodine, "Henry Bouquet and British Infantry Tactics," 53–54.
93. Letter from Camp at Bushy Run, August 6, 1763, Stevens, et al., eds., *Bouquet Papers* 6: 342–44, reprinted in Parkman, *Conspiracy of Pontiac* 2: 237–39.
94. Brodine, "Henry Bouquet and British Infantry Tactics," 43.
95. Extract from a letter, August 12. Pennsylvania Gazette No. 1810, quoted in Parkman, *Conspiracy of Pontiac* 2: 36.
96. "Bouquet Papers," *MPHC* 19: 268.
97. Boyd, ed., "From a Remote Frontier," 182.
98. Douglas Edward Leach, *Roots of Conflict: British Armed Forces and Colonial Americans, 1677–1763* (Chapel Hill: University of North Carolina Press, 1986), chs. 5–6; Fred Anderson, *A People's Army: Massachusetts Soldiers and Society in the Seven Years' War* (Chapel Hill: University of North Carolina Press, 1984).
99. Robert Scott Stephenson, "With Swords and Plowshares: British and American Soldiers in the Trans-Allegheny West, 1754–1774," Ph.D. diss., University of Virginia, 1998, 202–20.
100. E.g., *Pennsylvania Archives*, 1st series, 4 (1853), 251–52, 255, 283–85.
101. Walter S. Dunn, Jr., *The New Imperial Economy: The British Army and the American Frontier, 1764–1768* (Westport, Conn.: Praeger, 2001); John Shy, *Toward Lexington: The Role of the British Army in the Coming of the American Revolution* (Princeton, N. J.: Princeton University Press, 1965), 45–46, 52–83; Peter D. G. Thomas, "New Light on the Commons Debate of 1763 on the American Army," *William and Mary Quarterly*, 3rd series, 38 (1981), 10–12;

Peter D. G. Thomas, "The Cost of the British Army in North America," *William and Mary Quarterly*, 3rd series, 45 (1988), 510–16; John L. Bullion, "'The Ten Thousand in America:' More Light on the Decision on the American Army, 1762–1763," *William and Mary Quarterly* 43 (1986), 646–57.

102. *NYCD* 7: 570; Carter, ed. *Correspondence of General Gage*, 2: 3–4.
103. *WJP* 10: 925.
104. *WJP* 4: 341.
105. "Journal of John Bremner, 1756–1764," New-York Historical Society, Manuscript Division (typescript), 77.
106. Ward, "'The Indians Our Real Friends': The British Army and the Ohio Indians, 1758–1772."
107. Carter, ed., *The Correspondence of General Thomas Gage*, 1: 333, 335–36.

CHAPTER 4: SETTING BOUNDARIES

1. Peter C. Mancall, *Valley of Opportunity: Economic Culture along the Upper Susquehanna, 1700–1800* (Ithaca: Cornell University Press, 1991), ch. 4.
2. Richard White, *Middle Ground: Indians, Empires, and Republics in the Great Lakes Region, 1650–1815* (Cambridge: Cambridge University Press, 1991), ch. 7; Clarence Edwin Carter, ed., *Correspondence of General Thomas Gage*. 2 vols. (New Haven: Yale University Press, 1931–33), 2: 2. Jack M. Sosin, *Whitehall and the Wilderness: The Middle West in British Colonial Policy, 1760–1775* (Lincoln: University of Nebraska Press, 1961), ch. 3, traces the evolution of the Proclamation Line through British politics and imperial machinery.
3. White, *Middle Ground*, 269–71; Ian K. Steele, *Warpaths: Invasions of North America* (New York: Oxford University Press, 1994, part 3), 246–47; Jon William Parmenter, "Pontiac's War: Forging New Links in the Anglo-Iroquois Covenant Chain, 1758–1766," *Ethnohistory* 44 (1997), 638–39; William R. Nester, *"Haughty Conquerors:" Amherst and the Great Indian Uprising of 1763* (Westport, Conn.: Praeger, 2000), 223.
4. *WJP* 3: 457.
5. Verner Crane, ed., "Hints Relative to the Division and Government of the Conquered and Newly Acquired Countries in America," *Mississippi Valley Historical Review* 8 (1922), 367–73; Thomas Barrow, ed., "A Project for Imperial Reform: 'Hints Respecting the Settlement of our American Colonies,' 1763," *William and Mary Quarterly*, 3rd series, 24 (1967), 108–26; quotes at 116–17; Edward J. Cashin, *Governor Henry Ellis and the Transformation of British North America* (Athens: University of Georgia Press, 1994), quote re: Egremont at 153.
6. Egremont to Amherst, January 27, 1763, in "The Fitch Papers: Correspondence and Documents during Thomas Fitch's Governorship of the Colony of Connecticut, 1754–1766," *Collections of the Connecticut Historical Society*, 18 (1920), 224. See also Egremont to Lords of Trade, May 5, 1763, *NYCD* 7: 520–21.
7. Clarence Walworth Alvord, ed., *The Mississippi Valley in British Politics*. 2 vols. (Cleveland: Arthur H. Clark Co., 1917), 1: 148, 157–82, 203; R. A. Humphreys, "Lord Shelburne and the Proclamation of 1763," *English*

Historical Review 49 (1934), 241–64. Shelburne presided over the Board of Trade from April 23 to September 2, 1763.

8. The Proclamation was issued as a broadside and was also published in *The Gentleman's Magazine* in October 1763. It is reprinted in Adam Shortt and Arthur G. Doughty, eds., *Documents Relating to the Constitutional History of Canada, 1759–1791.* 2 vols. (Ottawa: Historical Documents Publication Board, 1918), 163–68, as well as in *WJP* 10: 977–85.

9. L. C. Green and Olive P. Dickinson, *The Law of Nations and the New World* (Edmonton: University of Alberta Press, 1989), 99–124; Robert A. Williams, Jr., *The American Indian in Western Legal Thought: The Discourses of Conquest* (New York: Oxford University Press, 1999), 229; Anthony Pagden, *Lords of All the World: Ideologies of Empire in Spain, Britain and France, c. 1500–c. 1800* (New Haven: Yale University Press, 1995), 85; Gregory Evans Dowd, *War under Heaven: Pontiac, the Indian Nations & the British Empire* (Baltimore: Johns Hopkins University Press, 2002), 177.

10. The following paragraphs rely heavily on John Borrows, "Constitutional Law from a First Nation Perspective: Self-Government and the Royal Proclamation," *UBC Law Review* 28 (1994), 1–47, and "Wampum at Niagara: The Royal Proclamation, Canadian Legal History, and Self-Government," in Michael Asche, ed., *Aboriginal and Treaty Rights in Canada* (Vancouver: University of British Columbia Press, 1997), 155–72; and "'Landed' Citizenship: Narratives of Aboriginal Political Participation," in Will Kymlicka and Wayne Norman, eds., *Citizenship in Diverse Societies* (Toronto: Oxford University Press, 2000), 326–42, esp. 334–35.

11. Borrows, "Wampum at Niagara," 162.

12. See also, Carter, ed., *Correspondence of General Thomas Gage*, 1: 37, for the figure of 2,000.

13. Brian Slattery, "The Land Rights of Indigenous Canadian Peoples, as Affected by the Crown's Acquisition of their Territories," Ph.D. diss., University of Oxford, 1979; Denning quoted in Pagden, *Lords of All the World,* 85.

14. D. W. Meinig, *The Shaping of America: A Geographical Perspective on 500 Years of History.* Vol. 1: *Atlantic America, 1492–1800* (New Haven: Yale University Press, 1986), 284.

15. Cashin, *Governor Henry Ellis and the Transformation of British North America,* 244.

16. Indian complaints in Croghan to Franklin, October 2, 1767, in Howard H. Peckham, ed., *George Croghan's Journal of his Trip to Detroit in 1767 with his Correspondence relating Thereto* (Ann Arbor: University of Michigan Press, 1939), 23.

17. Woody Holton, *Forced Founders: Indians, Debtors, Slaves, and the Making of the American Revolution in Virginia* (Chapel Hill: University of North Carolina Press, 1999), ch. 1, esp. 7–8, 29–31; Thomas P. Abernethy, *Western Lands and the American Revolution* (New York: D. Appleton-Century, 1937), ch. 2.

18. Washington to Crawford, quoted in Fred Anderson, *Crucible of War: The Seven Years' War and the Fate of Empire in British North America, 1754–1766* (New York: Alfred Knopf, 2000), 740.

19. Lawrence Henry Gipson, "Virginia Private Debts and the Government of

Great Britain," in Gipson, *The British Empire before the American Revolution.*
15 vols. (New York: Knopf, 1936–1970), 10, ch. 8; Holton, *Forced Founders.*

20. *WJP* 4: 264–66 (tavern meeting); 270–71 (memorial); 399 (quote from
    Croghan letter, which is also reprinted in Alvord and Carter, eds., *The
    Critical Period,* 221–24); *WJP* 10: 859 and *NYCD* 7: 569 (Amherst's
    disapproval); Abernethy, *Western Lands and the American Revolution,* 22–31;
    Sosin, *Whitehall and the Wilderness,* 145–46.

21. Peter Marshall, "Sir William Johnson and the Treaty of Fort Stanwix, 1768,"
    Journal of American Studies 1 (1967), 149–79; Carter, ed., *The Correspondence
    of General Thomas Gage,* 2: 71, 85, 98. The proceedings and deed of the
    Treaty of Fort Stanwix, October 24–November 6, 1768, are in *NYCD* 8:
    111–34.

22. *WJP* 6: 212; 12: 710; Carter, ed., *Correspondence of General Thomas Gage,* 1: 11,
    61, 91, 142–43; Peckham ed., *George Croghan's Journal of His Trip to Detroit,*
    16–17, 23–26, 33–35; White, *Middle Ground,* ch. 7; Michael N. McConnell,
    A Country Between: The Upper Ohio Valley and Its Peoples, 1724–1774
    (Lincoln: University of Nebraska Press, 1992), ch. 8; Francis Jennings,
    *Empire of Fortune: Crowns, Colonies and Tribes in the Seven Years War in
    America* (New York: W. W. Norton, 1988), chs. 20–21.

23. John Richard Alden, *John Stuart and the Southern Colonial Frontier* (Ann
    Arbor: University of Michigan Press, 1944), 183; James H. Merrell, "'Mind-
    ing the Business of the Nation': Hagler as Catawba Leader," *Ethnohistory* 33
    (1986), 55–70.

24. John T. Juricek, ed., *Georgia Treaties 1733–1763,* Vol. 11 in Alden T.
    Vaughan, gen. ed., *Early American Indian Documents: Treaties and Laws
    1607–1789* (Frederick, Md.: University Publications of America, 1989),
    348–450; Allen D. Chandler, ed., *Colonial Records of the State of Georgia*
    (Atlanta: Franklin Printing, 1904–06), 9: 9–17; Kenneth Coleman and
    Milton Ready, eds., *Colonial Records of the State of Georgia.* Vol. 28, pt. 1:
    Original Papers of Governors Reynolds, Ellis, Wright, and Others 1757–1763
    (Athens: University of Georgia Press, 1976), 405–6.

25. Steven C. Hahn, *The Invention of the Creek Nation, 1670–1763* (Lincoln:
    University of Nebraska Press, 2004), 1–2 (*Gazette* quote), 4, 264 ("bristled"),
    266.

26. Claudio Saint, *A New Order of Things: Property, Power, and the
    Transformation of the Creek Indians, 1733–1816* (Cambridge: Cambridge
    University Press, 1999), 48; Juricek, ed., *Georgia Treaties 1733–1763,* 351;
    Chandler, ed., *Colonial Records of the State of Georgia,* 9: 71–72; Coleman and
    Ready, eds, *Colonial Records of the State of Georgia,* 28, pt. 1: 429–30.

27. Coleman and Ready, eds., *Colonial Records of the State of Georgia,* 28, pt. 1:
    408–14, 427–30, quote at 429; Chandler, ed., *Colonial Records of Georgia,* 9:
    40–44.

28. Louis De Vorsey, Jr., *The Indian Boundary in the Southern Colonies,
    1763–1775* (Chapel Hill: University of North Carolina Press, 1961).

29. Cashin, *Governor Henry Ellis and the Transformation of British North
    America,* 171; George Reese, ed., *The Official Papers of Francis Fauquier,
    Lieutenant Governor of Virginia, 1758–1768.* 3 vols. (Charlottesville:
    University Press of Virginia, 1980–83), 3: 935–37; William L. Saunders and
    Walter Clark, eds., *The Colonial and State Records of North Carolina.* 30 vols.

(Raleigh: Secretary of State, 1886–1914), 6: 973. Alden, *John Stuart and the Southern Colonial Frontier,* ch. 11, traces the proceedings at Augusta. Stuart's "Journal of the Proceedings of the Southern Congress at Augusta" is in C. O. 5/65, pt. 2: 69–73 (with the presents distributed at 74), reprinted in Walter Clark, ed., *The State Records of North Carolina: Colonial Records,* 11 (1895), 156–205.

30. "Journal of the Proceedings of the Southern Congress at Augusta," 157; Hahn, *Invention of the Creek Nation,* 266–68 (Creek suspicions); Cashin, *Governor Henry Ellis,* 174; Edward Cashin, *Lachlan McGillivray, Indian Trader: The Shaping of the Southern Colonial Frontier* (Athens: University of Georgia Press, 1992), 220 ("debut").

31. Cashin, *Lachlan McGillivray,* 220–21, 274.

32. "Journal of the Proceedings of the Southern Congress at Augusta," 180–81.

33. "Journal of the Proceedings of the Southern Congress at Augusta," 183–92.

34. Coleman and Ready, eds., *Colonial Records of the State of Georgia,* 28, pt. 1: 453–60; "Journal of the Proceedings of the Southern Congress at Augusta," 199–203. The Creeks agreed to move their boundary with Georgia westward to "a Line extending up Savannah River to Little River and back to the Fork of Little River and from the fork of Little River to the ends of the South Branch of Bryar Creek and down that Branch to the lower Creek Path and along the lower Creek Path to the main Stream of Ogechee River, and down the main stream of that River just below the Path leading from Mount Pleasant and from thence in a straight Line cross to Santa Sevilla on the Altamaha River and from thence to the Southward as far as Georgia extends or may be extended."

35. Cashin, *Governor Henry Ellis,* 175–76; Joshua Piker, *Okfuskee, a Creek Indian Town in Colonial America* (Cambridge: Harvard University Press, 2004), 98.

36. Hahn, *Invention of the Creek Nation,* 3 (Chickasaw warning), 268–70, 274.

37. "Journal of the Proceedings of the Southern Congress at Augusta," 189, 198; James H. Merrell, *The Indians' New World: The Catawbas and Their Neighbors from European Contact through the Era of Removal* (Chapel Hill: University of North Carolina Press, 1989), 192–209, quotes at 200, 205; Treaty of Augusta in Coleman and Ready, eds., *Colonial Records of the State of Georgia,* 28, pt. 1: 458.

38. Juricek, ed., *Georgia Treaties 1733–1763,* 359–60; Stuart on Creek limits to settlement C. O. 323/17: 234, quoted in De Vorsey, *The Indian Boundary in the Southern Colonies,* 186.

39. Coleman and Ready, eds., *Colonial Records of the State of Georgia,* 28, pt. 2: 20, 23; "Journal of the Proceedings of the Southern Congress at Augusta," 204–5.

40. Coleman and Ready, eds., *Colonial Records of the State of Georgia,* 28, pt. 2: 52.

41. Juricek, ed., *Georgia Treaties 1733–1763,* 351–52; Chandler, ed., *Colonial Records of the State of Georgia,* 9: 71–73; "Journal of the Proceedings of the Southern Congress at Augusta," 177.

42. Juricek, ed., *Georgia Treaties 1733–1763,* 361.

43. Milo B. Howard, Jr., and Robert R. Rea, eds., *The Mémoire Justificatif of the Chevalier Montault de Monberaut: Indian Diplomacy in British West Florida,*

1763–1765 (Tuscaloosa: University of Alabama Press, 1965), 36–43, 83, 86, 158, 164.

44. Alden, *John Stuart and the Colonial Frontier,* 190; John T. Juricek, ed., *Georgia and Florida Treaties 1763–1776,* Vol. 12 in Alden T. Vaughan, gen. ed., *Early American Indian Documents: Treaties and Laws 1607–1789* (Frederick, Md.: University Publications of America, 2002), 14; Coleman and Ready, eds., *Colonial Records of the State of Georgia,* 28, pt. 2: 52–54.

45. Howard, Jr., and Rea, eds., *The Mémoire Justificatif of the Chevalier Montault de Monberaut,* 36–43, 93, 157–59, 167–70.

46. J. Russell Snapp, *John Stuart and the Struggle for Empire on the Southern Frontier* (Baton Rouge: Louisiana State University Press, 1996), 88; Coleman and Ready, eds., *Colonial Records of the State of Georgia,* 28, pt. 2: 113.

47. Joshua A. Piker, "'White & Clean' & Contested: Creek Towns and Trading Paths in the Aftermath of the Seven Years War," *Ethnohistory* 50 (2003), 315–47.

48. Juricek, ed., *Georgia and Florida Treaties 1763–1776,* 1–2, 8–12; Chandler, ed., *Colonial Records of the State of Georgia,* 9: 111–17; Coleman and Ready, eds., *Colonial Records of the State of Georgia,* 28, pt. 1: 457–58; pt. 2: 1–2, 21–23.

49. Dunbar Rowland, ed., *Mississippi Archives: English Dominion, 1763–1766* (Nashville: Barton Printing, 1911), 1: 12, 72, 114, 142.

50. Dunbar Rowland, A. G. Sanders, and Patricia Kay Galloway, eds., *Mississippi Provincial Archives, French Dominion, 1749–1763* (Baton Rouge: Louisiana State University Press, 1984), 5: 287.

51. James W. Covington, ed., *The British Meet the Seminoles* (Gainesville: University Press of Florida, 1961), 18–41; Saunt, *A New Order of Things,* 36.

52. James W. Covington, "Trade Relations between Southwestern Florida and Cuba, 1600–1840," *Florida Historical Quarterly* 38 (1959), 114–28; William Bartram, *Travels through North and South Carolina, East and West Florida* (London: 1792; Charlottesville: University Press of Virginia, 1980), 184.

53. Samuel Cole Williams, ed., *Adair's History of the American Indians* (New York: Promontory Press, 1930), 434–44; Snapp, *John Stuart and the Struggle for Empire,* 23.

54. Snapp, *John Stuart and the Struggle for Empire,* chap. 2; quotes at 35, 37; Galphin quote at 32; Coleman and Ready, eds., *Colonial Records of the State of Georgia,* 28, pt. 2: 50–52. Jefferson's private letter to Governor William Henry Harrison of Indiana territory, February 27, 1803, is reprinted in Francis Paul Prucha, ed., *Documents of United States Indian Policy* (Lincoln: University of Nebraska Press 1975), 22–23.

55. Robin A. Fabel, *The Economy of British West Florida, 1763–1783* (Tuscaloosa: University of Alabama Press, 1988), 49–61, for the importance and operations of the West Florida deerskin trade. Daniel H. Usner, Jr., *Indians, Settlers, and Slaves in a Frontier Exchange Economy: The Lower Mississippi Valley before 1783* (Chapel Hill: University of North Carolina Press, 1992), 122–30, 268–69; Richard White, *The Roots of Dependency: Subsistence, Environment, and Social Change among the Choctaws, Pawnees, and Navajos* (Lincoln: University of Nebraska Press, 1983), 69–87; Greg O'Brien, *Choctaws in a Revolutionary Age, 1750–1830* (Lincoln: University of Nebraska Press, 2002), 10, 47–48, 80–84.

56. *Pennsylvania Archive*, 1st series, 4 (1853), 182–92 (quote at 191); *NYCD* 7: 634–41. See also Peter Marshall, "Colonial Protest and Imperial Retrenchment: Indian Policy, 1764–1768," *Journal of American Studies* 5 (1971), 1–17.

57. Snapp, *John Stuart and the Struggle for Empire*, chaps 2–3.

CHAPTER 5: ENDINGS AND ENDURANCE IN FRENCH AMERICA

1. Quoted in Guy Frégault, *Canada: The War of the Conquest* (Toronto: Oxford University Press, 1969), 227.

2. Frégault, *Canada: The War of the Conquest*, x–xi.

3. Fred Anderson, *Crucible of War: The Seven Years' War and the Fate of Empire in British North America, 1754–1766* (New York: Knopf, 2000), xvi.

4. Robert V. Wells, *The Population of the British Colonies in America before 1776* (Princeton: Princeton University Press, 1975), 64.

5. Keith R. Widder, "The French Connection: The Interior French and Their Role in French-British Relations in the Western Great Lakes Region, 1760–1775," in David Curtis Skaggs and Larry L. Nelson, eds., *The Sixty Years' War for the Great Lakes, 1754–1814* (East Lansing: Michigan State University Press, 2001), 127.

6. Public Record Office, Colonial Office Records, C. O. 5/ 65, pt. 2: 87.

7. W. J. Eccles, *Essays on New France* (Toronto: Oxford University Press, 1987), 142–43.

8. Peter N. Moogk, *La Nouvelle France: The Making of French Canada—A Cultural History* (East Lansing: Michigan State University Press, 2000), 270.

9. W. J. Eccles, *The French in North America, 1500–1783*. 2nd ed. (East Lansing: Michigan State University Press, 1998), 240.

10. Quoted in Pierre Tousignant, "The Integration of the Province of Quebec into the British Empire, 1763–91," in *Dictionary of Canadian Biography*, 4: xxxiii.

11. Adam Shortt and Arthur G. Doughty, eds., *Documents Relating to the Constitutional History of Canada, 1759–1791*. 2 vols. (Ottawa: Historical Documents Publication Board, 1918), 1: 40–41; Tousignant, "The Integration of the Province of Quebec into the British Empire," xxii–xlix.

12. Clarence Edwin Carter, ed., *The Correspondence of General Thomas Gage*. 2 vols. (New Haven: Yale University Press, 1933), 1: 1; Murray to George Ross, January 26, 1764, James Murray Papers: Letterbook, 1763–1765, National Archives of Canada, MG A-1993, reel 2: 335.

13. G. P. Browne, "James Murray," *Dictionary of Canadian Biography* 4; 570–71.

14. Murray to George Ross, October 23, 1763; and Ross to Murray, n.d., James Murray Papers: Letterbook, 1763–1765, National Archives of Canada, MG A-1992 (reel 1).

15. R. Cole Harris, ed., *Historical Atlas of Canada*. Volume 1: *From the Beginning to 1800* (Toronto: University of Toronto Press, 1987), 117.

16. Philip Lawson, *The Imperial Challenge: Quebec and Britain in the Age of the American Revolution* (Montreal: McGill-Queen's University Press, 1989).

17. Moogk, *La Nouvelle France*, 271–73.

18. Shortt and Doughty, eds., *Documents Relating to the Constitutional History of Canada*, 1: 165, 181–205.

19. Murray to Halifax, October 15, 1764, Murray Papers, NAC, MG A-1993, 2: 124; Shortt and Doughty, eds., *Documents Relating to the Constitutional History of Canada*, 1: 211, 231.

20. Murray to Lords of Trade, April 24, 1764, Murray Papers NAC, MG A-1993, 2: 91.

21. Shortt and Doughty, eds., *Documents Relating to the Constitutional History of Canada*, 1: 115

22. Murray to Eglinton, October 27, 1764, Murray Papers, NAC, MG A-1993, 2: 131–33. Murray expressed similar sentiments to the lords of trade two days later; Shortt and Doughty, eds., *Documents Relating to the Constitutional History of Canada*, 1: 231

23. Tousignant, "The Integration of the Province of Quebec into the British Empire," xxxiii–xli; Lawrence Henry Gipson, *The British Empire before the American Revolution.* 15 vols. (New York: Alfred A. Knopf, 1936–1970) 9: 163–69; Allan Greer, *Peasant, Lord, and Merchant: Rural Society in Three Quebec Parishes 1740–1840* (Toronto: University of Toronto Press, 1985), 72–81; Shortt and Doughty, eds. *Documents Relating to the Constitutional History of Canada*, 1: 205–9, 236.

24. Browne, "James Murray," 572; Murray to Halifax, February 14, March 5, April 23, 1764, Murray Papers, reel 2: 44–47, 67, 92.

25. Browne, "James Murray," 576; Shortt and Doughty, eds., *Documents Relating to the Constitutional History of Canada*, 1: 232–35.

26. Browne, "James Murray," 578.

27. Quoted in Mason Wade, *The French Canadians, 1760–1967.* Rev. ed. 2 vols. (Toronto: Macmillan of Canada, 1968), 1: 61.

28. Moogk, *La Nouvelle France*, 272–73.

29. D. W. Meinig, *The Shaping of America: A Geographical Perspective on 500 Years of History.* Vol. 1: *Atlantic America, 1492–1800* (New Haven: Yale University Press, 1986), 279.

30. Patrick C. T. White, ed., *Lord Selkirk's Diary, 1803–1804: A Journal of His Travels in British North America and the Northeastern United States* (Toronto: Champlain Society, 1958), 217.

31. Wade, *The French Canadians*, 48; Frégault, *Canada: The War of the Conquest*, 342.

32. Wade, *The French Canadians*, 1: 65, 67.

33. Susan Sleeper-Smith, *Indian Women and French Men: Rethinking Cultural Encounter in the Western Great Lakes* (Amherst: University of Massachusetts Press, 2001), 56.

34. Quoted in Michael A. McDonnell, "Charles-Michel Mouet de Langlade: Warrior, Soldier, and Intercultural 'Window' on the Sixty Years' War for the Great Lakes," in Skaggs and Nelson, eds., *The Sixty Years' War for the Great Lakes*, 87.

35. Kerry A. Trask, "To Cast Out the Devils: British Ideology and the French Canadians of the Northwest Interior," *American Review of Canadian Studies* 15 (1985), 250–62.

36. Francis Parkman, *The Conspiracy of Pontiac*. 2 vols. (1851; New York: E. P. Dutton, 1908), 2: 161–62.
37. Eccles, *Essays on New France*, 85, 103.
38. Sleeper-Smith, *Indian Women and French Men*.
39. "Instructions of Villiers to Indian Nations," *WJP* 10: 819–21.
40. Helen Hornbeck Tanner, ed., *Atlas of Great Lakes Indian History* (Norman: University of Oklahoma Press, 1987), 92; Eric Hinderaker, *Elusive Empires: Constructing Colonialism in the Ohio Valley, 1673–1800* (Cambridge: Cambridge University Press, 1997), 176–77; "Journal of a Detachment of the 42nd Regiment from Fort Pitt down the Ohio to the Country of the Illenoise," National Archives of Scotland, DG298/196: 90, 94, 99.
41. "Bouquet Papers," *MPHC* 19: 40–42; "George Croghan's Journal, 1760–1761," in Reuben G. Thwaites, ed., *Early Western Travels, 1748–1846*. 32 vols. (Cleveland: Arthur H. Clark, 1904–07), vol. 1.
42. "Gladwin Manuscripts," *MPHC* 27: 613; "Bouquet Papers," *MPHC* 19: 40–45, 63–64.
43. Clarence Walworth Alvord and Clarence Edwin Carter, eds., *The Critical Period, 1763–1765* (Springfield: Collections of the Illinois State Historical Library, 1915), 10: 12.
44. Widder, "The French Connection: The Interior French and Their Role in French-British Relations in the Western Great Lakes Region, 1760–1775," 127; Sleeper-Smith, *Indian Women and French Men*, 61.
45. "Gladwin Manuscripts," *MPHC* 27: 632–34, 648–64 (reports of French involvement; quote at 658); Minavavana's speech in Milo M. Quaife, ed., *Alexander Henry's Travels and Adventures in the Years 1760–1776* (Chicago: R. R. Donnelley and Sons, 1921), 43–45; reprinted in Colin G. Calloway, ed., *The World Turned Upside Down: Indian Voices from Early America* (Boston: Bedford Books, 1994), 136–37; Parkman, *Conspiracy of Pontiac*, 1: 128–29; Gregory Evans Dowd, "The French King Wakes Up in Detroit; 'Pontiac's War' in Rumor and History," *Ethnohistory* 37 (1990), 254–78; Dowd, *A Spirited Resistance: The North American Indian Struggle for Unity, 1745–1815* (Baltimore: Johns Hopkins University Press, 1992), ch. 2. See also Michael N. McConnell, *A Country Between: The Upper Ohio Valley and Its Peoples, 1724–1774* (Lincoln: University of Nebraska Press, 1992), ch. 8, and Sleeper-Smith, *Indian Women and French Men*, ch. 4.
46. "Gladwin Manuscripts," *MPHC* 27: 664.
47. Milo M. Quaife, ed., *The Siege of Detroit in 1763: The Journal of Pontiac's Conspiracy and John Rutherfurd's Narrative of a Captivity* (Chicago: R. R. Donnelley and Sons, 1958), xxi, 94–96, 100.
48. "George Croghan's Journal, 1765," in Thwaites, ed., *Early Western Travels*, 1: 152.
49. Quaife, ed., *The Siege of Detroit in 1763*, liv.
50. "George Croghan's Journal, 1765," 150.
51. *NYCD* 7: 787–88, reprinted in Thwaites, ed., *Early Western Travels*, 1: 170–71.
52. Milo M. Quaife, ed., *Alexander Henry's Travels and Adventures in the Years 1760–1776* (Chicago: R. R. Donnelley and Sons, 1921), 78–85, 101–03.
53. *WJP* 10: 696; "Gladwin Manuscripts," *MPHC* 27: 631–32.

54. McDonnell, "Charles-Michel Mouet de Langlade," in Skaggs and Nelson, eds., *The Sixty Years' War*, 79–103; Quaife, ed., *Alexander Henry's Travels and Adventures*, 80n–81n.

55. Colin G. Calloway, *Crown and Calumet: British–Indian Relations, 1783–1815* (Norman: University of Oklahoma Press, 1987), ch. 2; Robert S. Allen, *The British Indian Department and the Frontier in North America, 1755–1830* (Ottawa: Department of Indian and Northern Affairs Canada, 1975; Canadian Historic Sites: Occasional Papers in Archaeology and History, no. 14).

56. William W. Warren, *History of the Ojibway People* (St. Paul: Minnesota Historical Society, 1984), 211.

57. Widder, "The French Connection," 126, 138; Carolyn Gilman, *Where Two Worlds Meet: The Great Lakes Fur Trade* (St. Paul: Minnesota Historical Society, 1982), 12.

58. Sleeper-Smith, *Indian Women and French Men*, 56–57, 62–63; Lucy Eldersveld Murphy, *A Gathering of Peoples: Indians, Métis, and Mining in the Western Great lakes, 1737–1832* (Lincoln: University of Nebraska Press, 2000).

59. Carl J. Ekberg, *French Roots in the Illinois Country: The Mississippi Frontier in Colonial Times* (Urbana: University of Illinois Press, 1998), 103.

60. Jay Gitlin, "Constructing the House of Choteau: St. Louis," in Common-Place (*www.common-place.org*) vol. 3, no. 4 (July 2003); William E. Foley and C. David Rice, *The First Chouteaus: River Barons of Early St. Louis* (Urbana: University of Illinois Press, 1983), ch. 1; John Francis McDermott, "Myths and Realities Concerning the Founding of St. Louis," in John Francis McDermott, ed., *The French in the Mississippi Valley* (Urbana: University of Illinois Press, 1965), 9–10.

61. Ekberg, *French Roots in the Illinois Country*, 96–101.

62. Foley and Rice, *The First Chouteaus*, 15.

63. Edgeley W. Todd, ed., *Astoria, or Anecdotes of an Enterprise beyond the Rocky Mountains by Washington Irving* (Norman: University of Oklahoma Press, 1964), 132–34.

64. *NYCD* 7: 777; my thanks to Jay Gitlin for this reference.

65. Lawrence Kinnaird, trans. and ed., *Spain in the Mississippi Valley, 1765–1794: Translations of Materials from the Spanish Archives in the Bancroft Library, University of California, Berkeley.* 3 vols. (Washington, D.C., 1946–49: American Historical Association, Annual Report for the Year 1945), 2, part 1: xviii–xix.

66. Foley and Rice, *The First Chouteaus*; Shirley Christian, *Before Lewis and Clark: The Story of the Chouteaus, the French Dynasty That Ruled America's Frontier* (New York: Farrar, Straus and Giroux, 2004).

67. *NYCD* 7: 776–777.

68. "Journal of Captain Henry Gordon, 1766," in Newton D. Mereness, ed., *Travels in the American Colonies* (1916; reprinted New York: Antiquarian Press, 1961), 476–77.

69. Christian Morissonneau, "The 'Ungovernable' People: French-Canadian Mobility and Identity," in Dean R. Louder and Eric Waddell, eds., *French America: Mobility, Identity, and Minority Experience across the Continent* (Baton Rouge: Louisiana State University Press, 1993), 15–32.

70. Peter C. Newman, *Empire of the Bay: The Company of Adventurers That Seized a Continent* (Toronto: Penguin, 1998), 167, quote at 219.

71. Jay Gitlin, "On the Boundaries of Empire: Connecting the West to Its Imperial Past," in William Cronon, George Miles, and Jay Gitlin, eds., *Under an Open Sky: Rethinking America's Western Past* (W. W. Norton, 1992), 71–89, esp. 77–78.

72. Patricia Galloway, "'So Many Little Republics': British Negotiations with the Choctaw Confederacy, 1765," *Ethnohistory* 41 (1994), 526; Milo B. Howard and Robert R. Rea, eds., *The Mémoire Justificatif of the Chevalier Montault de Monberaut: Indian Diplomacy in British West Florida, 1763–1765* (Tuscaloosa: University of Alabama Press, 1965), quote at 69.

73. Ekberg, *French Roots in the Illinois Country,* 2, 250–52.

CHAPTER 6 : LOUISIANA TRANSFER AND MISSISSIPPI FRONTIER

1. E. Wilson Lyon, *Louisiana in French Diplomacy, 1759–1804.* 2nd ed. (Norman: University of Oklahoma Press, 1974), 28, 33; Arthur S. Aiton, "The Diplomacy of the Louisiana Cession," *American Historical Review* 36 (1931), 701–20.

2. Daniel H. Usner, Jr., *Indians, Settlers, and Slaves in a Frontier Exchange Economy: The Lower Mississippi Valley before 1783* (Chapel Hill: University of North Carolina Press, 1992), quote at 105.

3. Dunbar Rowland, A. G. Sanders, and Patricia Kay Galloway, eds., *Mississippi Provincial Archives: French Dominion, 1749–1763* (Baton Rouge: Louisiana State University Press, 1984), 5: 284–85, 291, 293.

4. Letters from D'Abbadie, November 6, 1763, January 10, 1764, June 29, 1764, National Archives of Canada, MG 1, series C13A, vol. 43: 235–38, reel F-460; vol. 44: 21, 29–30, 74–77, reel F-461; Carl A. Brasseaux, trans. and ed., "The D'Abbadie Journal [1763–1764]," in *A Comparative View of French Louisiana, 1699 and 1762: The Journals of Pierre Le Moyne d'Iberville and Jean-Jacques-Blaise d'Abbadie.* rev. edn., (Lafayette: University of Southwestern Louisiana Center for Louisiana Studies, 1981), 96, 100–101, 102n, 107, 111–15.

5. Clarence Walworth Alvord and Clarence Edwin Carter, eds., *The Critical Period, 1763–1765* (Springfield: Collections of the Illinois State Historical Library, 1915), 10: 302.

6. Dunbar Rowland, ed., *Mississippi Provincial Archives: English Dominion, 1763–1766* (Jackson: Mississippi Department of Archives and History, 1911), 1: 10, 136–37.

7. Rowland, ed., *Mississippi Provincial Archives: English Dominion,* 1: 83–91; Rowland, Sanders, and Galloway, eds., *Mississippi Provincial Archives, French Dominion,* 5: 294–301.

8. Patricia Galloway, "'So Many Little Republics': British Negotiations with the Choctaw Confederacy, 1765," *Ethnohistory* 41 (1994), 513–37, esp. 513, 518–19.

9. Rowland, ed., *Mississippi Provincial Archives: English Dominion,* 1: 14; Galloway, "So Many Little Republics," 514, 519, 530.

10. John T. Juricek, ed., *Georgia and Florida Treaties, 1763–1776,* in Alden T. Vaughan, gen. ed., *Early American Indian Documents: Treaties and Laws,*

1607–1789 (Bethesda, Md.: University Publications of America, 2002), 12: 193–94.

11. Galloway, "So Many Little Republics," quotes at 519, 522.

12. Greg O'Brien, "Protecting Trade through War: Choctaw Elites and British Occupation of the Floridas," in Martin Daunton and Rick Halpern, eds., *Empire and Others: British Encounters with Indigenous Peoples, 1600–1850* (Philadelphia: University of Pennsylvania Press, 1999), 149–66.

13. Clarence Edwin Carter, ed., *Correspondence of General Thomas Gage.* 2 vols. (New Haven: Yale University Press, 1931–33), 1: 199; *NYCD* 7: 777.

14. Brasseaux, trans. and ed., "The D'Abbadie Journal [1763–64]," 86–87, 94; N. M. Miller Surrey, ed., *Calendar of Manuscripts in Paris Archives and Libraries Relating to the History of the Mississippi Valley.* 2 vols. (Washington: Carnegie Institute, 1928), 2: 1439–40, 1443–45, 1449.

15. Antonio de Ulloa, *Relacion historica del Viage de la America Meridional* (Madrid, 1748).

16. Lyon, *Louisiana in French Diplomacy, 1759–1804,* 45.

17. Louis Houck, ed., *The Spanish Regime in Missouri.* 2 vols. (Chicago: R. R. Donnelley and Sons, 1909), 1: 22.

18. William E. Foley and C. David Rice, *The First Chouteaus: River Barons of Early St.Louis* (Urbana: University of Illinois Press, 1983), 13 14.

19. Lawrence Kinnaird, trans. and ed., *Spain in the Mississippi Valley, 1765–1794: Translations of Materials from the Spanish Archives in the Bancroft Library, University of California, Berkeley.* American Historical Association, Annual Report for the Year 1945. 3 vols. (Washington, D. C.: 1946–49), 2, part 1: 59.

20. Foley and Rice, *The First Chouteaus,* 8–9; Houck, ed., *Spanish Regime in Missouri,* 63.

21. Foley and Rice, *The First Chouteaus,* 13–14.

22. Houck, ed., *Spanish Regime in Missouri,* 1: 78.

23. Kinnaird, trans. and ed., *Spain in the Mississippi Valley,* 2, part 1: 40.

24. John Preston Moore, *Revolt in Louisiana: The Spanish Occupation, 1766–1770* (Baton Rouge: Louisiana State University Press, 1976); Kinnaird, trans. and ed., *Spain in the Mississippi Valley,* 2, part 1; xxi–ii; 105.

25. Usner, *Indians, Settlers, and Slaves in a Frontier Exchange Economy,* 139.

26. Gilbert C. Din, *Spaniards, Planters, and Slaves: The Spanish Regulation of Slavery in Louisiana, 1763–1803* (College Station: Texas A & M University Press, 1999), esp. ch. 3.

27. Usner, *Indians, Settlers, and Slaves in a Frontier Exchange Economy.*

28. Stephen Webre, "The Problem of Indian Slavery in Spanish Louisiana, 1769–1803," *Louisiana History* 25 (1984), 117–35; Kinnaird, trans. and ed., *Spain in the Mississippi Valley,* 2, pt. 1: 125–26, 167–79.

29. Herbert Eugene Bolton, ed., *Athanase De Mézières and the Louisiana-Texas Frontier, 1768–1780.* 2 vols. (Cleveland: The Arthur H. Clark Co., 1914), 1: 67.

30. Luis Navarro García, "The North of New Spain as a Political Problem in the Eighteenth Century," in David J. Weber, ed., *New Spain's Northern Frontier: Essays on Spain in the American West, 1540–1821* (1979; Dallas: Southern Methodist University Press, 1988), 201–15; quote at 206.

31. Ulloa to the Marqués de Grimaldi, March 31, 1766, Archivo General de Indias: Audiencia of Santo Domingo, leg. 2585, cited in Charles A. Weeks, *Paths to a Middle Ground: The Diplomacy of Natchez, Boukfouka, Nogales, and San Fernando de las Barrancas, 1791–95* (Tuscaloosa: University of Alabama Press, 2005), 31, 254n.

32. Bolton, ed., *Athanase De Mézières and the Louisiana-Texas Frontier, 1768–1780*, 1: 18–28, 67–71, 89; Kinnaird, trans. and ed., *Spain in the Mississippi Valley*, 2, part 1: xviii, 15, 59–62, 154–55; "Instructions for Holding Council with the Indians," in Houck, ed., *Spanish Regime in Missouri*, 1: 46–48; Kathleen DuVal, *Native Ground: Indian Sovereignty and European Dependence in the Arkansas River Valley, 1500–1828* (University of Pennsylvania Press, forthcoming); DuVal, "The Education of Fernando de Leyba: Quapaws and Spaniards on the Border of Empires," *Arkansas Historical Quarterly* 60 (2001), 1–29; David La Vere, "Friendly Persuasions: Gifts and Reciprocity in Comanche-Euroamerican Relations," *Chronicles of Oklahoma* 71 (1993), 329.

33. Bolton, ed., *Athanase De Mézières and the Louisiana-Texas Frontier*, 1: 74.

34. Bolton, ed., *Athanase De Mézières and the Louisiana-Texas Frontier*, 1: 71–72, 83–84, 92–97, 113–14, 127–30, 135–36, 148–50, 206–27, 256–48 282–306; Todd Smith, *The Wichita Indians: Traders of Texas and the Southern Plains, 1540–1845* (College Station: Texas A & M University Press, 2000), 45–91; Elizabeth A. H. John, *Storms Brewed in Other Men's Worlds: The Confrontation of Indians, Spanish, and French in the Southwest, 1540–1795* (Lincoln: University of Nebraska Press, 1975), chs. 10–11; Gary Clayton Anderson, *The Indian Southwest 1580–1830: Ethnogenesis and Reinvention* (Norman: University of Oklahoma Press, 1999), 101–2, 166–70.

35. Willard H. Rollings, *The Osage: An Ethnohistorical Study of Hegemony on the Prairie-Plains* (Columbia: University of Missouri Press, 1992), 98–100; Garrick A. Bailey, *The Osage and the Invisible World, from the Works of Francis La Flesche* (Norman: University of Oklahoma Press, 1995), 27–28.

36. Rollings, *The Osage*, 69n; Bolton, ed., *Athanase De Mézières and the Louisiana-Texas Frontier*, 1: 304; Abraham P. Nasatir, ed., *Before Lewis and Clark: Documents Illustrating the History of the Missouri, 1785–1804*. 2 vols. Reprint ed. (Lincoln: University of Nebraska Press, 1990), 1: 51–52.

37. Rollings, *The Osage*, 82–95, 100–23, 282.

38. John Joseph Mathews, *The Osages: Children of the Middle Waters* (Norman: University of Oklahoma Press, 1961), 229–30.

39. Rollings, *The Osage*, 130–33; *WJP* 6: 391, 393.

40. Rollings, *The Osage*, 134–35; Gilbert C. Din and A. P. Nasatir, *The Imperial Osages: Spanish-Indian Diplomacy in the Mississippi Valley* (Norman: University of Oklahoma Press, 1983), ch. 3.

41. Smith, *The Wichita Indians*, 35–41.

42. F. Todd Smith, *The Caddo Indians: Tribe at the Convergence of Empires, 1542–1854* (College Station: Texas A & M University Press, 1995), 62–66.

43. John, *Storms Brewed in Other Men's Worlds*, 590–91; Colin G. Calloway, *One Vast Winter Count: The Native American West Before Lewis and Clark* (Lincoln: University of Nebraska Press, 2003), 291.

44. Alfred Barnaby Thomas, ed., *The Plains Indians and New Mexico, 1751–1778* (Albuquerque: University of New Mexico Press, 1940), 155–56.

45. Gerald Betty, *Comanche Society Before the Reservation* (College Station: Texas A & M University Press, 2002), 154–55.
46. Stanley J. Stein and Barbara H. Stein, *Apogee of Empire: Spain and New Spain in the Age of Charles III, 1759–1789* (Baltimore: Johns Hopkins University Press, 2003), 52–58, 351.
47. Lawrence Kinnaird, ed., *The Frontiers of New Spain: Nicolas De Lafora's Description 1766–1768* (The Quivira Society, 1958), 76–80, 94, 106, 185, 215–17. Lafora, an engineer, kept a detailed record of the tour. On frontier conditions in the 1760s and the role of Gálvez and Rubí in bringing about reform of military regulations in 1772, see Joseph P. Park, "Spanish Indian Policy in Northern Mexico, 1765–1810," *Arizona and the West* 4 (1962), 325–44 (reprinted in Weber, ed., *New Spain's Far Northern Frontier,* 217–34), and David Weber, *The Spanish Frontier in North America* (New Haven: Yale University Press, 1992), 204–20.
48. R. Douglas Hurt, *The Indian Frontier, 1763–1846* (Albuquerque: University of New Mexico Press, 2002), 37 ("European solution").
49. Arthur J. Ray, *Indians in the Fur Trade: Their Role as Hunters, Trappers, and Middlemen in the Lands Southwest of Hudson Bay, 1660–1870* (Toronto: University of Toronto Press, 1974), ch. 5; Peter C. Newman, *Empire of the Bay: The Company of Adventurers That Seized a Continent* (Toronto: Penguin, 1998), 167, quotes at 219.
50. For information on the exchange network that centered on the Upper Missouri, see W. Raymond Wood and Thomas D. Thiessen, eds., *Early Fur Trade on the Northern Plains: Canadian Traders among the Mandan and Hidatsa Indians, 1738–1818* (Norman: University of Oklahoma Press, 1985); Gary E. Moulton, ed., *The Journals of the Lewis and Clark Expedition.* 13 vols. (Lincoln: University of Nebraska Press, 1986–2001) 3: ch. 10; Nasatir, ed., *Before Lewis and Clark;* John C. Ewers, "The Indian Trade of the Upper Missouri before Lewis and Clark," in *Indian Life on the Upper Missouri* (Norman: University of Oklahoma Press, 1968), 14–34, and Roy W. Meyer, *The Village Indians of the Upper Missouri* (Lincoln: University of Nebraska Press, 1977).
51. Bolton, ed., *Athanase De Mézières and the Louisiana-Texas Frontier,* 1: 331.
52. Thomas, ed., *The Plains Indians and New Mexico,* 161–63; Bolton, ed., *Athanase De Mézières and the Louisiana-Texas Frontier,* 1: 76–77; Charles W. Hackett, ed., *Pichardo's Treatise on the Limits of Louisiana and Texas.* 4 vols. (Austin: University of Texas Press, 1931–46), 1: 392.
53. Henry Kamen, *Empire: How Spain Became a World Power, 1492–1763* (New York: HarperCollins, 2003), 485.

CHAPTER 7: EXILES AND EXPULSIONS

1. Helen Hornbeck Tanner, ed., *Atlas of Great Lakes Indian History* (Norman: University of Oklahoma Press, 1987), 64, 92; Emily J. Blassingham, "The Depopulation of the Illinois Indians," *Ethnohistory* 3 (1956), 370, 391.
2. Quoted in Lawrence Henry Gipson, *The British Empire before the American Revolution.* 15 vols. (New York: Alfred A. Knopf, 1936–1970), 8: 307.
3. Lord Adam Gordon, "Journal of an Officer who Travelled in America and the West Indies in 1764 and 1765," in Newton D. Mereness, ed., *Travels in the American Colonies* (New York: Macmillan, 1916), 394.

4. James Leitch Wright, *Anglo-Spanish Rivalry in North America* (Athens: University of Georgia Press, 1971), 110.

5. Quotes from D. W. Meinig, *The Shaping of America: A Geographical Perspective on 500 Years of History*. Vol. 1: *Atlantic America, 1492–1800* (New Haven: Yale University Press, 1986), 280. The transfer is covered in Robert L. Gold, *Borderland Empires in Transition: The Triple-Nation Transfer of Florida* (Carbondale: Southern Illinois University Press, 1969).

6. James W. Covington, ed., *The British Meet the Seminoles* (Gainesville: University of Florida Press, 1961), 6, 17.

7. Gold, *Borderland Empires in Transition*, 35–54; "Robertson's Report" in Covington, ed., *The British Meet the Seminoles*, 5–16 (no "publick houses" quote at 11).

8. "Robertson's Report" in Covington, ed., *The British Meet the Seminoles*, 6; Gold, *Borderland Empires in Transition*, 36, 133, 139 (quote).

9. Gold, *Borderland Empires in Transition*, p. 67 (table 4); Wilbur H. Siebert, "The Departure of the Spaniards and Other Groups from East Florida, 1763–1764," *Florida Historical Quarterly*, 19 (October 1940), 145–54.

10. Gold, *Borderland Empires in Transition*, 35, 68, and ch. 5 generally. Tables at 69–73.

11. Gold, *Borderland Empires in Transition*, 158.

12. Gold, *Borderland Empires in Transition*, 93–99.

13. Duvon C. Corbett, "Spanish Relief Policy and the East Florida Refugees of 1763," *Florida Historical Quarterly* 27 (July 1948), 67–82; quote at 67.

14. Paul David Nelson, *General James Grant: Scottish Soldier and Royal Governor of East Florida* (Gainesville: University Press of Florida, 1993), chs. 4–5; figures at 65.

15. Dunbar Rowland, ed., *Mississippi Provincial Archives: English Dominion, 1763–1766* (Jackson: Mississippi Department of Archives and History, 1911), 1: 136–37; *The Memoirs and Adventures of Robert Kirk, Late of the Royal Highland Regiment … Written by Himself* (Limerick: J. Ferrar printer, n.d.), 106.

16. Gold, *Borderland Empires in Transition*, 56, 101–2, 159–61; Wilbur H. Siebert, "How the Spaniards Evacuated Pensacola in 1763," *Florida Historical Quarterly*, 11 (October 1932), 48–57. A report compiled in August listed 722 persons, including the Yamassees, and mentioned additional refugees and their families (Siebert, 54); Gipson, *The British Empire Before the American Revolution*, 205.

17. Gold, *Borderland Empires in Transition*, 63–64.

18. A. Mackillop and Steve Murdoch, eds., *Military Governors and Imperial Frontiers c. 1600–1800: A Study of Scotland and Empires* (Leiden: Brill, 2003), xxi, 181.

19. Rowland, ed., *Mississippi Provincial Archives, 1763–1766: English Dominion*, xiv–xv.

20. Robin F. A. Fabel, *The Economy of British West Florida, 1763–1783* (Tuscaloosa: University of Alabama Press, 1988), ch. 1; "Englishmen" quote at 11; 1765 population at 18; Gold, *Borderland Empires in Transition*, 56.

21. Fabel, *Economy of British West Florida*, ch. 2, 205.

22. William V. Bangert, *A History of the Society of Jesus* (St. Louis: Institute of Jesuit Sources, 1972), 361, 372–83: Jean Delanglez, *The French Jesuits in Lower Louisiana, 1700–1763* (Washington, D.C.: Catholic University of America, 1935), 491–95.

23. P. Watrin "The Banishment of the Jesuits," translated in Reuben G. Thwaites, ed., *The Jesuit Relations and Allied Documents: Travels and Explorations of the Jesuit Missionaries in New France, 1610–1791.* 73 vols. (Cleveland: Burrows Bros, 1896–1901), 70: 212–301, and in Clarence Walworth Alvord and Clarence Edwin Carter, eds., *The Critical Period, 1763–1765* in *Collections of the Illinois State Historical Society Library,* 10 (1915), 62–133; quote at 63.

24. Lafrénière's decree to the Superior Council is in Delanglez, *The French Jesuits in Lower Louisiana,* 509–13; N. M. Miller Surrey, ed., *Calendar of Manuscripts in Paris Archives and Libraries Relating to the History of the Mississippi Valley* (Washington: G.P.O., 1928), 2: 1451; Brasseaux, trans. and ed., "The D'Abbadie Journal", 94–95.

25. Watrin, "The Banishment of the Jesuits," in Alvord and Carter, eds., *The Critical Period,* 100–101; Delanglez, *The French Jesuits in Lower Louisiana,* 527–28.

26. Watrin, "The Banishment of the Jesuits," in Alvord and Carter, eds., *The Critical Period,* 73–74.

27. "Father P. Watrin's Account (1763)," in Samuel Cole Williams, ed., *Early Travels in the Tennessee Country, 1540–1800* (Johnson City, Tenn.: Watauga Press, 1928), 198–200; Watrin "The Banishment of the Jesuits," in Alvord and Carter, eds., *The Critical Period,* 101–15.

28. E. Wilson Lyon, *Louisiana in French Diplomacy, 1759–1804.* 2nd ed. (Norman: University of Oklahoma Press, 1974), 16; Arthur S. Aiton, "The Diplomacy of the Louisiana Cession," *American Historical Review* 34 (1931), 711–12; Surrey, *Calendar of Manuscripts in Paris Relating to the History of the Mississippi Valley,* 2: 1394.

29. Geoffrey Plank, *An Unsettled Conquest: The British Campaign against the Peoples of Acadia* (Philadelphia: University of Pennsylvania Press, 2001); John Mack Faragher, *A Great and Noble Scheme: The Tragic Story of the Expulsion of the French Acadians from Their American Homeland* (New York: W. W. Norton, 2005); "cannot easily collect themselves" quote at 336; Robert G. Leblanc, "The Acadian Migrations," in Dean Louder and Eric Waddell, eds., *French America: Mobility, Identity, and Minority Experience across the Continent* (Baton Rouge: Louisiana State University Press, 1993), 164–90; Carl A. Brasseaux, *"Scattered to the Wind": Dispersal and Wanderings of the Acadians, 1755–1809* (Lafayette: University of Southwestern Louisiana, 1991); Brasseaux, *The Founding of New Acadia: The Beginnings of Acadian Life in Louisiana, 1765–1803* (Baton Rouge: Louisiana State University Press, 1987), esp. ch. 4 for the Acadians' experience in France; David Jaffee, *People of the Wachusett: Greater New England in History and Memory, 1630–1860* (Ithaca: Cornell University Press, 1999), 163 (7,000 New Englanders).

30. R. Cole Harris, ed., *Historical Atlas of Canada,* Vol. 1: *From the Beginning to 1800* (Toronto: University of Toronto Press, 1987), plate 30; Leblanc, "The Acadian Migrations," 177, provides more precise figures; Brasseaux, *"Scattered to the Wind,"* 8, 29; Faragher, *A Great and Noble Scheme,* 422.

31. Adam Shortt and Arthur G. Doughty, eds., *Documents Relating to the Constitutional History of Canada, 1759–1791.* 2 vols. (Ottawa: Historical Documents Publication Board, 1918), 115–16.

32. Brasseaux, *The Founding of New Acadia,* 58; Brasseaux, *"Scattered to the*

Wind," 22–24, 27, 33, 39–61; Faragher, *A Great and Noble Scheme,* 426, 428, 433.

33. Meinig, *The Shaping of America: A Geographical Perspective on 500 Years of History.* Vol. 1: *Atlantic America, 1492–1800,* 283.

34. Brasseaux, *"Scattered to the Wind,"* 61–65; Faragher, *A Great and Noble Scheme,* 428, 431 (Aubry quote); Surrey, ed., *Calendar of Manuscripts in Paris Archives and Libraries Relating to the History of the Mississippi Valley,* 2: 1483.

35. Brasseaux, *The Founding of New Acadia,* 89.

36. Lawrence Kinnaird, trans. and ed., *Spain in the Mississippi Valley, 1765–1794: Translations of Materials from the Spanish Archives in the Bancroft Library, University of California, Berkeley.* American Historical Association, Annual Report for the Year 1945. 3 vols. (Washington, D.C., 1946–49), 2, pt 1: xv–xx, quote at 41.

37. Brasseaux, *The Founding of New Acadia,* 47, 53, 72, and ch. 5; Brasseaux, *"Scattered to the Wind,"* 61–69.

38. Captain Philip Pittman, *The Present State of the European Settlements on the Mississippi* (Cleveland: Arthur H. Clark, 1906), 60, 123.

39. Brasseaux, *The Founding of New Acadia,* 131–36.

40. Leblanc, "The Acadian Migrations," 188.

41. W. J. Eccles, *The French in North America, 1500–1783.* 2nd ed. (East Lansing: Michigan State University Press, 1998), 269.

42. Brasseaux, *The Founding of New Acadia,* 198.

EPILOGUE

1. Quoted in Robert L. Gold, *Borderland Empires in Transition: The Triple-Nation Transfer of Florida* (Carbondale: Southern Illinois University Press, 1969), 16.

2. W. J. Eccles, "The Role of the American Colonies in Eighteenth-Century French Foreign Policy," in Eccles, *Essays on New France* (Toronto: Oxford University Press, 1987), 144–55, quote at 148; Arthur Herman, *To Rule the Waves: How the British Navy Shaped the Modern World* (New York: HarperCollins, 2004), 112.

3. Quoted in Edward J. Cashin, *Henry Ellis and the Transformation of British North America* (Athens: University Press of Georgia, 1994), 211.

4. Stephen Hornsby, *British Atlantic, American Frontier: Spaces of Power in Early Modern British America* (Hanover: University Press of New England, 2004); Elizabeth Mancke, "Negotiating an Empire: Britain and Its Overseas Peripheries, c. 1550–1780," in Christine Daniels and Michael V. Kennedy, eds., *Negotiated Empires: Centers and Peripheries in the Americas, 1500–1820* (New York: Routledge, 2002), 235–65.

5. Eccles, "The Role of the American Colonies," 154.

6. Colin G. Calloway, *Crown and Calumet: British-Indian Relations, 1783–1815* (Norman: University of Oklahoma Press, 1987), 5–12.

7. Quoted in Jon Kukla, *A Wilderness So Immense: The Louisiana Purchase and the Destiny of America* (New York: Alfred A. Knopf, 2003), 256.

8. David Hackett Fischer and James C. Kelly, *Bound Away: Virginia and the Westward Movement* (Charlottesville: University of Virginia Press, 2000), 299.

Index

Boston
  population of, 35
  smallpox in, 45
Boswell, James, 3, 57
Bougainville, Louis Antoine de, 6, 162, 168
Boundaries
  Florida and, 93, 94, *95,* 107, 108–10
  Royal Proclamation on Appalachian
    Mountains, 16, 17, 92–100, *95,* 102,
    109, 116–20, 121, 123, 152, 169
  Treaty of Augusta as, 17, 100–108,
    196*n*34
Bouquet, Henry, 73, 74, 76, 80, 81, 85,
  86, 87–90
Braddock, Edward, 4, 90
Bradstreet, John, 5, 75, 91
Brasseaux, Carl, 163
Bremner, John, 91
Britain. *See also* American colonies
  Acadians and, 160–62, 163
  Articles of Capitulation and, 93, 96
  in Canada, 5–6, 8, 9, 25, 112–22, 132,
    174*n*10
  Catholicism and, 118–19, 152
  Charles II as king of, 147
  Charlotte as queen of, 19
  Cherokees in, 23–24
  Cuba and, 7, 9, 46, 72, 82–83, 84, 85,
    147, 152–55
  emigration from, 57–59
  financial crisis in, 11–14, 67–68, 90
  Florida and, 136, 142, 151, 152–57
  Franklin, Benjamin, in, 23
  French and Indian War and, 4–14,
    48–50, 69, 133, 168
  George III as king of, 10, 19, 47, 99,
    118, 124, 125, 132
  Germany as ally of, 5
  Indians and, 15–18, 24, 25–29, 35–37,
    47–56, 82–91, 102, 103, 104, 105,
    106–7, 108–9, 111, 120, 132,
    134–38, 140, 144, 160, 178*n*17
  interior French and, 122–32
  Louisiana and, 133–40, 142
  Molasses Act by, 13
  North American empire of, 168
  Peace of Paris of 1763 and, 3, 8–18,
    19, 25, 41, 66, 69, 103, 109, 112–14,
    118–19, 123, 133, 134–35, 138, 152,
    154
  Peace of Paris of 1783 and, 168–69

  in Philippines, 7, 9
  in Pontiac's War, 82–91, 120
  Protestant, 150
  as Redcoats in American colonies,
    81–91
  Royal Proclamation on Appalachian
    Mountains by, 16, 17, 92–100, *95,*
    102, 109, 116–20, 121, 123, 152, 169
  Stamp Act by, 14, 178*n*17
  Stuart as Indian Superintendent for,
    24, 37, 102, 103, 104, 105, 106–7,
    108–9, 111, 132, 137–38
  taxes imposed by, 12–14, 165, 178*n*17
  trade and, 94, 101, 110–11, 130–31,
    134, 137–38, 143, 145, 147–48, 149,
    169
  Treaty of Augusta by, 17, 100–108,
    196*n*34
  in War of Independence, 168
  wars in identity of, 11
British Army, 46, 81–91
British Royal Navy, 47, 51, 168
Broadsides, 20
Bull, Captain, 54–55
Burd, James, 44–45
Burke, Edmund, 165–68
Burlington Company, 99
Burton, Ralph, 114, 117
Bushy Run, Battle of, 87–88, *89*
Bute, Earl of. *See* Stuart, John

Cachupin, Thomas Vélez, 146
Caddos (confederacies), 146
Cadotte, Jean Baptiste, 128
Cahokia, 123, 124
Campbell, Donald, 85–86, 125
Canada, 123. *See also* Quebec
  Amherst on, 113, 114
  Britain in, 5–6, 8, 9, 25, 112–22, 132,
    174*n*10
  Catholicism in, 114, 117, 118–19, 121,
    122, 152, 158
  French defeated in, 5–6, 8, 9, 112–22,
    132, 174*n*10
  Indians in, 65, 74, 93, 96–98, 112,
    113, 118
  Peace of Paris of 1763 on, 165–68
  population in, 35, 113
  Royal Proclamation and, 96–99,
    116–20, 121
  Scots in, 58

About the Author

Colin G. Calloway is Professor of History and Samson Occom Professor of Native American Studies at Dartmouth College. A native of England, he received his Ph.D. from the University of Leeds in 1978. After moving to the United States, he taught high school in Springfield, Vermont, and was a professor of history for seven years at the University of Wyoming. Calloway has written many books on Native American history, including *One Vast Winter Count: The Native American West Before Lewis and Clark*, which won numerous awards, including the Organization of American Historian's Ray Billington Prize as well as its Merle Curti Award.

About the Typeface

This book is typeset in 11.5/14 Adobe Caslon using old-style figures. William Caslon released his first typefaces in 1722. Caslon's types were based on seventeenth-century Dutch old style designs, which were then used extensively in England. Caslon's typefaces were popular throughout Europe and the American colonies. As a printer, Benjamin Franklin hardly used any other typeface. The first printings of the American Declaration of Independence and the Constitution were typeset in Caslon. For her Caslon revival, designer Carol Twombly studied specimen pages printed by William Caslon between 1734 and 1770.

Printed in Great Britain
by Amazon.co.uk, Ltd.,
Marston Gate.